Issues and Challenges of Immigration in Early Childhood in the USA

Immigration and Childhood Education

This series addresses the realities, challenges and developmental experiences of immigration from the perspective of the young child and their families. Using a forward-thinking approach, the series examines current and existing realities about immigration and reflects on its impact on childhood. Titles provide viewpoints and research-based implications of experiences and circumstances surrounding immigrant and refugee child and families leading readers to consider and ponder their implications for socially just practice. Each title is also intended to stimulate discussion and further awareness about immigration issues facing the young child in contemporary society.

Series Editor:
Wilma Robles-Meléndez (Nova Southeastern University, USA)

Editorial Board:
Mari Riojas-Cortez (California State University System-Channel Islands, USA)
Ramon Ferreiro (Nova Southeastern University, USA)
Clodie Tal (Lewinsky College of Teachers' Education, Israel)
Kenya Wolff (Mississippi State University, USA)

Issues and Challenges of Immigration in Early Childhood in the USA

Wilma Robles-Meléndez and Wayne Driscoll

BLOOMSBURY ACADEMIC
LONDON • NEW YORK • OXFORD • NEW DELHI • SYDNEY

BLOOMSBURY ACADEMIC
Bloomsbury Publishing Plc
50 Bedford Square, London, WC1B 3DP, UK
1385 Broadway, New York, NY 10018, USA

BLOOMSBURY, BLOOMSBURY ACADEMIC and the Diana logo are trademarks of
Bloomsbury Publishing Plc

First published in Great Britain 2021

For legal purposes the Acknowledgments on p. xv constitute an extension
of this copyright page.

Series design by Adriana Brioso
Cover image © Misty Smith: Immigrant preschoolers at the RCMA
program in rural southwest Florida

A catalogue record for this book is available from the British Library.

Library of Congress Cataloging-in-Publication Data
Names: Robles-Meléndez, Wilma, author. | Driscoll, Wayne, author.
Title: Issues and challenges of immigration in early childhood in the
USA / Wilma Robles-Melendez, Wayne Driscoll.
Description: New York : Bloomsbury Academic, 2020. | Series: Immigration
and childhood education | Includes bibliographical references and index.
Identifiers: LCCN 2020023052 (print) | LCCN 2020023053 (ebook) |
ISBN 9781350099999 (hardback) | ISBN 9781350100008 (ebook) |
ISBN 9781350100015 (epub)
Subjects: LCSH: Children of immigrants–United States–Social conditions. |
Children of immigrants–Education (Early childhood)–United States.
Classification: LCC JV6600 .R63 2020 (print) | LCC JV6600 (ebook) |
DDC 362.7/79120973–dc23
LC record available at https://lccn.loc.gov/2020023052
LC ebook record available at https://lccn.loc.gov/2020023053

ISBN: HB: 978-1-3500-9999-9
ePDF: 978-1-3501-0000-8
eBook: 978-1-3501-0001-5

Series: Immigration and Childhood Education

Typeset by Newgen KnowedgeWorks Pvt.Ltd., Chennai, India

To find out more about our authors and books visit www.bloomsbury.com
and sign up for our newsletters.

To all the children of immigration whose dreams of a future continue to grow and unfold in our classrooms and communities; to our early childhood educators whose efforts give children a future; and to my family who made me know that dreams of equality are what inspire our work and lives.

—W. R.-M.

To all the courageous children and adult immigrants whose voices and stories provided unique insights into their initial and continuing experiences as students in the U.S. educational system.

—W. T. D.

Contents

Illustrations

Figures

Photos

Tables

Boxes

Preface

During the summer of 2014, we all became shockingly aware of the desperate situation of thousands of unaccompanied children who poured through the borders of the United States. In the years to follow, this became a grim reality as children migrating and escaping from throughout the globe continue to be in the front pages. During the last days of fall 2019, as we completed our writing, the images of children, some still in their infancy, crossing the borders alone or with their families continue to reveal a dimension of the story about immigration that many had ignored. In the midst of the pandemic in 2020, their images and calls for action for children remain asking everyone's attention. The saga of children venturing out and becoming immigrants has captured the media's attention. Beyond the photos and newscasts, the reality of young children as protagonists in the immigration process became clear. Thousands of questions arose about children and immigration. Listening to the discourse and comments, sometimes egregiously misinformed, ignoring the richness that immigrants bring to society, was among the reasons that led to the writing of this book. No doubt many more stories will continue to emerge as the immigration circumstances remain a puzzling factor in our country and in the global community. Meanwhile, we both hope to add to the conversation by focusing attention on children and the promise that they represent. In particular, we hope to bring a voice to the story followed throughout time by thousands of immigrant children whose silent voices plead to be heard. Their stories are both accounts of difficult realities and of successful triumph. Their contributions are among the most significant in our country and in society.

Writing this book has been a highly personal and a professional experience, one that has allowed us to add to the efforts of advocates and professionals working in support of immigrant children. Both of us share in common personal and first-hand experiences with immigration, growing up proud of our immigrant heritage and learning from our families about the opportunities and challenges. What we present was born out of the shared concern for our immigrant children who are arriving and who are growing up in our communities. Our concerns grew out of our experiences as educators, who continue to support and advocate for young children through our work. This book is also rooted in our own personal stories and experiences with immigration. It gathers stories personally collected about preserving our cultures, languages, and traditions under the umbrella of a nation defined by its diversity and by immigration. For one of us, it is a story of coming to live in the US mainland and experiencing what it means to be an immigrant. Though our own immigration stories are different, as educators, we are joined by our professional aspirations for a better life and a firm belief in equity for all children. We have experienced the challenges and difficulties of children and families coming from other cultures as they bravely build a future for their children. In particular, we both share hopes for understanding and appreciation for what each immigrant brings and contributes to society. Their contributions continue to make us into a proud nation rich in heritage, with ideals of fairness, equality, and justice.

Purpose

This book is aimed at early childhood professionals—classroom teachers, program directors, and preservice and graduate early childhood teachers— whose work brings hope and equity into the lives of children. It is also aimed at advocates and all those individuals who care and contribute to the defense of the immigrant child. Throughout these pages, they will find an emphasis on the child as the protagonist in the immigration process, a fact long ignored as emphasis has been on the adult immigrant. Viewed from the perspective of fairness, discussion brings attention to the need for concerted efforts to appreciate the diversity of experiences and realities of child immigrants and respectively support their rights to optimize their development.

The general purpose of this book is intended to explore immigration from the perspective of young children and the ensuing implications in early childhood education. Its primary purpose is to serve as a text for teacher candidates or practicing early childhood teachers who already have some knowledge about developmental practices. The text will engage readers in exploring issues of diversity and social justice with consideration to young children and immigration. A secondary purpose is to serve as reading to stimulate further inquiry into early childhood practice and issues of diversity within the context of current times. Each chapter engages readers to examine topics, issues, factors, and circumstances leading to immigration, guided at understanding and exploring current and unfolding events in the context of the United States.

Organization and contents

The content for this book is the result of our research, personal interactions, and experiences that continue to give us first-hand knowledge about immigration and about immigrant children. The book is organized into six chapters, with each placing emphasis on the presence of children as a protagonist in the immigration process. Chapter 1 presents an overview about immigration as a societal process and its defining characteristics. Details and current information about immigration are discussed, providing a background on the historical trajectory of immigration within the context of the United States. It also introduces readers to the presence of children as immigrants and the ethical implications for early childhood education. Chapter 2 focuses on the child as an immigrant. The discussion traces the presence of children in immigration from a historical perspective establishing their participation as protagonists. It also highlights attention to the well-being of child immigrants with consideration to the realities and circumstances they experience. Issues about the undocumented population and arrival of child immigrants through the southern borders are discussed from the perspective of ethics. Chapter 3 examines social justice and its implication in the context of immigration and children. This chapter presents a discussion on a multifocal approach to examine realities of immigration in early childhood through four lenses. Chapter 4 examines issues about education, care, and attention to the early childhood needs of immigrant children. Culture serves as the lens guiding the discussion. Chapter 5 examines aspects about practices and experiences and discusses some of the existing educational inequities that impact the education of immigrant children. Chapter 6 discusses the need and role of advocacy in support of child immigrants and their families. It also addresses issues calling for advocacy and action and presents an action agenda to support socially just practices for children of immigrants.

Special features

We include a section, *Key points*, in each chapter highlighting the main topics and concepts discussed. In order to further reflect and apply topics, the section *Things to reflect and do* is included in each chapter. Reflection on main issues is encouraged throughout each chapter in the *Time to reflect on* boxes, intended at building deeper consciousness about immigration issues in early childhood. Because narratives are a powerful source of personal experiences, accounts of immigration experiences shared and learned from our research are integrated into each chapter. It was our goal to also give a voice to the many experiences of immigrants during their childhood as well as of early childhood educators. We chose to safeguard the privacy of everyone who shared his or her stories. For that reason, all names throughout the chapters are pseudonyms.

Everyone recognizes the role of stories for conveying difficult topics and situations such as those presented in children's stories. Given their powerful way to present ideas, we incorporated children's books related to immigration topics throughout the chapters. They are intended to further underline immigration aspects using related stories. Those included were carefully selected following recommendations from immigrant early childhood educators. We also included those we have used in our teaching to engage discussions of immigration and diversity topics. You are urged to add those you already know to engage discussions about immigration and diversity topics.

Because the book is intended as a text and resource in teacher education and professional development programs, chapter topics were aligned with the professional teacher preparation standards from the National Association for the Education of Young Children (NAEYC).

A word to our readers

We leave you with what it is hoped will contribute to build and expand ideas about immigration and young children. Much is still to be done to achieve justice and a hopeful future for our youngest immigrants. We count on you and your commitment for young children.

Wilma Robles-Meléndez and Wayne T. Driscoll

Acknowledgments

Every work is always possible whenever you find support and collaborators. This one was not different, and we are grateful for the support received. A very special thank you to our colleague and friend, Dr. Audrey Henry, for her careful and detailed editing of the manuscript. Her comments helped us to expand and bring clarity to our thoughts. We also want to thank all the teachers, students, parents, and immigrants who shared their stories and experiences. Through their accounts, we learned about their ongoing journeys, struggles, and successes. More importantly, we learned about the courageous ways in which they continue to build their future and that of their children and families. Our book could have never been possible without the stories, experiences, and anecdotes shared. To them, our heartfelt thank you. Sincere thanks to Misty Smith for her assistance and for the photo that became the cover for the book.

We both want to say thank you to our families for their support and understanding especially while researching and writing. Thank you for the encouragement and thoughtful ways staying with us during the many hours spent during the long evenings, weekends, and holidays. A special thanks from Wayne to the professor who provided the collegial spirit and scholarly guidance, Dr. Michael Simonson, throughout the process of writing this book.

Special thanks to our colleagues Dr. Berta Capo, Prof. Mabel Valdés, and Carmen Delgado for sharing their insights and experiences. A special thank you to Barbara Mainster, Isabel Garcia, Judy Burleson, Lourdes Villanueva, and Gladys Montes for their inspiring work with immigrant children and for sharing their concerns, comments, and hopes. We also want to express our most sincere thanks to our editor, Mark Richardson, whose encouragement and support have been invaluable to make this idea about a publication become possible. Mark, thank you! ¡Gracias!

The Landscape of Immigration

Chapter objectives

Through this chapter, we will

- Define immigration
- Explore the leading factors for immigration
- Explore some of the historical tenets about immigration in the United States
- Identify the implications of immigration on early childhood education

Key terms

- Immigration
- Migrants
- Immigrants
- Push and pull factors

NAEYC standards

- NAEYC #1 Promoting Child Development
- NAEYC #6 Becoming a Professional

Sharing stories: *"We came because of a dream"*

I still remember how papito, my dad, would tell us that someday we would be taking a "big trip" to where we would have everything we wanted. That day came when I was seven. He came home excited showing my Mom a letter that brought tears to her eyes. But he never told us that our lives would soon change. My parents had talked about that big trip so many times but never thought it would be that night. My mother who was wearing her flowery dress was holding my younger brother in her arms. Together with my five-year-old sister, we followed our parents and jumped into our uncle's truck. We drove and drove and only remember that the scent of the orange blossoms was strong and so soothing. I remember how my papito touched my arm reassuring us that everything would me fine, "nuestro sueño está cerca, ya verán," our dream is getting closer you'll see, he said when we arrived at the airport. The rest was just like a dream. It was not until years later that I would understand why we left that night. Every time I smell the orange blossoms again, it takes me back to that night remembering his words and all that he did for us, what he wanted for us, a future. (Rosario [pseudonym])

The ever-presence of immigration

During a recent visit to a classroom in a rural community, we were happily welcomed by a group of kindergartners. They were planning an upcoming event where they would parade their favorite story characters. Busily working, giggling, and engaged in what they were creating, their conversation was a blend of voices in English, Spanish, and Mixtec, an indigenous language from Mexico. So were their ethnic and cultural roots. Looking at the group of children one could not help but realize their diversity and how together they were a sample of what our country's people are as well. How and why it happens that we became culturally and ethnically diverse is the story itself of immigration in a nation undeniably anchored on the efforts and spirit of immigrants.

Reading the news in recent years about the thousands of children and families on the move to other countries because of a multitude of circumstances in their homelands clearly brought the face of children to immigration. For everyone since 2014, images of children crossing the Mediterranean, unaccompanied children crossing the nation's borders, and caravans across Central America and Mexico have intensified the discussion on the realities of immigrants. More recently, with the pandemic of 2020, the plight of immigrants remains in the humanitarian agenda calling for action and attention. Calls for understanding and compassionate actions continue as faces of the youngest immigrants remind everyone of their presence and their hopes in society to respond to their plea. Listening to the impassioned arguments about immigration from some, it seems people have forgotten that immigration has always been part of the very soul of the nation and of humanity. The facts shows that of the population in the United States, "one-quarter is foreign-born or native born with at least one foreign-born parent" (Trevelyan et al. 2016, 3). Two facts are important to remember. Immigrants have always been present in our communities and, certainly, in our classrooms. Today, the many reasons that made people leave their countries, seeking dreams of freedom, stability, and a better life, remain the same. Now, however, what everyone seems to realize is that children are also the protagonists in the continuing event of immigration.

Time to reflect ... *Immigration in the news*

In recent years, immigration has become a topic present in the daily news. Take a moment to consider how much you know about the now ongoing immigration discussion. As an early childhood educator, what do you need to know? What is particularly relevant for you to know?

Immigration has always been part of the story of humanity. To many of us, it is what defines the experiences and the very nature of who we have become. Many are the stories born out of immigration and many more are yet to be written as people continue to cross borders driven by multiple reasons. To so many of us, immigration is part of our own soul and story. Like so many before us, we came from other countries and places hopeful and encouraged by the dreams of our parents or those of our own. Like the scenario opening this chapter, images of families together with their children remind us that immigration is also part of the life events of countless children.

In search of dreams

Following a dream, just like the family in the opening vignette, has led immigrants for decades to embark on a hopeful journey taking them away to other lands. We learn about Rosario's[1] story, talking with our students, and learned that the impressions remained as vivid as when they were experienced as a child. Such is the enduring reality of immigration stories and experiences that always stay with you. For a child, they are instances that shape and influence life in more ways than one can say. Rosario kept alive her memories about that moment when her family left and came to live in the United States. Her father's words continue to resound for her, grateful for what remains in her mind as the journey that took everyone to find the dream he had for them. To many of us, participants

---

[1] Pseudonym. To protect their privacy and keep their confidentiality, throughout all the chapters, names of all people who shared their stories and accounts as immigrants are pseudonyms. We thank them for opening their hearts sharing their experiences.

in the immigration journey, this is a familiar story we continue to live, in our communities and in our classrooms. Immigration remains at the core of what constituted the United States and continues today as one of its most dynamic shaping forces.

Time to reflect ... *Immigrants*

In a nation of immigrants, what are some of your personal experiences related to immigration in your community? In your family? What do your personal experiences convey to you about coming to live in the United States?

New faces seeking the same goals: A better life

In the early part of the twenty-first century, the enduring reality of immigration continues to shape the nature of society as the nation grows more diverse. Stories of families and individuals arriving into the country may vary. Yet, aspirations seem to resemble those of a century and a half ago when the country experienced an immigration boom (McLemore and Romo 2005). Today, families with children or children coming alone increasingly reflects the profile of immigrants coming through the borders of the nation from all parts of the world (UNICEF 2016). This fact raises the need to focus on childhood and the multiple implications and realities, in particular, of young children and immigration. They are now the face of immigrants summoning everyone to be mindful of their needs and future.

Immigrants in our classrooms

As immigration advances to the forefront, today it is one of the topics challenging society in the early decades of this century. In education, the increasing child immigrant population in the nation's classrooms, representing over 26 percent of students (Zong and Batalova 2019), elevates attention on immigration as one of the priority topics. The presence of child immigrants in schools and programs everywhere continues to focus our attention, demanding practices that fairly and responsibly respond to children of immigrants in our classrooms. Though much has been learned and advanced about teaching and addressing the needs of young immigrants over the past decades (Nieto and Bode 2018; Sánchez-Suzuki and Adair 2014), there is still much more to be learned and changed to fully and equitably respond to children's needs. We are not there yet. It is precisely the call for just and equitable practices for the youngest immigrants that drives the authors to delve into and bring forward the challenges faced by young child immigrants in our classrooms and communities. Unquestionably, the discourse on immigration has become a many-sided issue. The need for unclouding the realities that surround immigrant young children and their families is now vital for everyone (Abo-Zena 2018; Adair 2015). This is especially relevant for us as early childhood educators in whose hands are the future and hopes of the youngest immigrants.

Time to reflect … *What do we know about immigration and childhood?*

As we begin to examine topics about immigration, reflect on what you already know about immigration. Consider what else you would need to explore to equitably address the needs of children during the early years. What other factors would you need to expand and explore further?

Child immigrants: A priority for everyone

We see the unfolding stories of immigrants every day in our classrooms and in our communities. In classrooms everywhere in the country, the growing diversity of students' ethnicities, cultures, and languages is evidence of the continuing and integral presence of immigrants. As we teach, the young faces of children are a reminder of the hopeful dreams of so many families that courageously decided to start over in other places and of those that continue the trajectory of preceding generations. Perhaps you or your families are immigrants. We may know of families, colleagues, or even the children that we teach every day who came from so many close and distant places. For many of us, dreams of hope and of the future are what still resonate as the driving force to migrate. This is what is gathered by Morales, who came with her young child, in her children's book *Dreamers* (2018), when she says, "we enter a new country carried by hopes and dreams, and carrying our own special gifts, to build a better future" (n.p.). Whenever asked, access to quality educational experiences remains as a main motivation for families arriving as immigrants. Their aspiration is for their children to find educational opportunities to build their path for a successful future. Turning into a reality the aspirations of immigrant families cannot be ignored. There is a multitude of questions surrounding the topic of immigration. They are all relevant to be explored to fully grasp their complexity and implications during the early childhood years. In the pages ahead, we explore some of the factors, elements, facts, and realities that can help us in building knowledge about immigration.

Immigration: Reflections and implications in early childhood practices

What has driven immigrants to our nation? What has defined the experience of immigration? This is what we will explore in this chapter as we delve into the nature of immigration to get a perspective on the defining trends of current times not only in our country but also globally. This will help us in understanding some of immigration's character and of the pressing needs of families and children who continue to move seeking opportunities in other lands. As you read, we invite you to reflect on the implications of their needs and realities on our practices as early childhood educators. Reflections will also lead us to building and becoming consciously aware about the needs and aspirations of children. It will also guide us to identify inequities and to find ways to address these within our classrooms and programs (Freire [1974] 2013). Throughout the pages ahead, consider and thoughtfully reflect on the topics and how they further an understanding of immigration. The intention is to also deepen the call to ensure equity and socially just actions for our youngest immigrants.

Time to reflect ... *Families and children on the move*

Records from immigration entries for fiscal year 2019 reveal that almost half a million families with their children entered through the southern borders of the United States. As an early childhood educator, reflect on the conditions and realities forcing families to enter the nation. What are the realities they confronted? What are the implications for their children?

Immigration as a constant in society

Immigration is part of our own history. A look at events of the past help us understand some of the facets of this very complex phenomenon. As stated earlier, through humanity's history, immigration, the movement of people across lands, has always been an experience shared by many families. It is inscribed in the stories and soul of society throughout the world. Immigration is one of the ongoing elements contributing to the change and transformation of regions, nations, and communities everywhere. Because of its influence and vitality, it remains a topic of interest to everyone. This has become particularly evident in the twenty-first century where its presence has been launched as the focus of attention, vividly broadcasted by the media and openly debated by people.

The landscape of immigration in recent times has been spurred by discussions about young immigrant children. It is important to state that, though they have always been present in the story of immigration, children have suddenly come to the forefront, mostly because of the dire situations of thousands arriving in Europe and through the borders of the United States. Yet, the impact of immigration is an everyday reality in early childhood as seen in the faces of young children and their families. Whether recently arrived or children of immigrant families, they all accentuate the continuing need to understand and respond to the realities of immigration.

Defining immigration

Immigration is the movement of people across borders and throughout geographical areas. It happens every day all over the global community. It is part of the continuum of forces of change inherent to societal growth and development. As a multifaceted social element, immigration is a voluntary process where individuals freely make the decision to leave their homes and relocate across borders in places different from those of their birth (United Nations High Commissioner for Refugees [UNHCR] 2018). Difficult circumstances can also force people to leave their countries. Such is the case of refugees and of those seeking asylum. Whether voluntary or forced, migrant population data show that about 3.4 percent of the global population are immigrants (The World Bank 2019). In 2019, it was estimated that every 33 minutes one international migrant was entering the United States (U.S. Census Bureau 2019). People from virtually every country in the global community lives in the United States, something evidenced throughout the country's communities and school classrooms.

Who are the immigrants?

As we begin to explore the realities of immigration and their implications in early childhood, it is relevant to clarify who is considered as an immigrant. In general, *immigrants* designate those who leave their homelands and travel

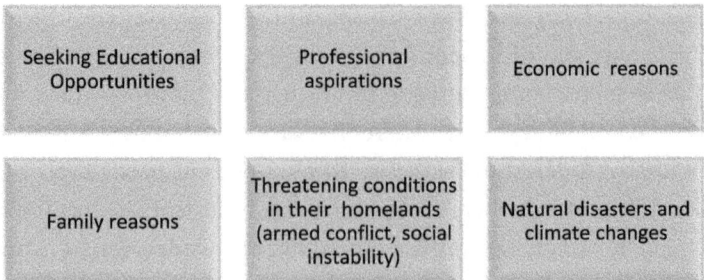

Figure 1.1 Main motivations leading people to migrate.
Source: UN (2017); Valdez, Valentine, and Padilla (2013).

across international borders. They settle in a country different from the place where they are born (International Organization for Migration 2019). Those who immigrate, whether young or adults, individuals or families with or without children, share in common the fact that they have left their home countries and moved to other places. In the United States, immigrants are considered as individuals born in a foreign country now living in the nation's communities (U.S. Census 2019a). Some have entered officially while others, driven by different circumstances, enter unofficially. The term "immigrant" is also used to refer to those born in the United States and who have at least one parent who is foreign born.

Overall, motivations guiding people to leave their homelands are very personal, sometimes guided by individual aspirations, personal circumstances, or conditions in their homelands placing their safety at risk and threatening their future (Figure 1.1). Among the main reasons to migrate, children continue to be at the top as a major motivator (Valdez, Valentine, and Padilla 2013).

Estimates from demographers point out to the increasing diversity across the nation mostly due to the ongoing immigration. Across the nation, immigration continues to be a common experience in US society. For many in our classrooms and communities, immigration is what defines their own personal story. The gradual increase in the number of children of immigrants, who in 2018 represented, 25 percent of the child population (Urban Institute 2019) is evident in US schools. Classroom enrollments already reflect the multiethnic nature of immigrant students (U.S. Census Bureau 2018a). Working in classrooms with young children, the journey and stories of immigration that drove them and their families become a daily experience for educators of young children.

A global reality

Immigration happens every day, a shared and common process in every nation. As a global reality, immigration remains today as a societal factor contributing to the changing nature of communities and countries. In 2019, the United Nations reported an upward immigration trend with the world immigrant population reaching 272 million (UN 2019a). Both Europe and Northern America emerged as the two main destinations for immigrants. While people movement is a continuous process, the impact of human mobility is now more noticeably perceived in the social and economic landscape of nations throughout the globe. To add to our knowledge on immigration, in the following sections, we look at it using the lens of the global community. An understanding about immigration and its main defining traits will help us as early childhood educators to broaden perspectives about a process, intrinsic to society, followed by so many families and children in our classrooms and communities.

Views about immigration: A polarizing issue

Similar to the United States, across the global community, immigration is today a widely debated topic by everyone. While many continue to advocate and provide support to immigrants in our classrooms and communities, immigration, particularly unauthorized immigrants, has been turned into a highly polarizing topic (Goodwin 2017). Divisive opinions together with long-held biases and misinformed views cloud the lived experiences and contributions of thousands of immigrants. Unfortunately, many of the arguments degrade the realities of immigration for both incoming immigrants as well as of those long established across the nation's communities. The xenophobic and racist tone of some of the discourse misleads the nature of immigration, a process continuing to be intrinsically relevant to the growth and development of the nation.

Many early childhood educators would agree that immigration in the United States is an ongoing experience, now more clearly evidenced by the changing diversity of children and families they teach. Similarly, the same is happening in other countries continuing to receive thousands of immigrants. European nations, for instance, have seen an increase in recent years that surpasses expectations. Meanwhile, many of the immigration arguments have soured as people seeking opportunities arrive into the continent.

Thousands of these are children. Unfounded comments and assumptions, however, are obscuring conversations about immigrants, who, overall, represent over 3.5 percent of the global population (United Nations 2019b). Exodus of families and children seeking opportunities or escaping from crisis in their home countries has raised the need to address immigration, with an emphasis to deliver education that equitably responds to what every child needs. Responding to their realities and providing equal and quality experiences still challenges the education and social agenda of many local, state, and national agencies. The United States has seen unprecedented influx of immigrants since the latter part of the twentieth century and the recent decades of this century (Pew Research Center 2015). Answers await as society is pressed for more socially appropriate and fair attention to the needs of the incoming immigrants and of those who are already integral members of our communities (Box 1.1).

Box 1.1 Connecting ideas: *Growing immigration trends*

Globally, immigration trends have evidenced an increasing pattern since the 1990s. In 2005, records of global immigration showed 195 million migrants, which at the time was "an all-time high" in comparison to what was registered in 1960 and 1990 (Fix et al. 2009). As shown in Table 1.1, global immigration trends indicate a gradual increase, soaring in 2019 when 272 million were reported as living in countries other than those where they were born (International Organization for Migration 2018; United Nations 2019a).

Table 1.1 Global immigration growth trends (1990–2019)

Year	Number of international immigrants (millions)
1990	152
2005	195
2013	232
2017	258
2019	272

Source: United Nations (2017a, 2019b).

Factors leading to people movement in the global context

Migration—both forced or voluntary—is bringing the world ever closer together. (UNICEF 2016)

For centuries, people's journeys and relocation have contributed to forming, shaping, and expanding communities. Beyond demographic lines, since ancient times to this day, human migration continues to be an instrumental force in society, bringing to their new home societies their work, culture, skills, knowledge, and wisdom. Many are the reasons behind human migration. In general, they all reveal the circumstances society experiences at a given time where the desire for freedom, stability, and safety continues to persuade people to leave behind their homelands. As in the past, the urge to migrate is rooted in the realities experienced and the anticipation of brighter beginnings.

The urge to migrate: A multidimensional reality

Why do people migrate? Decisions to migrate respond to a variety of multidimensional factors. Push and pull factors contribute to drive decisions to migrate. Many of these factors continue to be the same that drove people decades before. Others emerge out of contemporary realities. Currently, situations of the past two decades threatening children and families in some parts of the world have contributed to the increasing flow of immigration. Among the key push factors, the following can be considered as the main reasons (Burrone, D'Costa, and Holmqvist 2018; International Migration Report 2020; McLemore and Romo 2005):

1. *Social and economic challenges*: Serious economic challenges particularly after the recession earlier in the century led to instability and a loss of employment and opportunities. This resulted in countless people being forced into poverty, pressuring many to leave their homelands.
2. *Civil conflict and political unrest*: Life-threatening realities emerging out of armed and political conflict in some parts of the world, like Africa and the Middle East and in some Latin American nations, have forced many to choose migration options.
3. *Societal violence*: Serious levels of societal violence in some cities and communities, threatening the quality of life and opportunities for safe livelihood, is also another factor influencing decisions to migrate.

4. *Natural disasters*: Climate changes and the increasing intensity of weather events such as hurricanes in economically challenged regions have forced migration decisions for many individuals and families.

Time to reflect ... *Push and pull factors*

Push–pull factors is a way to identify forces driving people to migrate. Push factors refer to those circumstances that may adversely influence the life of individuals and their families. Poverty, armed conflict, violence, and persecution are examples of factors pushing people to leave their homelands. Pull factors, on the other hand, are those prospects for better opportunities of employment, education, and overall quality of life attracting people to migrate.

Reflect for a moment about some of the situations that may push or pull you to make a decision to migrate.

Rising global immigration: Who is immigrating?

Since the 1990s, the rate of immigration experienced globally was considered as following a stable rate (United Nations 2018). However, this has dramatically changed as socioeconomic and political circumstances, particularly during the 2010 decade, have driven thousands to leave their countries. In 2019, the international migrant population reached a high of 272 million migrants (United Nations 2019a). Two of the traits defining the increasing global migrant population (Figure 1.2) accentuate the nature of those who are migrating. Globally, almost half of the migrants, 48 percent, are women and 14 percent are children. Though children have always been present in immigration, this large number of children who are leaving their homelands significantly changes the face of immigration in current times. It has especially brought to light the participation of the child in a process seen mostly as one pertaining to adults. Implications for educators are obvious.

Children and families living with the threat of conflict and violence: The surge in global immigration

News about immigrants has become part of the everyday dialogue and agenda during the second decade of the twenty-first century. The surge in the number of

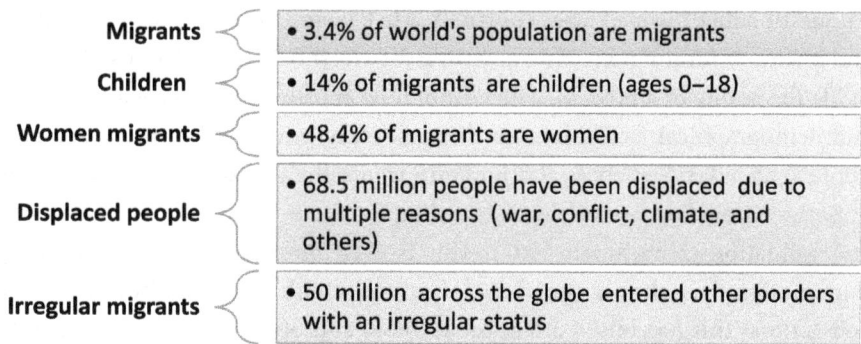

Figure 1.2 Selected traits of the global migrant population (2017–18).
Source: International Organization for Migration (2018).

immigrants witnessed across the world has brought attention to internal unrest and conflict in many countries and the ensuing exodus of families and their children, many of whom are children leaving unaccompanied. The escalation in conflicts and violence against civilians in various parts of the world has threatened thousands of families and children who opted for migration as an answer to their situations. Some of the threatening conditions still present in 2020 include the Syrian crisis, the Middle East conflicts, the political issues and social violence in Venezuela and in other Latin American nations, and the Rohingya refugee crisis in Asia. In the foreword to UNICEF's report on the migrant and refugee crisis, Anthony Lake noted that "Many are trapped in horrific conflicts in their home countries—forgotten or, often beyond the reach of humanitarian assistance" (2016, 1).

Time to reflect … *Building awareness about children living in crisis*

Several reports continue to expose the threatening circumstances forcing children and their families to leave. Some families and children may already live in some of our communities. Considering their situation, what efforts would be required to build greater awareness about their needs and realities?

News media and electronic communication have revealed the realities and continuing immigration incidents experienced by children and their families in many regions worldwide. Since the second decade of this century, these realities and incidents have signaled the human rights dimension of immigration.

Unquestionably, the media has contributed to keeping the presence of challenges and realities of immigrants as a human issue (Kosho 2016). It has also brought to life the reality of a process, which until now, mostly seen as a socioeconomic and demographical factor, had not been fittingly prioritized in the social and political agendas. Society is at a juncture where the role of immigration as an important transformational force is calling for further analysis, consideration, and validation (Hirschman 2007). This is even more pressing when current immigration has shown the faces of young children demanding attention and action. This has raised attention as views and opinions about immigrants continue to be the topic of arguments and discussions.

Views and attitudes about immigration

We all have views about immigration, some from our own experiences. The truth is that there are a multitude of opinions about immigrants. A report from the Pew Research Center revealed that the majority of people in the United States had favorable views about immigrants, considering them as a force strengthening the country (Jones 2019). Reports from the Gallup Survey found similar results, with 75 percent of people considering immigration "is a good thing for the U.S." (Brennan 2018, n.p.). Similar opinions gathered from a United Nations survey showed that, overall, views about immigrants across the globe tend to be positive (International Organization for Migration 2015). Yet, results also exposed clear differences in opinions across world regions including the United States, indicating a serious concern as the number of immigrants increased in many communities. We cannot set aside the host of views and opinions about immigration that thus far, rather than inviting understanding, have led to discordant positions.

The lingering shadow of discrimination

Despite the positive views that many have about immigrants, others do not. These continue challenging impartial views about immigration. Presently, differences in attitudes about immigrants held by some seem to obscure perceptions about the positive role that immigration has on society as a whole (Pew Research Center 2015). Despite the outcomes from recent surveys, acknowledging positive consideration about immigrants, opinions and actions from some individuals and groups disclose a different panorama of views about immigrants. Not all are welcoming words or objective valuation about the role immigration plays in the country. Rooted in old notions about diversity and race, hateful conversations and ideas continue (Suárez-Orozco 2017). Unjustified attacks deny the contributory force of immigrants. We have seen the rhetoric of hate and discrimination, and some of us have personally experienced it. Unfounded fears and misleading views have tarnished discussions about immigration, creating a challenging discourse that hurts everyone, including children. This cannot be ignored. Awareness about current discourse is relevant, particularly considering the long-lasting impact on children. We heard repeatedly how those voices and incidents of rejections experienced in childhood linger with people. What is more, research has confirmed persisting discriminatory practices continued to be experienced by children of immigrants (Adair 2015; Suarez-Orozco, Yoshikawa, and Tseng 2015).

At present, anti-immigration voices have resurfaced, uncovering the prejudiced and discriminatory narrative fermenting through decades. Discrimination, persisting in society, has obscured realities, placing political views ahead of the humanitarian needs of children and families. These positions also affect immigrants who are already members of communities in the nation. Sadly, "old ideas about superiority of some racial and ethnic groups have poisoned the minds of many" (Robles-Meléndez and Beck 2013, 70) and presently call for these to stop.

Today, amid the debate, individuals and families leaving their communities and planting their roots in places close and remote continue the story of immigration in our times. Once again, they continue underlining the essential need for fairness and consideration to people's realities.

Time to reflect … *Hurtful comments and views*

Unfounded views about individuals have long plagued society. With children possibly exposed to comments and actions from those holding distorted ideas, reflect on ways to address those who may be hurt by these harmful comments. Consider also how to respond to children who may be exposed to this type of comments. How would you ensure an antibias environment where diversity is valued?

United States: A main destination for immigrants

Immigration is a constant factor in the nation. As one of the main destinations for global immigrants, the United States has the "biggest international migrant population in the world" (Bolter 2019). In 2018, immigrants living across the nation constituted 44.7 million of its population, while 26 percent of the country's children were children of immigrants (Batalova, Blizzard, and Bolter 2020).

Time to reflect ... *About immigration*

Immigration is a continuous reality in communities across the United States. Take a moment to consider the demographic traits of your community, where you live or teach. Find out how immigration is reflected in your own community. What examples denote the presence of immigrants in your setting or classroom?

Over a million immigrants continue to arrive annually into the United States (Radford 2019). The steady flow of immigrants into the nation has remained as a contributing factor in our society. Though growth in the immigrant population continues, it has slowed down (Zong, Batalova, and Burrows 2019). During the period of 2010–17, reports indicate a slower growth in immigration into the country, due particularly to lower numbers of unauthorized immigrants from Mexico, which has traditionally had a higher percentage entering the United States (Radford 2019). Still, demographical projections demonstrate that immigration remains as a main factor contributing to the nation's population growth in the coming decades. These projections also imply the continuing presence of child immigrants in classrooms in the years ahead.

Diversity: A profile of immigrants today

Perhaps what best characterizes the profile of immigrants in the United States is its diversity. Actually, the profile has grown even more diverse in the past decades. Immigrants come from all parts of the world, with people living in the nation basically representing every continent and country. Essentially, immigrants are a multiethnic, multicultural, multilingual, and socially and economically diverse group. Socioeconomically, immigrants represent all levels, including many who are wealthy and others with limited resources. The contrast is evident and particularly observed in the case of some individuals and families arriving unofficially and whose opportunities for employment and access to services are limited due to their immigration status (Robles-Meléndez and Driscoll 2018).

The diversity of languages is another distinctive characteristic. Linguistically, they represent a myriad of languages. Some immigrants come from English-speaking countries while others speak English along with their home languages. Others speak multiple languages including their primary language. Yet others speak their indigenous heritage languages as in the case of some people from Mexico, Central and South America, and Asia. Their language diversity is already evident in early childhood classrooms. Reports from Head Start, the federally funded early childhood education program, revealed an increase in the number and diversity of languages spoken by children attending their programs (Aikens et al. 2017).

Diversity also characterizes the educational levels of immigrants. Many immigrants continue to arrive with lower educational levels and emerging skills. However, contrary to those in the past, today a larger number of immigrants arrive with stronger levels of educational preparation and professional experiences (Radford and Krogstad 2019). Despite their characteristic diversity, still, what immigrants all have in common is their desire for a stable and safe place, and for a better future. There is also commonality in their cultural and family values that strongly tie their commitment to their children. In fact, this is one of the important protective factors that immigrant children find from their families.

A note about terminology

Terminology about immigration is at times confusing. For that reason, it is important to mention that throughout this book, *child immigrant, children of immigrants,* and *immigrant children* will be used to refer to young children born in other countries or born in the United States to immigrant parents. They will also be used as umbrella terms to include children who have entered as asylees and refugees. Though the nature of their entries may differ, their lived experiences share much in common across all these designations.

What has changed today that makes immigration such a relevant issue in early childhood education?

The need for greater understanding about immigrants, particularly children and families, is paramount in our society. Never before has society seen such a surge in immigration featuring children. In fact, it has been said that "the 21st century will be the century of the children of immigrants" (Suárez-Orozco and

Suárez-Orozco 2018). Globally, childhood immigration has shaken up the very soul of this century's society. The scenes of Syrian children fleeing violence and conflict by crossing the perilous waters of the Mediterranean clearly shocked everyone and troubled society. The same is true about the infants and young children driven away from Myanmar. Their plight has not ceased as they continue to face the ravaging effects of conflict. In the borders of the United States, during 2018 and 2019, young children in long caravans from Central America trying to find a safer place to live drove attention to their difficult conditions. Together, these young immigrants have caught everyone's attention about the reality of children as participants in the unending journey of immigration. Responses to their situation have been mixed, challenging what is socially just and fair for children, demanding clear insights into their realities and circumstances. These experiences of immigrant children have led to an increased need to learn and gain an understanding about immigration and its influence on early childhood. With society's eyes on immigration, attention is called on the nature and diversity of experiences that characterize children of immigrants in our communities and classrooms.

Beyond labels: Seeing the child

Faces of young immigrant children greet teachers every day across classrooms in early childhood programs. Their families have placed their hopes and trust in education to make their dreams come true. No less different are the aspirations of families and children arriving or already established in the country. Neither are of those at the borders of the United States or of those risking their lives seeking a future in other nations. Beyond geography or nationalities, they are children who need from society the same opportunities for a successful future.

A humanitarian issue

Interest on children and immigration has become an issue of attention not only in the United States but also globally. Answers to the reasons and experiences of children moving across borders have puzzled people and continue today to challenge the international agendas. The same is happening in our country where immigration is integral to the essence of its society. The circumstances forcing many and the decisions of others to leave in search of a future has reached critical levels, changing the scope of the conversation about immigration. The fact is that the vast flow of immigrants arriving in the United States and Europe has become a humanitarian issue for the world. At stake are the rights and survival of thousands including young children. Responses to the crisis have raised tensions according to Crawford (2017), who sees these arising between what is ethical and compassionate actions and the established immigration policies. Undoubtedly, attention is needed on the circumstances driving many to seek opportunities for a future (Box 1.2). This is irrespective of labels describing immigrants, whether these are voluntarily relocating or forced to migrate.

Box 1.2 Connecting ideas: *Everyone is talking about immigration*

It seems that everyone today is talking about immigration. Though an ongoing experience and societal process, the media outlets and modern technology have directed everyone's attention to immigration. Current immigration debates have been focused on the high numbers of people leaving their countries, which has virtually turned into an exodus in some parts of the world. Responses and treatment of immigrants has placed the eyes of the public on immigration, not just of those arriving today but as an ongoing reality. Amid the discussions, misinformed opinions, unfair statements, and arguments have tainted views about immigrants in our global society. New policies and restrictions are being enacted while immigrants continue waiting for clear direction about their future. Some comments have clouded the relevant and contributory force of immigrants in US society, a nation continually built by immigrants. Moreover, the arguments have reached the doors of our schools and classrooms. Evidently, the need for clarity and understanding is urgent. At stake is the need for securing equity and fairness in assessing and determining actions and practices for immigrants, including young children. Education is, after all, a way to ensure social justice for the youngest members of society.

Education: A main influencer in the lives of immigrant children

If you ever moved to another community, those impressions and experiences at school still stay with you. This is simply because what is experienced at school continues to be a relevant and influential force for children. Essentially, interactions and experiences are a source addressing children's social and emotional needs as they adjust to new realities. This is undeniably critical, as Hek (2005) stated in her analysis of experiences of child refugees in the United Kingdom. Clearly, what is experienced is what gives children a sense of belonging and stability, a fact well known to educators working with immigrant children (Amigó 2012; Suárez-Orozco and Suárez-Orozco 2001). Whenever we asked immigrants about their memories growing up in our country, comments always referred to what they experienced in schools. Images of teachers that kindly responded to their needs brought smiles to their faces. They also shared about the kindness and empathy received when they needed it the most. However, others continue to remember the inexcusable ways they were treated that still hurt.

Because of the irrefutable influence of education during the most vulnerable years, as authors, we hope to share and engage you in exploring and reflecting on the realities of children and immigration through the following chapters. For years, we have been working, and continue today, teaching and mentoring immigrant students and teachers of young children. Learning their stories and experiencing their numerous successes and challenges have taught us much about the individual side of immigration that for so many of us is personal. Ahead, in this chapter we explore the nature of immigration globally and in this country. It is our hope that this will provide a perspective about its roots, realities, and implications for educators teaching and working with young immigrant children today.

Time to reflect ... *Understanding immigration*

Current times demand early educators to understand the implications of immigration for young children. Reflect on your own knowledge of immigration and consider what aspects of immigration are critical to be more fully understood.

This is a call for early childhood educators

Child immigrants have always been present in classrooms throughout the United States. Many and diverse are the stories of each child immigrant in classrooms still calling and waiting for everyone to hear and understand. In education, just as Sarah Dryden-Peterson stated, "Every child in every classroom brings a history to school" (2015, 2). In each story, events and incidents marking their experiences reveal the nature of their life trajectory as young child immigrants, whether they come from other countries or are born here. Thousands of young children continue to attend private and public preschool programs across the nation. With their families placing their hopes on early childhood educators, the question arises as to how well we do know them or if we are responding to their individual realities and needs.

Responding with empathy and professionalism

Reports show that a quarter of children in our country are children of immigrants (Zong, Batalova, and Burrows 2019), with most born in the United States. Through the years, their presence has been signaling for attention to their realities and needs. It especially calls for a focus on their personal stories and experiences (Dryden-Peterson 2015; Suárez-Orozco and Suárez-Orozco 2001). The diversity of cultures and languages that these children bring to our classrooms and programs has been and remains as the focus for those advocating for fairness and valuing of diversity (Moll 1992). Working with immigrant students and professionals, we have learned about their aspirations, efforts, and strengths. Some of us, immigrants ourselves, still remember the experiences and recognize the need for attention to the unique realities of immigration. Overall, whenever we delve into their stories, we realize there is a call for a thoughtful understanding of the circumstances and life experiences of child immigrants and their families. Many would ask why attention should be placed on immigrants. The answer is evidenced by the fact that immigration remains as an ongoing constituent component in our society. For educators, this underlines the due consideration into its multiple realities and its implications on planning, working, and responding to immigrant children. The stories learned about the youngest immigrants and their families call for empathy and thoughtful attention from everyone. Irrespective of their ethnicity, culture, or languages, children's future remains at stake. They await and count on society to respond with honest understanding, fairness, and equity to their needs (Box 1.3).

Box 1.3 Children and immigration: *Equity matters*

Through the pages in this chapter we have begun to examine the relevant need to learn about children and immigration. However, it still becomes pertinent to reiterate why educators must delve into this reality. Voices of children and their families resonate asking for understanding and for the support of educators and society. Responding to their needs is a matter of equity calling to inform and direct practices for young children. Immigration is a constant in the history of the country and reflected in the profile of many students in our classrooms. Whether they are newcomers or have lived for generations in the country, their immigrant stories remain individual, characterizing the children we teach and their own experience with immigration. Yet, we must honestly ask ourselves how much we know about what immigration entails. Experiences as teacher educators have shown us that while references to immigrants may be included in the content of coursework, delving into its realities requires more in-depth knowledge to build understanding. With thousands of children of immigrants in our classrooms, the need to explore and learn about the factors, motivations, experiences, and needs is heightened. Different from past decades when immigrants gravitated to traditionally known destinations in the country, today they live in most communities throughout the nation. This fact further alerts educators to be mindful about immigration and its implications in the education of young immigrants. Far from the discussions in the media, it is pertinent to build our knowledge about immigration to help us understand and appreciate its significance in the lives of children in our classrooms and communities. It may also contribute to understanding our own experience for those of us who are immigrants teaching and working in different capacities with and for young children.

Today, working with child immigrants calls for objective knowledge about the child's and their families' diverse realities. This is fundamental to cement practices in what is responsive and socially just for children. This is, in essence, another goal of this book, to support your work as an early childhood educator in gaining knowledge and encouraging you to explore immigration and its multifocal implications on the young child and family.

Families and children: A growing face of immigration

News about waves of immigrants leaving their homelands and of the perils experienced by hundreds of families and children has become a continual issue since the beginning of this century. Multiple crises have forced thousands to go beyond their borders (Taylor 2015). Groups of families currently lead the exodus, driven away to elude critical and dangerous realities in different parts of the world, including the Americas. What we have heard from many early childhood professionals is that their stories reveal the human dimension about immigration, calling for due diligence, attention, and compassionate understanding. Many early childhood professionals have also pointed out that current experiences also bring attention to the presence of immigrant families and their children that for generations have been present in our classrooms. Even in the midst of the 2020 pandemic, immigrants have continued their search for the well-being of their families and children.

While responses to the arriving immigrants continue to be determined, the call for attention to families and children loudly resounds in the world community. It also resonates for educators of young children advocating for fair and appropriate answers to their needs. Their circumstances are a reminder, as well, about the more than five million immigrant children from birth to age 5 living in the country (Migration Policy Institute 2017).

The drive to migrate

As mentioned earlier, motivations to migrate vary and are very personal. Many may find motivation in how relocating in other countries meets the needs and aspirations of their families. For many, this is part of the expectations of families where immigration is the option followed to realize goals of a better life (International Organization for Migration 2020; Suárez-Orozco and Suárez-Orozco 2001). The experience of the authors gathered from conversations with a group of Hispanic families, who shared why they moved, indicated how coming to the United States continues to be seen as the path to a better life. "Allá es donde hay esperanza," that's where there is hope, was the comment more commonly shared. Some were encouraged by relatives and friends who had migrated, a fact also identified by some researchers of the immigration process (Fratzke and Salant 2018; Valdez, Valentine, and Padilla 2013). Several of those interviewed by the authors mentioned encouragement from relatives as a leading reason to migrate as well. One person whose father came after his uncles who had previously immigrated shared how that created a trend in his family. Similar to his father, other relatives relocated to the United States. Still others came attracted by their professional aspirations and seeking opportunities. Overall, the ideal of freedom and opportunities remains as a strong motivator for thousands in this century just as it was before. Waves of current violence drive countless today to leave their country, seeking safety as expressed by many immigrants coming through the southern borders of the United States. Fear of current personal and social circumstances has been cited as a main motivation to leave their countries (Chishti and Hipsman 2014).

Immigration as a personal life event

Just as in the past, undeniably, today the experience of immigration is a personal and individual life event. Not all those who are immigrants share the same motivation or goal. Not all their stories are the same. Their destinies are shaped by their own individual circumstances. Some people are driven freely by their desire of a better life, pursuing employment, educational and professional opportunities in other countries, and hoping for a promising future. Political uncertainty and unrest drive many to leave their countries in search of stability for their families. This is what drove thousands in the past to leave their countries, who never thought they would become immigrants. It continues today. Serious and difficult circumstances in communities caused by extreme poverty, impact of natural disasters, and social insecurity may also motivate others to migrate (UNHCR 2018). In those cases, immigration is forced due to the severity of the circumstances. Ongoing efforts and responses from humanitarian organizations and government continue to assist in relocation of those forced to find new places due to extreme conditions and living circumstances (United Nations 2018). Recent natural disasters and circumstances in some parts of the world have highlighted the need for relocation of thousands of families and children.

Voices of Immigration: *I never thought we would become immigrants*

For many immigrants, the thought of leaving their homes was never something contemplated. Yet, as you will find in this account, with changing circumstances families seeking their children's well-being will find immigration as the option to safeguard their children.

In the 1960s and 1970s many Jamaicans felt that to succeed they had to migrate to the United States. The man on the street believed that the US streets were paved with gold and all they had to do was get here so they could share in the wealth. My husband and I had no intention of migrating. In the early 1970s he attended the University of Florida as part of an exchange program with the Jamaica School of Agriculture. After earning his doctorate, he returned to Jamaica.

When the political climate began to change, my husband who was dead set against migrating decided it was time to leave. There were two main reasons for this decision, our children would have more opportunities and the future

---

of the country was uncertain. This is our story and this story is a personal one and in no way represents the experience of all migrants.

The children were 8 and 10 and in the fifth and seventh grade when we migrated. Their first experience in the school system was when they were given a standardized test to determine if they were ready for the aforementioned grades. Because they scored higher than expected, they were given the test again with the same results. My husband and I did not know what to make of it. We wondered whether it was because they were Jamaicans and not expected to score that high or whether there was an error with the test. Needless to say, we never learned the reason.

Another incident which stood out for me was when my 10-year-old came home from middle school asking what it meant to be a wetback, because that is what he was being called by his classmates. At the time, we did not give the incident a serious thought, passing it off as kids' prank. Luckily for us there was no further incident.

As the years went by, our boys learned to code switch. When they were playing with the neighborhood kids they talked like them, but at home they reverted to the Jamaican accent, much to the amazement of parents of the American kids.

The next few years passed uneventfully until the then 15-year-old was in high school and we received a call from the principal. We panicked, thinking our son was not doing well in school, only to be told that he had been named a National Merit Scholar and the principal wanted to verify that we had permanent resident status.

My husband and I looked back at the decision we had made several years prior and determined we had made the right decision.

Immigrant population living in the United States

Why migrate? Every day we learn more about the reasons continuing to attract people to migrate. The answer may lie in the fact that the unending search for progress and a better life remains as a driving force, leading people to go beyond their homelands. Even with changes in immigration policies, immigration into the United States remains as a constant (Valdez, Valentine, and Padilla 2013). Thousands of immigrants arrive into the United States hopeful to achieve their dreams. In 2017, reports showed that approximately forty-five million foreign-born people (Table 1.2) were living in the country (Batalova and Alperin 2019), representing almost 14 percent of the nation's overall population (Radford and Noe-Bustamante 2019).

Table 1.2 Facts about immigrant population in the United States

Facts	
Total immigrant population	44.6 million
Unauthorized immigrant population	12 million
Immigrant children in the United States (under age 5)	0.7%
Immigrant children (ages 5–17)	5.1%

Source: Baker (2015); U.S. Census Bureau (2017).

Immigration status: A multiple reality

Access to education services and programs has brought attention to the immigration status of families and their children. Today, the fact that not all who migrate share the same immigration status has become even more accentuated. It is not uncommon to read or hear people talking about legal and illegal immigrants. Beyond geographical lines, existing laws in each country determine the status of those crossing its borders. Reasons forcing individuals to cross borders also affect the nature of their status as they arrive. Some will enter as *legal or authorized* immigrants, as it is designated in the United States. Those entering officially follow the country's prescribed process to enter accordingly with the respective immigration laws. Estimates show that annually about a million people arrive officially into the country (Table 1.2). In cases where others choose to circumvent the process, their entry is described as *illegal or undocumented* immigration. They are considered as nonauthorized immigrants in the United States, with reports estimating that about twelve million unauthorized immigrants live in the country. Because the authors believe in the dignity of every individual, the term "illegal" will not be used to refer to immigrants who entered unofficially.

Immigrants arriving unofficially

Estimates show that over 3 percent of the foreign born are unauthorized immigrants (Krogstad, Passel, and Cohn 2019). A large number of the unauthorized population have been residents in the country for over a decade and are parents of US-born children (Goo 2015; Krogstad, Passel, and Cohn 2019). Many of them opted to enter unofficially, driven away by difficult social, political, and economic realities in their countries. For many the incentive of finding better conditions for their families continues as a main motivation. In desperation, they opt for unauthorized channels to migrate, following what others have done. Recent years saw an increase in the numbers of immigrants and especially families crossing undocumented through the southern borders of the country (Table 1.3), with staggering numbers

Table 1.3 Migrants entering through the US southwest border (2017–19)

Year	Total
2017	415,517
2018	521,090
2019	977,509

Source: U.S. Department of Homeland Security (2019).

during 2018 and 2019 (U.S. Department of Homeland Security 2019). This trend, however, changed in the latter early part of 2019 with the implementation of new policies for those entering through the southern borders.

In recent times, reports show that many undocumented immigrants initially entered officially and stayed after their visas expired. Current debates on immigrants with unauthorized entry persist while calling for solutions. Advocates continue demanding actions to address their status, particularly when many have been residing in the nation for years.

Forced migration: The case of refugees and asylees

A variety of circumstances force some people to leave their countries. This is the case of refugees and asylees. Refugees and asylees are also included among those legally entering the country. The dangerous nature of their living circumstances forces them to seek protection in other places. Many of those who are forced to migrate today are escaping from violence, armed conflict, and life-threatening circumstances. Severity of conditions impede people from returning to their countries and make some unwilling to go back. In these cases, they take refuge by entering as *refugees*. They do not choose the country where they are relocated. Cases are reviewed by the United Nations High Commission for Refugees (UNHCR), the agency responsible for making recommendations for relocation as refugees to selected countries. In the United States, the Office of Refugee Resettlement provides assistance including transitional services to those arriving as refugees. Support services, including medical and social services, are intended to assist individuals and their families as they adjust to life in the United States (Congressional Research Service 2018). Since 1975, over three million people have been granted entry as refugees in the United States (USA for UNHCR 2019). Thirty thousand refugees were admitted during the fiscal year 2019 (Figure 1.3). Today, many individuals and their families continue to enter as refugees in the United States, including numerous children attending Head Start programs (Head Start 2018).

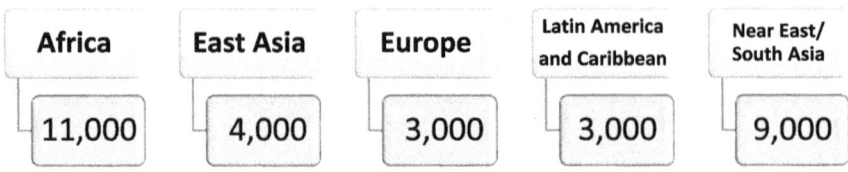

Figure 1.3 Refugees admitted into the United States (FY 2019).
Source: U.S. Department of State, Bureau of Population, Refugees and Migration. Refugee Processing Center (2019).

Those leaving because of political or religious persecution may seek asylum by entering as *asylees*. Humanitarian protection is granted to people in these situations. Their cases are reviewed and those found to be eligible are granted entry as asylees. Such was the case of many of the families who crossed the borders of the nation and applied for asylum into the United States in recent years. Various agencies provide services and programs to facilitate the adjustment of families and children into the country. International agencies such as the United Nations Refugee Agency protect and advocate for the rights of migrants, refugees, and asylees.

Growing diversity: The invaluable impact of immigration in the nation's communities

Immigration is a subject inherent in all facets of society in the United States. The energy and motivation of people who over the almost three hundred years have chosen to settle in the country are ingrained in its continuing history. History reveals the United States is a nation of immigrants, the heart and core of what the country is today and where immigrants continue to be the force building the nation and writing its story (Handlin 2002). Today, immigration remains as the source for the growing diversity characteristic of the nation. Reports show immigrants from new countries of origin are emerging as a new trend, denoting the changing ethnic diversity of the nation (Zong and Batalova 2019).

Time to reflect … *A nation of immigrants*

Whenever one hears the phrase "a nation of immigrants" referring to the United States, what images does it evoke for you? What experiences does it remind you of?

Immigration is an active and significant factor contributing to effect change beyond demographics. It influences the social, economic, and cultural trajectory of the receiving country as has been the case of the United States, whose own history emerges from the waves of immigration (Takaki 2008). Presently, the nation continues to experience a trend of growth that is further defining its social and cultural diversity. The influential vigor that immigrants bring to a country is appreciated whenever one considers all that is culturally infused into our communities. As in the past, immigrants today are contributing to the rich culturally diverse character of the nation. The wisdom, skills, and knowledge brought by its growing population continue to shape and enhance the future of the nation. Collectively, immigrants share their cultural heritage while they adjust to the culture of the country. The exchange embeds new skills, ideas, and behaviors that through time has become part of the country's cultural framework. Infusion of new views, opinions, and visions continues to maintain the dynamism of the country's overall culture.

Time to reflect … *Cultural contributions*

Immigrants bring to every community their heritage, cultural traditions, and practices. Take a moment to consider the cultures of immigrants in your community. What cultural elements have they shared and contributed to your community? If you are an immigrant, what has your culture contributed in your community?

Changing cultural diversity landscape

Today, the multiplicity of cultural groups that make up the United States reflect the global nature of society. Its more culturally diverse character has become evident in the last few decades across the nation's communities. Census data reveal that besides the traditional immigrant destination states, many others have become new destinations (Jacobs 2019). Among these, some states in the southern part of the nation like Georgia and North Carolina have multiplied their immigrant population. Language diversity has increased its presence, becoming now more evident across communities. It is not uncommon today to find signage and local publications in languages other than English. In education, the student population virtually representing the world is present in classrooms everywhere in the country. An estimated 25 percent of the nation's student population is of immigrant roots, numbers that showed an increase of 51 percent during the period of 1995–2014 (Camera 2016). Some states like California, Florida, Texas, New York, and New Jersey are known for their high concentration of immigrant student population. The past decades show that during 1980–2010, more newcomers arrived from Asia, Central America, and Africa, all adding to the country's increasing cultural and social diversity (Zong and Batalova 2019).

Time to reflect ... *Diversity in your community*

Diversity is a common parameter in many cities. Take a moment to reflect on the diverse elements that are characteristic of your own neighborhood or community. Consider which ones they are and how they influence the character of your community.

Immigrant destination states

Traditionally, some states have served as the main destination for immigrants arriving in the United States. A large immigrant population already describes people in states such as California, Florida, New York, New Jersey, and Texas. These states have served as destinations for immigrants for decades. Many immigrant groups live in communities in large metropolitan areas such as New York, New Jersey, Los Angeles, Dallas, and Miami. These cities are also known as having the largest immigrant population in the country (Zong and Batalova 2019). Immigrant presence has added a unique social and cultural flair to the cities, communities, and neighborhoods of the country. *Calle Ocho*, Eighth Street, and Little Haiti in Miami and the Chinatowns found in cities like New York or San Francisco are among other ethnic neighborhoods that are a vibrant reminder of the immigrant presence in the country. How the nation gained its immigrant character is briefly sketched in Box 1.4.

Box 1.4 Connecting ideas: *Snapshot of the immigration trajectory in the United States*

When did immigration start or what led to the growing immigrant character of the United States? A brief look at the past will help answer some of these questions to better appraise some of the current realities. Since the seventeenth century, when history recorded the arrival of the first groups of pilgrims, thousands have contributed to writing the history of the United States as a nation, formed by immigrants in this part of North America. With a population of 328 million, in 2018, 14 percent of people living in the country were foreign born, a term used in the United States to designate immigrants and their descendants (U.S. Census Bureau 2018a). With a new population census scheduled for 2020, projections estimate that the portrait of the nation will continue to affirm its deep immigration roots.

Historically, three main waves of immigration account for the nation's diverse population (Chishti, Hipsman, and Ball 2015; McLemore and Romo 2005). Table 1.4 shows the timelines of these waves and the ethnic nature of each one. Population increased significantly with the impact of the first two waves of immigrants that took place during the end of the nineteenth and early part of the twentieth centuries. Most of the immigrants who arrived during this time were European, particularly from the United Kingdom, Germany, and Scandinavian countries. Immigrants from Asia also arrived during the nineteenth century and settled in the West. Chinese immigrants, mostly coming as workers, came during the mid-nineteenth century, settling mainly in the western United States. Records also show Japanese immigrants arriving during the latter part of the 1800s. Mexicans came through the southwest borders where they had long historical ties to the region (McLemore and Romo 2005). The second immigration wave continued to maintain a mainly European origin for most of those that arrived, though this time coming from other European regions.

Table 1.4 Immigrant waves in the United States

First immigration wave (1820–89)	Second immigration wave (1890–1924)	Third immigration wave (1946–present)
• People from western and northern Europe	• People from southern and eastern Europe	• People from Latin America and Asia particularly after 1965
• Some Asian immigrants from China and Japan	• Some immigrants from Asia, mainly Japan and China	

Source: Daniels (2004); McLemore and Romo (2005).

Immigrants coming during the first two waves of immigration were predominantly European. However, the ethnic profile of the third and most recent immigration wave dramatically changed, leading to an increasing ethnic diversity in the nation. The third immigrant wave was significantly influenced by the passage of the new Immigration and Nationality Act of 1965, still current today. This new regulation dramatically transformed the ethnic character of those immigrating to the United States and "cleared the way for immigration from non-European countries" (Pew Research Center 2015, 65). Regulation changes also favored those with families already living in the country. Family reunification was one of the target goals of the 1965 Immigration Act that served as a boost for the arriving immigrants, which continues till date. Though the 1965 Act was originally intended to maintain the same ethnic composition of the nation and expected European immigration to continue, the outcome was a wave of ethnically diverse immigrants that led to the intense diversity of current times (Zolberg 2006). With a lower influx of immigrants from Europe, half of those entering the country were people from Latin America, with about a quarter of newcomers from Asia (Pew Research Center 2015). Present projections by demographers point to a higher incidence of people from Asia to characterize future immigrants to the United States (López, Ruiz, and Patten 2017). This is already evident, with reports showing that countries of origin of the largest immigrant groups arriving during 2010–17 were India and China (Zong and Batalova 2019). Estimates indicate that, overall, immigrants arriving into the United States in the coming years will become as the most influential factor in the future population growth (Vespa, Armstrong, and Medina 2018).

Who is coming?

Immigration legislation has dramatically influenced entry into the nation. It continues today and explains the diversity present in our classrooms. A highly contentious topic, regulations on border entries evolved from a rather open-door policy until after the Civil War, to one of centralized control by the federal government (Zolberg 2006). Events since 9/11 have intensified immigration enforcement and scrutiny (Chishti and Bergeron 2011). Since then, some consider that there has been a reemergence of prejudiced attitudes and views about immigrants from some parts of the world. It evidently made it more an issue of *who* is coming.

Until the 1880s, most of the people in the United States had roots in the western and northern European regions, characterizing the nation's population as mostly homogenous. However, this began to change with the arrival of

European immigrants from other parts of the continent. Economic issues, social changes, and crisis in Europe during the nineteenth century motivated many to sail to the United States in the hopes of finding better opportunities. This time, immigrants were coming from other regions of the world, which some groups saw as a threat to the nation's racial homogeneity that until then was depictive of the US society. Views about racial differences, sadly, generated actions and practices that challenge equity ideals, integral to US societal principles. Box 1.5 further discusses some of the factors concerning views about race differences.

Box 1.5 Connecting ideas: *Race and immigration: Influence on immigration policies*

Perceptions and views about race have also influenced the immigration process. Despite the faulty ideas about racial differences, it is pertinent to mention its impact in the immigration policies and practices. From a social justice perspective, this would explain some of the preceding events still influencing views about immigrants. Historically, as the nation began to experience a larger influx of people coming from eastern and southern Europe and some from Asia, restrictive regulations began to be considered. At the core of concerns was the impact of the race factor in the immigration process fueled by the concern about who was coming to settle in the country. With people arriving from southern and eastern Europe, views about their cultural and ethnic differences soon gave way to prejudice and unfair concerns. The alluded concerns emerged out of the influence of ideas about race grounded on social Darwinism. This view claimed the preeminence of certain racial groups for the success of society (McLemore and Romo 2005). For the proponents of such views, the newcomers were seen as not sharing the common racial traits and heritage that defined the mostly western and northern Europeans from previous immigrations. The open discriminatory racist views of the influential group resulted in restrictive regulations that limited or excluded some of the ethnic groups from entering the United States. Driven by fear of change and by unfounded ideas about race superiority, their persisting influence led to the enactment of restrictive and exclusionary immigration regulations. In 1882, the Chinese Exclusion Act became the first legislation controlling immigration into the country. The infamous regulation openly closed the country's doors to Chinese immigrants (Zolberg 2006). Rising immigration during the 1920s mobilized around the race ideological views, and supporters, putting pressure on the government, called for further restrictions. Their efforts led to the Immigration Act of 1924, which imposed annual national-origin quotas. The quota formulas restricted the number of people allowed to enter from certain countries given, in what was considered as a step to preserve the character of the US society at the time. Sadly, this trend distanced itself from the welcoming mission proclaimed by many who stood and continue today to advocate for the rights of immigrants.

Impact of new regulations: A changing ethnic landscape

More and more, immigration of families and children to the United States over the past few years reveals its diverse and multicultural nature. This has given a significantly different character to immigration patterns from previous decades. How did this happen, one would question, as children and families in our classrooms and communities confirm the diversity of the country's population.

Dramatic changes came with the signing of a new immigration law in 1965. The Immigration and Nationality Act of 1965, known as the Hart–Celler Act for the legislators who served as its sponsors, opened doors to a more diverse ethnic profile of immigrants, transforming the cultural landscape of the country. Signed by President Lyndon Johnson on October 3, 1965, it changed the regulations for entering the country. Different from the previous immigration laws, the 1965

Photo 1.1 President Johnson signing the 1965 Immigration Act.
Source: U.S. National Archives. Photograph A1421-33A; Photograph of President Lyndon B. Johnson Signing the Immigration Act; 10/3/1965. [Online Version, https://www.docsteach.org/documents/document/lbj-immigration-act, July 21, 2019]

Immigration and Nationality Act repealed the national-origin quotas, which, in the opinion of Chishti, Hipsman and Ball (2015), kept immigration into the nation to be mostly European. Instead, the 1965 law favored prioritizing admission of immigrants with family members already living in the country, encouraging many to bring their family members. Though, as posited by some, its goal was to attract further European immigration into the United States, however, it had little effect.

With the elimination of the quota systems and of Asian exclusionary regulations, ethnic and cultural diversity of immigrants denoted those arriving (Zolberg 2006). Changes in the immigration regulations together with rising difficult sociopolitical and economic conditions in Latin America and Asia gave people from these continents an impetus to immigrate into the United States (Daniels 2014; McLemore and Romo 2005). The result was a third immigration wave with a stream of people representing a multitude of diverse cultures and places that enriched and changed the ethnic and cultural nature of US immigration. This continues today. Diversity was further emphasized with the signing of the Immigration Act of 1990. Signed by President George Bush, the law boosted immigration and created the diversity immigrant visas for individuals from countries where immigration was lower (S.358-Immigration Act of 1990).

United States: A nation of ongoing immigration

Immigration remains as a dynamic force in the nation, which, already present in classrooms serving young children, reflects itself throughout the country. Recent census records showed over 44.5 million of foreign born living in communities across the nation (U.S. Bureau of the Census 2017). Beyond states traditionally serving as main destinations for immigrants like California, Florida, and Texas, other states have observed a significant growth in their immigrant population during recent years. During the period of 2000–17, North Dakota, Delaware, Tennessee, South Dakota, and Kentucky experienced an immigrant population growth of over 100 percent (Zong, Batalova, and Burrows 2019). Reports reveal that in 2017, 56 percent of child immigrants lived in California, Texas, New York, Florida, and New Jersey (Zong, Batalova, and Burrows 2019).

At the national level, people with immigrant roots marked its "highest share since 1910" (Tavernise 2018). Estimates indicate that over the coming decades, it is expected that the United States will continue to be characterized by its diverse immigrant population (Colby and Ortman 2015). By 2050, it is projected that

82 percent of the population increase will be as a result of incoming immigrants and their descendants (Passel and Cohn 2008).

Continuing arrival of immigrants

Social and political realities since the beginning of this century together with lingering inequalities in some parts of the world continue driving people to leave their homes. For many of these immigrants, the United States has been their targeted destination. The search for opportunities and a future for their families remains as a driving force. The glimpse of hope and the accounts from those who preceded them continue to fuel their energies to migrate, leading to the continuous arrival of immigrants. Severity of circumstances in some areas may also explain the growing immigration experienced during the past decades of some ethnic groups. This was particularly observed by those arriving through the southwest borders of the nation adding up to almost a million during the 2019 fiscal year (U.S. Department of Homeland Security 2019). Thousands of immigrant families arriving with their children have called attention to their needs and circumstances. This has also given emphasis to the realities experienced by children of immigrants already living across the nation.

Time to reflect … *The personal and human side of immigration*

People movement or immigration is more than just a demographical reality. For so many it is what defines their very individual story. Take time to think about yourself, your family, or someone you know with immigrant experiences. Remember some of the stories shared about those experiences and consider what made it become a very personal experience.

In our classrooms: A growing diverse and multicultural immigrant population

Today, classrooms and communities across the nation are a reflection of the diversity of immigrants arriving after 1965. This was further expanded by the 1990 Immigration Act that opened the doors to diversity of immigrants through its visa program still continuing today. Indeed, it could be affirmed that while the country continued to be a nation of immigrants, it actually became the home of the most ethnically diverse immigrant population. School enrollment has become more ethnically diverse than ever, showing an increase of students from countries such as Nepal, Myanmar, and African nations.

Two main ethnic groups have significantly contributed to transforming the ethnic character of the nation, Hispanics or Latinos and people of Asian origin. Though both groups already had a long-time presence in the nation, they both experienced a substantial growth since the 1960s. That growth continues today, with both becoming the largest number of immigrant ethnic groups in the nation. Their presence is already evident in classrooms throughout the nation.

Immigrants in our nation: The growing Hispanic or Latino population

A large majority of immigrants arriving in recent decades are Hispanic. At present, Hispanics or Latinos are the largest ethnic minority in the United States. Hispanic population accounts for almost fifty-nine million (Zong, Batalova, and Burrows 2019), representing 18 percent of the national population in 2018. In classrooms throughout the nation, 25 percent of the K-12 students are of Hispanic descent (López, Krogstad, and Flores 2018). Ethnically, Hispanics are a very heterogeneous group. With a variety of cultures and indigenous languages, they are an example of diversity in itself. Their cultures are as diverse as they are as an ethnic group. Under the term "Hispanics," we find people with roots and heritage from every country in Latin America including the Spanish Caribbean. Though many Latinos speak indigenous languages, Spanish is the common language shared by most as an ethnic group.

Mexicans are the largest Hispanic immigrant group in the nation, representing 63 percent of people with Hispanic roots (Flores 2017). They are followed by Puerto Ricans[2] representing almost 10 percent of the total Hispanic population. Cubans comprise about 4 percent of the population. In recent years, people from both Central and South America have increased their presence. This has been due to the growing arrival of people particularly from Guatemala, Honduras, and El Salvador.

Long-time presence of Hispanics in the United States

Presence of Hispanics is evident in classrooms throughout the nation as well as in communities. By now the largest ethnic group, Hispanics have a

---

[2] People born in Puerto Rico are US citizens at birth.

long historical trajectory in the United States dating back particularly to the 1800s. During the 1860s, records show that 155,000 Hispanics were living in the nation. Of these, 81 percent were of Mexican roots (Flores et al. 2017). Different from other immigrant groups, historically there has been a standing relationship between Mexicans and the United States. This relationship evolved out of their geographical location, shared economic interests, and historical events. Agricultural interests, among others, laid the ground for Mexican workers to come since the nineteenth century. During the 1940s, an agreement between the United States and Mexico led to the *bracero* program. The agreement brought thousands of Mexicans to work in US farms, contributing to the vital success of agriculture and of the economy during the war years. This set a trend for thousands of immigrants who became seasonal workers still traveling today with their families to work in the fields throughout the country.

Cubans constitute another large immigrant group representing close to 3 percent of the immigrant population. Since 1959, when the Castro regime took over power in Cuba, thousands were forced into exile. About 1.3 million Cubans live in the United States (Blizzard and Batalova 2020), with a large number living in Florida. The Pedro Pan flights, which are discussed in Chapter 2, took hundreds of children from Havana to Florida, sent away by their desperate families to escape the Castro regime. Hundreds of others have continued to flee the island. Recent decades have witnessed large numbers from the Dominican Republic, with many arriving in search of better social, educational, and economic opportunities. Immigration of Hispanics continues, though a slight decrease has been observed in recent years, particularly of people from Mexico (Zong, Batalova, and Burrows 2019).

Time to reflect ... *The immigrant experience*

In the children's book *A Piece of Home* (Watts 2016), the author shares the following impressions:

> In swift movements and rapid time, I found my world packed into three boxes and one suitcase.

What are the impressions about the experience of immigration revealed in this quote? What are the emotions that are reflected?

Table 1.5 Estimates of the ten main Asian immigrant groups in the United States (2017)

Ethnicity	Number
China	4,888,040
Asian India	4,121,944
Filipino	3,912,921
Vietnamese	2,067,527
Korean	1,816,567
Japanese	1,469,637
Pakistani	500,433
Thai	300,319
Hmong	296,890
Laotian	263,296

Source: Adapted from U.S. Census Bureau (2018c).

Growing Asian immigrant population

Today, the presence of children and families from Asia has become more familiar across communities. In the past decade, Asians have become the second largest growing immigrant group in the nation. A substantial increase in Asian immigrants emerged after the passing of the 1965 Act, which presently continues. With an estimated population of twenty-one million (Census Bureau 2018), Asians are another heterogeneous group that includes a diversity of ethnicities, cultures, and languages. In 2017, students of Asian roots accounted for 5 percent of the US public school enrollment (de Brey et al. 2019). For Asian immigrants, the United States is their main immigration destination. Projections estimate a continuous growth, with Asians becoming the largest ethnic minority in the nation by 2055 (Zong and Batalova 2016). Recent influx of immigrants from Asia placed Chinese as the leading group followed by immigrants from India (Table 1.5).

Immigration and education: With eyes on equitable educational practices for all

In a society grounded on immigration, issues and topics about immigrants are never absent from the education agenda in the United States. Their presence is a reminder about the need for attention to their experiences, realities, and needs. Two-and-a-half percent of the world's child immigrants live in the United States. At present, young immigrant children constitute almost 6 percent of the nation's population. In classrooms throughout the nation, voices of children and families with immigrant backgrounds blend along with those speaking in languages other than English. They evidence the reality of a society with continuously growing roots in immigration and the ever-changing nature of the country's national demographics. Already, immigrant children in the United States have shown a steady increase since the 1990s, with close to 24 percent of young children having immigrant parents (Fortuny, Hernandez, and Chaudry 2010; Park and McHugh 2014). Projections predict that in the coming decades, immigrants will be a significant factor contributing to the nation's population growth. In fact, it is expected for the foreign-born population "to rise from 44 million people today to 69 million in 2060, growing from 14 percent to 17 percent of the population" (Vespa, Armstrong, and Medina 2018, 4). These projections carry relevant implications for everyone, and especially for educators. Societally, the notion of an immigrant majority tacitly indicates the higher level of diversity of an already multicultural society. Further impact is clearly seen on education where the increasing diversity of students demands attention to how well programs and services offered respond and address their well-being. An issue of equity, voices of educators and advocates have raised the need to consider their development and education with fairness. The reality of a growing immigrant student population reminds everyone that beyond their immigrant realities, "*A child is a child, no matter why she leaves home, where she comes from or where she is and how she got there. And every child deserves protection, care and all the support and services she needs to thrive*" (UNICEF 2020, n.p. [emphasis added]).

Fairness in early education demands attention to the cultures, personal circumstances, and diversity of experiences of the youngest immigrants attending programs across the country. At the heart of the experiences of every child, equity continues as the marker for what education owes to them. This is precisely what the National Association for the Education of Young Children (NAEYC 2019) called for in its position statement on equity. The dignity and the rights of every child to receive and experience the same quality is at stake as society faces an increased presence of immigrants. This time the challenge is to move the discourse into concrete actions for the thousands of immigrant children and their families already in our programs and for the many yet to come.

Early childhood: Children's most vulnerable years

The early childhood years are times where every child waits and relies on society as their development unfolds. These are also the times of greatest vulnerability. Studies have revealed that experiences and conditions during early childhood demand consideration to ensure children's successful development. This premise emphasizes consideration to the experience of immigration and its implications on the child's developmental well-being. The fact that they are more ethnically, linguistically, and culturally diverse has made them become "more visible minorities" (Suarez-Orozco, Yoshikawa, and Tseng 2015), leading many to experience discrimination, even when almost 90 percent of child immigrants are born in the United States. In particular, reports from studies have revealed that anti-immigrant rhetoric and the hostility characterizing some environments negatively impact the young child (American Psychological Association 2012; Rojas-Flores and Medina-Vaughn 2019). Many young immigrant children continue to be exposed to traumatic experiences caused by the instability of their family's legal status and the fear of family separation that many have come to experience. Still others have been victimized by the experience of immigration itself and the response from practices many have endured (Henderson and Baily 2016). No less harmful is the derogatory tone of conversations and name-calling, which, propelled by an anti-immigrant climate, some experience. Some adults born to immigrant parents that the authors interviewed still remembered with sadness the offensive words and epithets they heard during their childhood. Their voices evidence and support the calling for addressing their diversity and realities with respect and responsive attention.

At stake is the fact that experiences, programs, and services demand consideration of the needs of a developing child, times marking the most critical period for their individual future success. Children's rights to feel pride in their heritage and experiencing opportunities that contribute to their optimal development go beyond frontiers and political agendas, clearly affirmed by the Convention of the Rights of the Child (United Nations 1989). These rights are what mark the agenda for equitable attention to immigrant children in every society. They also underline the need for advocacy efforts to bring forward the voice of children and their families and their calling for socially just experiences.

Social justice: A cornerstone for equity

The life realities of immigrants and ethnic groups are a constant reminder about the persistent need for fairness that everyone living in a democratic society is entitled to enjoy. As a long-standing topic in the education agenda of the United States, interest on issues and services for students with immigrant roots has intensified. Emphasis on social justice has permeated discussions refocusing attention on equity and fair educational experiences, revisiting practices for immigrants in schools and programs throughout the nation (Abo-Zena 2018; Robles-Meléndez, Valdés, and Robles 2018). However, obstacles still prevent many young immigrant children from receiving equitable experiences. Educators, advocates, and the public continue to call out for ensuring socially just experiences and policies inclusive of and for all children.

With the public eye centered on the conditions and experiences of immigrants, the successful development of young children and their families has also made it into a subject of critical interest in early childhood education. Ethically, as a core value for early childhood educators, we are called to respect the child's dignity, uniqueness, and diversity underlying the expectations of the profession (NAEYC 2011, 2019). Clearly, in early childhood education, the need is for driving the social justice agenda into action for young children and families with immigrant backgrounds.

The growing number of immigrant young children in our classrooms demands greater emphasis and attention in the educational agenda. Several issues remain waiting for appropriate answers to equitably respond to the needs of children. Among the issues, language diversity particularly due to the highly multilingual student population requires a more holistic and equity grounded consideration. Similarly, discriminatory practices experienced by many children and their families because of their culture and immigrant status urgently demand attention (Casas and Cabrera 2011; Philbin and Ayón 2016). While debates continue, we must make sure that the rights and well-being of child immigrants are safeguarded. A long-standing reality and priority for responsive and socially just early childhood educational experiences, consideration to the needs of young child migrants will be the focus of the chapters ahead.

Time to reflect ... *Growing immigrant population*

You may already work in a highly culturally diverse community or in one with emerging diversity. With projections for the country to increase its immigrant character, as an early childhood educator, what considerations are implicit to you in this reality?

An enduring reality: Immigrant children

The news media has opened the eyes of society to a continuing immigrant reality. They are the faces of young child immigrants. Those we have seen in recent years have transformed society's views on immigration. To most, immigrants have the face of adults. The fact is, as most would agree, that through time, children have been a continuous part of immigration across the world just as it has been in the United States. Some of us may have experienced it as part of our own personal history. Indeed, so many of us in early education worked and continue to work today with child immigrants and their families from a diversity of ethnic roots. Their story is ongoing.

To a large extent, the majority of studies about immigrants have placed attention on the adult or family. Some researchers even posited that the focus was more on the immigrant impact on the employment and socioeconomic fabric of the country rather than on children (Forbes and Simes 2016). Typically, it is mostly adults who venture migrating into other places; yet, the presence of children is recorded in the historical chronicles about immigration. Meanwhile, experiences of children were kept rather shrouded by their invisibility. The spotlight was never as clearly targeted on child immigrants as it is today. Events of recent years in the early part of the century have shifted the focus, bringing up for consideration the impact of the immigration process for a child. They have also revealed the severity of circumstances alerting every one of their experiences. Today, with attention focused on the child immigrant, the imperative is for addressing the childhood experience of those coming today and of the thousands already living in our communities. They all deserve to receive quality and responsible services and programs.

Time to reflect … *The youngest immigrants in our classrooms*

Today, hundreds of children continue as in the past to arrive in new lands. Many of them may live in your community. Imagine being a child arriving into a new country and think about what some of your most pressing needs would be. What would make you feel welcome into a new country or community?

Hope and a future for children

Practices addressing the needs of families and children with immigrant roots have been an area of concern in education for many decades and especially in early education. Social, political, and armed conflict particularly since the 2010 decade in some parts of the world have created difficult and threatening situations for many families and children. Images of families and children risking their lives as they cross the sea or walk thousands of miles have brought the enduring realities of immigrants to everyone. For early childhood educators, the grim situation experienced by children and families has raised attention to the realities of immigration and the need for action and reasonable attention to all children of immigrants. In particular, it has made everyone aware about the need to consider the appropriateness and fairness of responses and practices for the immigrant child and their families. This is an imperative not only for those arriving today but also for the thousands already living and attending our programs.

An urgent call for action

that every child has an inherent right to life. (Article 6, Convention on the Rights of the Child [United Nations 1989])

A community of voices has formed, rising to denounce their critical situations and the need to address the immigrant children's well-being and future. As the epigraph states, advocates for children recognize what the Convention of the Rights of the Child asserted, calling for everyone to safeguard children's future. Questions arise as to the reasons and conditions forcing increased number of immigrants with young children to leave their countries. Concerns are particularly with the many unauthorized immigrants arriving through the US border areas. In the latter part of 2018 and 2019, images of caravans of migrants from Central America on their way to the United States, many with children, elevated the need for attention and responsive attention to their realities. Meanwhile, society must also look for answers to the circumstances leading to the tragedies experienced by young children and their families in some parts of the world. As answers are sought, it is relevant for early childhood educators to delve into some of the conditions and factors depicting immigration within the scope of the global society.

In the midst of a globalized society, the first decades of the century continue to witness the increasing number of people leaving their birthplaces and moving across borders (Connor 2016b). Some of the factors driving their migration discussed earlier highlight the magnitude of human rights issues, above all affecting the well-being of young children and their families. Children cannot wait, as childhood demands actions promptly and fairly.

Beyond statistical data, the voices of children resonate, calling for support and action. For early childhood educators, questions remain as to the needs and practices that will best address the realities and needs of children and their families. To that end, in the chapters that follow we will focus on examining and deepening discussions about their realities.

Key ideas

- Immigration, the movement of people across borders, is an integral phenomenon to society. It impacts the social, economic, and cultural dimensions of a country.
- People movement is caused by a variety of reasons. It can be a voluntary decision or forced due to the severity of circumstances. There are push and pull factors that influence immigration.
- Immigration in the twenty-first century has become the subject of heated debates by the public and governments. In some countries, immigration has reached crisis levels demanding humanitarian efforts and socially just decisions.
- The presence of children as immigrants has become the focus of attention during the 2010 decade. Their needs call for concerted efforts focused on ensuring their rights and protection. Social justice provides emphasis on ensuring children receive equal and appropriate services and programs.
- Attention to the needs of children and their families immigrating into the United States has brought to light the reality of life as immigrants.

To think, do, and reflect ...

1. Considering the factors motivating individuals and families to immigrate, which ones would you say are those that led people you know to immigrate?

2. In what ways has immigration changed and transformed the landscape of countries and communities?
3. Think about your own community. In what ways has the character of your community changed over the past several years?
4. As an early childhood educator, what are the main implications of immigration in your community?

References

Abo-Zena, Mona. 2018. "Supporting immigrant-origin children: Grounding teacher education in critical developmental perspectives and practices." *Teacher Educator* 53(3): 263–76.

Adair, Jennifer. 2015. *The Impact of Discrimination on the Early Schooling Experiences of Children from Immigrant Families*. Washington, DC: Migration Policy Institute.

Aikens, Nikki, Emily Knas, Lizabeth Malone, Louisa Tarullo, and Jessica Harding. 2017. *A Spotlight on Dual Language Learners in Head Start: FACES 2014, OPRE Report 2017-99*, Washington, DC: Office of Planning, Research, and Evaluation, Administration for Children and Families, U.S. Department of Health and Human Services.

American Psychological Association. 2012. *Crossroads: The psychology of immigration in the new century. APA Presidential Task Force on Immigration*. Retrieved from http://www.apa.org/topics/immigration/report.aspx.

Amigó, Maria. 2012. "Liminal but competent: Latin American migrant children and school in Australia." *Child Studies in Asia-Pacific Contexts* 2(1): 61–75.

Baker, B. 2015. *Estimates of the Unauthorized Illegal Alien Population Residing in the United States: January 2015. Population Estimates*. Washington, DC: Office of Immigration Statistics, Department of Homeland Security.

Batalova, Jeanne, and Elijah Alperin. 2019. *Immigrants in the U.S. with the Fastest Growing Foreign-Born Populations*. Migration Policy Institute. Retrieved from https://www.migrationpolicy.org/article/immigrants-us-states-fastest-growing-foreign-born-populations.

Batalova, Jeanne, Brittany Blizzard, and Jessica Bolter. 2020. *Frequently requested statistics on immigrants and immigration in the United States*. Migration information source. Retrieved from https://www.un.org/development/desa/en/news/population/international-migrant-stock-2019.html.

Bolter, Jessica. 2019. "Explainer: Who is an immigrant." *Explainers*. Retrieved from https://www.migrationpolicy.org/content/explainer-who-immigrant.

Brennan, Megan. 2018. "Record-high 75% of American say immigration is good thing." *Gallup Poll*. Retrieved from https://news.gallup.com/poll/235793/record-high-americans-say-immigration-good-thing.

aspx?g_source=link_NEWSV9&g_medium=TOPIC&g_campaign=item_&g_
content=Record-High%252075%2525%2520of%2520Americans%2520Say%2520Im
migration%2520Is%2520Good%2520Thing.

Burrone, Sara, Bina D'Costa and Goran Holmqvist. 2018. *Child-related concerns and migration decisions: Evidence from the Gallup world poll*. Office of Research, Innocenti Working Paper. WP2018-17. December. Retrieved from https://www. unicef-irc.org/publications/pdf/Child-related-concerns-migration-decisions- evidence-gallup-poll.pdf.

Camera, Lauren. 2016. "The increase in immigrant students test tolerance." *US News*. Retrieved from https://www.usnews.com/news/blogs/data-mine/ articles/2016-01-05/number-of-immigrant-students-is-growing.

Casas, J. Manuel, and Ana Cabrera. 2011. "Latino/a immigration: Actions and outcomes based on perceptions and emotions or facts?" *Hispanic Journal of Behavioral Science* 33(3): 283–303.

Chishti, Muzzafar, and Claire Bergeron. 2011. "Post-9/11 policies dramatically alter the U.S. immigration landscape." *Policy Beat*. September 8. Migration Policy Institute. Retrieved from https://www.migrationpolicy.org/article/ post-911-policies-dramatically-alter-us-immigration-landscape/.

Chishti, Muzaffar, and Faye Hipsman. 2014. *Dramatic Surge in the Arrival of Unaccompanied Children Has Deep Roots and No Simple Solutions*. Washington, DC: Migration Policy Institute.

Chishti, Muzaffar, Faye Hipsman, and Isabell Ball. 2015. *Fifty Years on, the 1965 Immigration and Nationality Act Continues to Reshape the United States*. Washington, DC: Migration Policy Institute. Retrieved from https://www.migrationpolicy.org/ article/increased-central-american-migration-united-states-may-prove-enduring- phenomenon.

Colby, Sandra, and Jennifer Ortman. 2015. *Projections of the Size and Composition of the U.S. Population: 2014–2060*. Current Population Reports, P25-1143. Washington, DC: U.S. Census Bureau.

Congressional Research Service. 2018. *Refugee Admissions and Resettlement Policy*. Washington, DC: CRS. Retrieved from https://fas.org/sgp/crs/misc/RL31269.pdf.

Connor, Phillip. 2016a. "Migrant remittances worldwide drop in 2015 for first time since the Great Recession." *Fact Tank*. Pew Research. Retrieved from http://www.pewresearch.org/fact-tank/2016/08/31/ migrant-remittances-worldwide-drop-in-2015-for-first-time-since-great-recession/.

Connor, Phillip. 2016b. "International migration: Key findings from the U.S., Europe and the world." *Fact Tank*. December. Pew Research. Retrieved from http://www.pewresearch.org/fact-tank/2016/12/15/ international-migration-key-findings-from-the-u-s-europe-and-the-world/.

Crawford, Emily. 2017. "The ethic of community and incorporating undocumented immigrant concerns into ethical school leadership." *Educational Administration Quarterly* 53(2): 147–79.

Daniels, Roger. 2004. *Guarding the Golden Door. American Immigration Policies and Immigrants since 1882*. New York: Hill and Wang, a division of Farrar, Straus and Giroux.

de Brey, Cristobal, Lauren Musu, Joel McFarland, Sydney Wilkinson-Flicker, Melissa Diliberti, Anlan Zhang, Claire Branstetter, and Xiaolei Wang. 2019. *Status and Trends in the Education of Racial and Ethnic Groups 2018* (NCES 2019–038). U.S. Department of Education. Washington, DC: National Center for Education Statistics. Retrieved from https://nces.ed.gov/pubsearch/.

Dryden-Peterson, Sarah. 2015. *The Educational Experiences of Refugee Children in Countries of First Asylum*. Washington, DC: Migration Policy Institute.

Duta, Ana Maria, Sonia Kalamntaryan, Simon McMahon, Francesco Sermi, D. Tarchi, and Giuliana Urso. 2018. *Atlas of Migration 2018*. Luxembourg: Publications Office of the European Union.

Fix, Michael, Demetrios Papademetriou, Jeanne Batalova, Aaron Terrazas, Serena Lin, and Michelle Mittelstadt. 2009. *Migration and the Global Recession: A Report Commissioned by the BBC World Service*. Washington, DC: Migration Policy Institute.

Flores, Antonio. 2017. *How the U.S. Hispanic Population Is Changing*. Washington, DC: Pew Research Center.

Flores, Antonio, Gustavo López, and Jynnah Radford. 2017. *Facts on U.S. Latinos, 2015: Statistical Portrait of Hispanics in the United States*. Washington, DC: Pew Research Center.

Forbes, Joan, and Daniela Simes. 2016. "Relations between child poverty and new migrant child status, academic attainment and social participation: Insights using social capital theory." *MDPI Journal Education Sciences* 6(24): 1–5.

Fortuny, Karina, Donald Hernandez, and Ajay Chaudry. 2010. *Young children of immigrants. The leading edge of America's future*. August, Brief no. 3. The Urban Institute.

Fratzke, Susan, and Bryan Salant. 2018. *Moving beyond Root Causes: The Complicated Relationship between Development and Migration*. Policy Brief. January. Washington, DC: Migration Policy Institute.

Freire, Paulo. [1974] 2013. *Education for Critical Consciousness*. London: Bloomsbury.

Global Migration Group. 2008. *International Migration and Human Rights. Challenges and Opportunities on the Threshold of the 60th Anniversary of the Universal Declaration of Human Rights*. Retrieved from http://www.globalmigrationgroup.org/system/files/uploads/documents/Int_Migration_Human_Rights.pdf.

Goldin, Ian. 2016. *How Immigration Has Changed the World—For the Better*. World Economic Forum. Retrieved from https://www.weforum.org/agenda/2016/01/how-immigration-has-changed-the-world-for-the-better/.

Goo, Sara. 2015. *Unauthorized Immigrants: Who They Are and What the Public Thinks*. Pew Research Center. Retrieved from https://www.pewresearch.org/fact-tank/2015/01/15/immigration/.

Goodwin, Lin. 2017. "Who is in the classroom now? Teacher preparation and the education of immigrant children." *Educational Studies* 53(5): 433–49.

Handlin, Oscar. 2002. *The Uprooted: The Epic Story of the Great Migrations That Made the American People* (2nd ed.). Philadelphia: University of Pennsylvania Press.

Head Start. 2018. *Integrating Refugees into the Head Start Community.* Retrieved from https://eclkc.ohs.acf.hhs.gov/culture-language/article/integrating-refugees-head-start-community.

Hek, Rachel. 2005. "The role of education in the settlement of young refugees in the UK: The experiences of young refugees." *Practice* 17(3): 157–71.

Henderson, Schuyler, and Charles Baily. 2016. "In their own words: Immigration and pediatric mental health in 2016." *Journal of the Academy of Child & Adolescent Psychiatry* 55(10): 833–4.

Hirschman, Charles. 2007. "The impact of immigration on American society: Looking back to the future." *Transit-Europaische Revue, 32*. Retrieved from https://faculty.washington.edu/charles/new%20PUBS/A110.pdf.

International Organization for Migration. 2015. *How the World Views Migration.* Geneva, Switzerland: Global Migration Data Analysis Centre. International Organization for Migration. Retrieved from https://publications.iom.int/system/files/how_the_world_gallup.pdf.

International Organization for Migration. 2018. *Global Migration Indicators 2018.* Berlin, Germany: Global Migration Data Analysis Centre. International Organization for Migration. Retrieved from https://publications.iom.int/system/files/pdf/global_migration_indicators_2018.pdf.

International Organization for Migration. 2019. *Key Migration Terms.* Retrieved from https://www.iom.int/key-migration-terms.

International Organization for Migration. 2020. *World Migration Report 2020.* Retrieved from https://publications.iom.int/books/world-migration-report-2020.

Jacobs, Paul. 2019. *Where the Foreign-Born Lives Has Changed over Time.* U.S. Census Bureau. Retrieved from https://www.census.gov/library/stories/2019/05/where-nations-foreign-born-live-has-changed-over-time.html.

Jones, Bradley. 2019. *Majority of Americans Continue to Say Immigrants Strengthen the U.S. Fact Tank. News in Numbers.* Washington, DC: Pew Research Center.

Jordan, Miriam. 2019. "Family separation may have hit more migrant children than reported." *New York Times.* January 17. Retrieved from https://www.nytimes.com/2019/01/17/us/family-separation-trump-administration-migrants.html.

Kates, Graham, and Camilo Montoya-Galvez. 2020. "Officials ignored child separation warnings, report finds: 'I was called a broken record.'" *CBS News.* March 5. Retrieved from https://www.cbsnews.com/news/officials-ignored-child-separation-warnings-report-finds/?intcid=CNI-00-10aaa3a.

Kosho, Joana. 2016. "Media influence on public opinion attitudes toward the migration crisis." *International Journal of Scientific & Technology Research* 5(5): 86–91. Retrieved from http://www.ijstr.org/final-print/may2016/Media-Influence-On-Public-Opinion-Attitudes-Toward-The-Migration-Crisis.pdf.

Krogstad, Jens Manuel, Jeffrey Passel, and D'Vera Cohn. 2019. "5 facts about illegal immigration in the U.S." *Fact Tank*. Pew Research Center. Retrieved from https://www.pewresearch.org/fact-tank/2019/06/12/5-facts-about-illegal-immigration-in-the-u-s/.

Krogstad, Jens Manuel, Ana González-Barrera, and Hugo López. 2014. "Children 12 and under are fastest growing group of unaccompanied minors at U.S. border." *Fact Tank*. Pew Research Center. Retrieved from http://www.pewresearch.org/fact-tank/2014/22/children-12-and-under-are-fast-growing-group-of-unaccompnied-minors-at-u-s-border/.

López, Hugo, Jens Manuel Krogstad, and Antonio Flores. 2018. "Facts about young Latinos, one of the nation's fastest-growing populations." *Fact Tank*. Pew Research Center. Retrieved from http://www.pewresearch.org/fact-tank/2018/09/13/key-facts-about-young-latinos/.

López, Gustavo, Neil G. Ruiz, and Eileen Patten. 2017. "Key facts about Asian Americans, a diverse and growing population." *Fact Tank*. Pew Research Center. Retrieved from https://www.pewresearch.org/fact-tank/2017/09/08/key-facts-about-asian-americans/.

McLemore, S. Dale, and Harriet Romo. 2005. *Racial and Ethnic Relations in America* (7th ed.). Boston, MA: Pearson.

Migration Policy Institute. 2017. *Children in U.S. Immigrant Families.* Retrieved from https://www.migrationpolicy.org/programs/data-hub/charts/children-immigrant-families?width=1000&height=850&iframe=true.

Moll, Luis. 1992. "Bilingual classroom studies and community analysis: Some recent trends." *Educational Researcher* 21(2): 20–4.

National Association for the Education of Young Children. 2011. *Code of Ethical Conduct and Statement of Commitment. Position Statement. Reaffirmed and Updated.* Washington, DC: Author.

National Association for the Education of Young Children. 2019. *Advancing Equity in Early Childhood Education. Position Statement.* Washington, DC: Author.

Nieto, Sonia, and Patty Bode. 2018. *Affirming Diversity: The Sociopolitical Context of Multicultural Education* (8th ed.). Boston, MA: Pearson.

Nixon, Ron. 2018. "Agency's computer could not track separated families." *New York Times* (October 8): 9.

Park, Maki, and Margie McHugh. 2014. *Immigrant Parents and Early Childhood Programs. Addressing Barriers of Literacy, Culture, and Systems Knowledge.* Washington, DC: Migration Policy Institute.

Passel, Jeffrey, and D'Vera Cohn 2008. *U.S. Population Projections: 2005–2050.* Washington, DC: Pew Research Center.

Pew Research Center. 2015. *Modern Immigration Wave Brings 59 Million to U.S. Driving Population Growth and Change through 2065: Views on Immigration's Impact on U.S. Society Mixed.* Washington, DC: Author.

Philbin, Sandy, and Cecilia Ayón. 2016. "Luchamos por nuestros hijos: Latino immigrant parents strive to protect their children from the deleterious effects of anti-immigration policies." *Children and Youth Services* 63: 128–35.

Portes, Alejandro, and Rubén Portes. 2014. *Immigrant America: A Portrait* (4th ed.). Oakland: University of California Press.

Radford, Jynnah. 2019. "Key findings about U.S. immigrants." *Fact Tank. News in the Numbers.* Retrieved from https://www.pewresearch.org/fact-tank/2019/06/03/key-findings-about-u-s-immigrants/.

Radford, Jynnah, and Jens Manuel Krogstad. 2019. "Recently arrived U.S. immigrants, growing in number, differ from long-term residents." *Fact Tank. News in the Numbers.* Pew Research Center. Retrieved from https://www.pewresearch.org/fact-tank/2019/06/03/recently-arrived-u-s-immigrants-growing-in-number-differ-from-long-term-residents/.

Radford, Jynnah, and Luis Noe-Bustamante. 2019. *Facts on U.S. Immigrants, 2017. Statistical Portrait of the Foreign-born Population in the United States.* Pew Research Center. Retrieved from https://www.pewhispanic.org/2019/06/03/facts-on-u-s-immigrants/.

Robles-Meléndez, Wilma, and Vesna Beck. 2013. *Teaching Young Children in Multicultural Classrooms: Issues, Concepts and Strategies* (4th ed.). CA: Cengage.

Robles-Meléndez, Wilma, and Wayne Driscoll. 2018. "Poverty and immigrant children: Moving ahead with *esperanza*, with hope." *Dimensions of Early Childhood* 46(2): 21–4.

Robles-Meléndez, Wilma, Mabel Valdés, and Eric Robles. 2018. "Explorando conceptos de justicia social y equidad en el nivel preescolar." [Exploring social justice and equity in the preschool classroom.] Paper presented at the National Association for the Education of Young Children. November 16. Washington, DC.

Rojas-Flores, Lisbeth, and Jennifer Medina-Vaughn. 2019. *Determinants of Health and Well-Being for Children of Immigrants: Moving from Evidence to Action.* Foundation for Child Development. Retrieved from https://www.fcd-us.org/determinants-of-health-and-well-being-for-children-of-immigrants/.

S.358-Immigration Act of 1990. 101st Congress (1989–90). Retrieved from https://www.congress.gov/bill/101st-congress/senate-bill/358.

Sánchez-Suzuki, Kiyomi, and Jennifer Adair. 2014. "Countering deficit thinking: Agency, capabilities and the early learning experiences of young children." *Contemporary Issues in Early Childhood* 15(2): 122–35.

Silverstein, Paul. Immigrant racialization and the new savage slot: Race, migration, and immigration in the New Europe. *Annual Review of Anthropology* 34(1): 363–84. Retrieved from https://www.annualreviews.org/doi/full/10.1146/annurev.anthro.34.081804.120338.

Suárez-Orozco, Carola. 2017. "The diverse immigrant student experience: What does it mean for teaching?" *Educational Studies* 53(5): 522–34.

Suárez-Orozco, Marcelo, and Carola Suárez-Orozco. 2001. *Children of Immigration.* Cambridge, MA: Harvard University Press.

Suárez-Orozco, C., Hirokazu Yoshikawa, and Vivian Tseng. 2015. *Intersecting Inequalities: Research to Reduce Inequality for Immigrant-Origin Children and Youth.* New York: William T. Grant Foundation.

Suárez-Orozco, Marcelo, and Carola Suárez-Orozco. 2018. "Like it or not, immigrant children are our future." *WorldPost Opinion. Washington Post.* Accessed May 18, 2019. Retrieved from https://www.washingtonpost.com/news/theworldpost/ wp/2018/09/20/immigrant/?noredirect=on&utm_term=.ebd1e3569d7f.

Takaki, Richard. 2008. *A Different Mirror: A History of Multicultural America.* New York: Back Bay Books.

Tavernise, Sabrina. 2018. "U.S. has highest share of foreign-born since 1910, with more coming from Asia." *New York Times.* Retrieved from https://www.nytimes. com/2018/09/13/us/census-foreign-population.html.

Taylor, Alan. 2015. "Fleeing by the millions: Migration crises around the world." *Atlantic.* Retrieved from https://www.theatlantic.com/photo/2015/06/ fleeing-by-the-millions-migration-crises-around-the-world/394805/.

Trevelyan, Edward, Gambino Christine, Thomas Gryn, Luke Larsen, Yesenia Acosta, Elizabeth Grieco, Darryl Harris, and Nathan Walters. 2016. *Characteristics of the U.S. Population by Generational Status: 2013.* Washington, DC: U.S. Census Bureau.

UNICEF. 2016. *Uprooted: The Growing Crisis for Refugee and Migrant Children.* New York: United Nations Children's Fund. Retrieved from https://www.unicef.org/ children-uprooted.

UNICEF. 2017. *Child Migration-UNICEF Data.* Retrieved from https://data.unicef.org/ topic/child-migration-and-displacement/migration/.

UNICEF. 2020. *Children uprooted.* Retrieved from https://www.unicef.org/ children-uprooted.

UN. 2017. Migration and population change—drivers and impacts. December. *Population facts.* No. 2017/8. Retrieved from https://www.un.org/en/ development/desa/population/migration/publications/populationfacts/docs/ MigrationPopFacts20178.pdf.

United Nations. 2017a. *International Migration Report 2017.* New York: United Nations.

United Nations. 2017b. "Mediterranean crossing still world's deadliest for migrant." *UN Report.* Retrieved from https://news.un.org/en/story/2017/11/637162- mediterranean-crossing-still-worlds-deadliest-migrants-un-report.

United Nations. 2018. *Migration Data Portal: The Bigger Picture.* United Nations. Retrieved from https://migrationdataportal.org/?i=stock_abs_&t=2017.

UN Department of Economic and Social Affairs. 2019a. The number of international migrants reaches 272 million, continuing an upward trend in all world regions, says UN. *News.* September 17. Accessed April 22, 2020. Retrieved from https://www. un.org/development/desa/en/news/population/international-migrant-stock-2019. html.

United Nations 2019b. Number of migrants now growing faster than world population, new UN figures show. *UN News*. Retrieved from https://news.un.org/en/story/2019/09/1046562.

UN High Commissioner for Refugees (UNHCR). 2018. *"Refugees" and "Migrants"— Frequently Asked Questions (FAQs)*, August 31. Accessed January 9, 2019. Retrieved from https://www.refworld.org/docid/56e81c0d4.html.

UN Human Rights Office of the High Commissioner. 2019. *Migration and Human Rights*. Retrieved from https://www.ohchr.org/EN/Issues/Migration/Pages/MigrationAndHumanRightsIndex.aspx.

UN Refugee Agency. (2018). *Refugee Facts*. Retrieved from https://www.unrefugees.org/refugee-facts/what-is-a-refugee/.

U.S. Census Bureau. 2017. *Selected Characteristics of the Native and Foreign-Born Populations*. American Community Survey 1-Year Estimates. Retrieved from https://factfinder.census.gov/faces/tableservices/jsf/pages/productview.xhtml?src=bkmk

U.S. Census Bureau. 2018a. "More than 76 million students enrolled in U.S. schools, Census Bureau reports." *Newsroom*. CB18-192. December 11. Retrieved from https://www.census.gov/newsroom/press-releases/2018/school-enrollment.html.

U.S. Census Bureau. 2018b. "Community facts. Population." *American Fact Finder*. Retrieved from https://factfinder.census.gov/faces/nav/jsf/pages/community_facts.xhtml.

U.S. Census Bureau. 2018c. *Asian and Pacific Islander Population in the United States*. Retrieved from https://www.census.gov/library/visualizations/2018/comm/api.html.html.

U.S. Census Bureau. 2019. *U.S. and World Population Clock*. Retrieved from https://www.census.gov/popclock/.

U.S. Department of Homeland Security. 2019. *Southwest Border Migration*. Retrieved from https://www.cbp.gov/newsroom/stats/sw-border-migration.

U.S. Department of State, Bureau of Population, Refugees and Migration. Refugee Processing Center. 2019. *Admission reports*. Retrieved from https://www.wrapsnet.org/admissions-and-arrivals/.

USA for UNHCR. 2019. *Refugee Facts*. Retrieved from https://www.unrefugees.org/refugee-facts/usa/.

Urban Institute. 2019. Part of us: A data driven look at children of immigrants. Shedding light on the children of immigrants who are shaping this country's future. March 14. *Features*. Retrieved from https://www.urban.org/features/part-us-data-driven-look-children-immigrants/.

Valdez, Carmen, Jessa Valentine, and Brian Padilla. 2013. "'Why we stay': Immigrants' motivation for remaining in communities impacted by anti-immigration policies." *Cultural Diversity Ethnic Minority Psychology* 19(3): 279–87.

Vespa, J., A. Armstrong, and L. Medina. 2018. *Demographic Turning Points for the United States: Population Projections for 2020–2060. Population Estimates and*

Projections. Current Population Reports. P25-1144. Washington, DC: U.S. Census Bureau.

Watts, Jeri. 2016. *A Piece of Home*. New York: Candlewick Books.

World Bank. 2019. *International Migrant Stock (%Population)*. Retrieved from https://data.worldbank.org/indicator/SM.POP.TOTL.ZS.

Zolberg, A. 2006. *Rethinking the Last 200 Years of U.S. Immigration Policy*. Feature. Migration Policy Institute.

Zong, Jie, and Jeanne Batalova. 2016. *Asian Immigrants in the United States*. Washington, DC: Migration Policy Institute.

Zong, Jie, and Jeanne Batalova. 2019. "Immigrants from new origin countries in the United States." *Spotlight*. Migration Policy Institute. Retrieved fromhttps://www.migrationpolicy.org/article/immigrants-new-origin-countries-united-states.

Zong, Jie, Jeanne Batalova, and Micayla Burrows. 2019. *Frequently Requested Statistics on Immigrants and Immigration in the United States*. Migration Policy Institute. Retrieved from https://www.migrationpolicy.org/article/frequently-requested-statistics-immigrants-and-immigration-united-states.

2

Children and the Immigration Experience

Chapter objectives

Through this chapter, we will

- Discuss who are child immigrants
- Identify some of the historical events ascertaining the presence of children as immigrants
- Discuss the factors driving families and children to migrate
- Identify some of the main characteristics of children who are immigrants.
- Explore the impact of immigration entry status on children.
- Consider some of the humanitarian actions on behalf of children.
- Reflect on the ethical responsibilities toward children and families with immigrant roots

Key terms

- Immigrant child
- Immigrant families
- Forced immigration
- Ethics
- Children's well-being

Related standards

- NAEYC #1 Promoting Child Development and Learning
- NAEYC #2 Building Family and Community Relationships
- NAEYC #6 Becoming a Professional

Sharing stories: Memories that never leave me

It was snowing outside, and during those first days, I remember sitting in the classroom staring at the white covering everything. I have never seen snow and it kept falling like soft rain. I was six and could only think that it was always so cold. Two months since we came and my whole life changed. At home, I remember saying to myself, it was so warm and green. My abuela, mi nana, was there and she would always braid my hair singing that song that is still in my heart. And I knew what people were saying. Here, I would just smile not knowing what they were saying. To this day, those memories are still with me. Why did we have to come here? It would be years later when I understood why my mother took us to this country. How brave of her! This is home now, but I still think about the home that was once ours far, far away. (Bibiana [pseudonym], personal communication)

Children: Our youngest immigrants

Every time we meet a child, we are seeing the seed of society. Their needs are many and they call for everyone's attention. This call resonates in the words of Nobel poet laureate Gabriela Mistral when she stated: "Many things can wait. Children cannot ... To them we cannot say 'tomorrow.' Their name is today," reminding us to prioritize children's needs if we are to safeguard their well-being. Far beyond their origins, cultures, or experiences, a child is a child and society has placed in children its own hope for a new beginning.

When Bibiana came to the United States, she was a young child. For the 6-year-old arriving from the Caribbean, everything was so different from the green and the beaches of the town where she lived. The language also sounded so strange! Looking back from the classroom where she teaches kindergartners, with many children just like her who came from other countries, memories always came rushing back. For her, the children are a reminder of the journey and struggles she endured together with her family. Learning to be a part of new realities as immigrants is a journey they embark on as they arrive into our communities. When asked about her childhood experiences, she shrugged, telling one of the authors that she would always remember those who saw her just as another child, not a stranger. *Son niños y así es como siempre veo a mis estudiantes*, "they are children and that's how I always see my students."

The foundational influence of the early years

We all remember experiences from our childhood. Those impressions stay forever as lessons and moments lived. Both positive and negative, the impressions shaped and linger to be present in each of us just like they remained for Bibiana. The influence and vivid presence of experiences during the early childhood years remain as one of the landmark times for every individual. All children have a right to a childhood where experiences are rich, welcoming, and conducive to their maximum overall development. This is at the core of practices in early childhood education rooted in developmental appropriateness and equity (Copple and Bredekamp 2009; NAEYC 2019). It is as well what is aspired as we recognize and respect the rights of children to find support from society to grow and develop (Convention of the Rights of Children 1989). Ensuring that their experience becomes an equally inclusive parameter shared by all is essential in education, particularly in early childhood. Those formative years are precious times that cannot be replaced. They are the cornerstone of how we develop and become who we are. The magnitude of what happens during those milestone early years places greater responsibility on early childhood education to deliver experiences and attention centered on what is individually and developmentally essential for children's holistic development. Just take a moment and consider the memories child immigrants in many communities or in your own community are experiencing. What will they bring from those early childhood years? What will their memories and experiences be like? What images will endure in their memories? A mindful awareness is fundamental to recognize the importance of experiences, opportunities, and of environments where children of immigration grow up. How these will contribute to foster appropriate development remains as a central goal of early childhood professionals. Evidence of the commitment of early educators has been witnessed for decades. Today, children of immigrants continue urging us to respond with vigor to their needs.

Responding to the needs of the child immigrants in early childhood education

As we explore the experience of immigration from the perspective of the child, it is relevant to consider the overall realities of children as immigrants. They are a vital source revealing to early educators the life experiences of our young students. In early childhood education, informing our practice is critical to ensuring we meet the individual child's needs. Developmentally based practices remind us that as a premise, experiences must anchor on knowledge about the child. They need to be responsively centered on their individual social and cultural realities (Copple and Bredekamp 2009). In fact, it is an ethical responsibility that we must uphold as we work with children and their families. What has been their prior experiences is relevant to better understand responses to the youngest immigrants. They also guide us to consider how appropriately we have responded to their needs. Have these been centered on equity? Have they responded to what every child conscientiously need? Answering these and many other questions makes it pertinent to explore some of the events and efforts from the past and factual realities about immigration. They will help us build and deepen our professional knowledge and practice about immigrants.

Through the lens of ethics: Addressing the needs of the immigrant child

Recently visiting a classroom of young children in one of our urban communities, their faces spoke loudly about the diversity of our nation. Most of them were children of immigrants including some who had arrived in the United States a few months earlier. Talking and seeing them play and be simply children brought to mind the lines from the children's book *Whoever You Are* (Fox 2006). Indeed, whoever they are, whatever their language, or wherever they came from, they are just children. Their trust is on us. Child immigrants are part of yesterday and continue today as a vibrant reality. More importantly, they are also relevant for the future reality of the country. As their teachers and professionals, we are committed to make it possible for children to find what each one, equitably, needs to grow and develop.

To fully appreciate the magnitude and implications of immigration on young children, it is critical to see them through the eyes of professional ethics. Professionally, we are called to respond to their needs and to identify ways to effectively support and optimize their development (Copple and Bredekamp 2009; NAEYC 2011). In our hands we also have the responsibility to address their circumstances with equity. Equity and ethics are both interwoven in our work with children. Both also denote the significance and responsibility entrusted in each one as early childhood educators. In the next sections, while we explore some of their characteristics, experiences, and circumstances, the lens of ethics paired with a focus on equity will serve to understand and consider children and the experience of immigration.

Immigration as a childhood life event

Everyone experiences defining events during childhood. In many ways, these events define us and plot the course of our lives as we grow up. Immigration is one of those experiences that today, just like yesterday or in times to come, influences the lives of child immigrants. Whether you came along with families from another land or were born to parents who immigrated to a new country, the experience of immigration is a major life event. For young immigrants, the moments lived, the memories of experiences here and there, and encounters with people and realities are shaping forces as children build their life in new or familiar contexts. In many ways, moving and growing up in towns different from those where you were born, the experience of immigration, is a major episode in the life of children. The same applies to children of immigrants born in the United States, who navigate between the realities of their home culture and that of the communities where they live. For them, the experience of growing up as an immigrant also marks their young lives.

Comments from adults who came as immigrants during their childhood reveal the memories still vividly alive of their arrival and living in communities so different from those they used to call home. In many instances, we heard immigrants who grew up in the United States recall the places and folk games of their childhood. More than one immigrant adult shared that even when they learned to play other games and sing in another language, the memories stay with them. Some of us, adults now, continue to hold these memories as reminders of times never to forget.

Immigration is a life-changing experience for everyone as they leave and begin life in another context. It is a highly emotionally charged event, crossing and entering into other cultural contexts and landscapes. If you have moved to another community, you probably know how a child feels entering into a different reality. Think what it would be for you to leave behind what you have known, and take a moment to consider what it may mean for a child. You probably would feel like the young child character in the children's story *A Piece of Home* (Levitin 1996), who faced with the need to choose something to take with him to America, "does not want to leave anything behind ... and cannot decide what to take." Similar feelings are probably common to most. Simply imagine what it entails for a young child.

Time to reflect … *Moving, memories from childhood*

Most of us may have experienced moving to a new place or country as a child. Think about some of your lasting memories about coming to live in another place. We invite you to reflect on some of your memories from childhood about moving. What memories are still with you from moving to another part of town, city, or state? Do you remember who or what made them special?

A life-changing experience for families and children

People moving to other countries remain as a continuing reality and an enduring phenomenon in society (International Organization for Migration 2017; McLemore and Romo 2005). Children will also continue to be present as active participants in the experience of immigration. Even though the presence of children has not been given a clear emphasis in the study of immigration (Turney and Kao 2009; Zayas et al. 2017), their story demands attention. A major life experience for everyone, for children, it is a life-changing experience as they begin to find themselves in other realities. This is what scholars of immigration have found (International Organization for Migration 2020; Suárez-Orozco and Suárez-Orozco, 2001). It is also what we heard from adults born to immigrant parents and from those who came during childhood and grew up in the United States. Growing up in a different landscape, culture, and many times language are all among the multiple factors influencing one's life during childhood. As one young adult immigrant shared, "it is a transformational experience." For early childhood educators, awareness about the events children experience is vital. Developmentally speaking, being cognizant about their realities and needs contributes to making informed decisions guiding us to determine practices and actions for children (Copple and Bredekamp 2009). More importantly, it awakens our professional responsiveness to the child as an individual.

How much do we know about immigrant children?

The presence of children in immigration has always been a reality. Participants in the immigration process and journey, over a quarter of the children living in the nation are immigrants (Child Trends 2018a). Despite the long-time presence of child immigrants in society, they have become more evident to everyone in recent years. Sadly, their presence has emerged clearly, given the perils that many in different parts of the world including the US borders have being experiencing. This has brought their needs and vulnerability to the forefront. It has aroused interest along with empathy and consideration toward young children turned into immigrants. This has also served as a reminder of society's responsibility to childhood and to all the circumstances impacting a child. Immigration is one of those. The unavoidable question is, thus, how much do we know about immigrant children? Much of the literature about immigration, with very few exceptions, has focused on adults, with children mentioned occasionally as part of details characterizing families or data collected. As Zayas et al. stated, "The children of immigration are typically insufficiently understood and tangential to the debate, and to a large extent in the scientific literature" (2017, 1). Clearly, the call to place attention on their realities is obvious, especially as we attempt to better address and respond to their needs both individually and collectively. Though immigrant children and their families have always been integral in early childhood practices and efforts, current circumstances are asking for attention and action to their specific realities. Moreover, it calls for delving into the multiple experiences of children who are immigrants. This is what we envision through these pages.

Our youngest immigrants

Whenever we see the faces of children, they remind us that we must ensure their future as an integral part of the world's reality. Far from rhetoric, without any doubts, children are the future of our society and are also a vital element of the present. Constituting a large portion of the world's population, more than a quarter of the global population, 26 percent, are children under age 15. In a global society where a large proportion of its population are young, caring and unselfish attention to the needs and welfare of children is paramount. The need is heightened as one learns that many of the world's children are also immigrants. Today, "1 in every 70 children worldwide lives outside their country of birth" (UNICEF 2016), which underlines the need for concerted efforts centered on addressing their realities as immigrants.

All for the well-being of children

Recently, we heard people ask, why do we have so many child immigrants? The fact is that children have always been part of the immigration journey. The reasons for their presence as immigrants are clear. For families throughout the world, children are always their major concern and priority. Guarding the future and well-being of a child continues today as a driving force leading a family to migrate. Outcomes from a Gallup survey conducted in over 150 countries over the span of a decade, 2006–16, revealed that people were more inclined "to move not only for their own wellbeing but for that of children" (Burrone, D'Costa, and Holmqvist 2019, 2). These findings confirm the fact that for families, aspirations to give their children a better life continue as a main motivation driving them to consider immigration as part of their choices and options. It may also explain the reasons followed by the countless immigrants already living in other countries and for the many who are considering immigrating.

We continue to learn about what drives families arriving today. "Por mis niños," for my children, is what we have heard in the past and it is also what we continue to hear families say. Through informal interviews, conducted by one of the authors with a group of migrant Hispanic families in 2018, when asked as to the reasons that led them to migrate, the main reason was their children. It was also what they stated that kept motivating them despite challenges. "No importa lo que tengamos que hacer para que salgan adelante." It doesn't matter what we may need to do to help them move forward, was their response. Anchored in their strong values, for families of all cultures the need to secure the future for their young remains as their leading aspiration. The same aspirations for their children guided families in the past.

Time to reflect … *For children*

For families, seeking to secure their children's well-being is a priority identified as a major factor leading to immigration. Take a moment to consider the implicit responsibilities for early childhood education professionals. How could early educators ensure immigrant families that their children's needs would be met? Try to see yourself in their position and think about the actions that you would like to recommend for your child.

Children and families on the move As in the past, decisions are made every day by thousands of families to start their lives anew in other countries where their children will find better opportunities. Immigrant families represent multiple realities and socioeconomic levels. They cannot be viewed with only one lens or criteria. No one is excluded from immigration, as this is a decision someone could make as aspirations emerge or forced by circumstances as these change. The fact is that the image of immigrants is as diverse as their realities are, too. Immigrant families and children already living in the nation as well as those recently arriving are portrayed by their diversity of backgrounds, social and cultural.

Recent years have shown thousands of families who opted to migrate after experiencing serious circumstances either because of natural disasters, like the earthquake in Haiti in 2010, or because of social and political conditions such as the Syrian conflict or the recent Venezuelan crisis. In conversations with a group of immigrants recently arrived from South America, one of them mentioned that for her and her family the decision to come was made after they found themselves unable to buy what they needed for their infant son. Never before did they consider leaving their country until events changed. Similarly, immigrants from Central America shared their urgent need to leave came after experiencing violence and personal threats. They did not wait and a few days after receiving threats, they left.

Who are immigrant families and their children?

A diversity of experiences, aspirations, and circumstances characterize families and children who are immigrants. Officially, in the United States, immigrants are foreign-born individuals or US-born persons who have at least one foreign-born parent (US Department of Homeland Security 2020). Families and children who are considered as immigrants include a variety of circumstances describing their official or unofficial status in the nation. Among those considered as immigrants, included are the following (American Immigration Council 2020; Breiseth 2018; Department of Homeland Security 2020):

People with official entry into the nation:

- Individuals (adults and children) born in other countries officially entering through the nation's borders.
  - Some may be permanent residents. Others are naturalized, that is, applied for citizenship and became US citizens. In 2018, 22.7 percent of immigrants had naturalized.
- Children born in the United States with one foreign-born parent.
- Families and children entering as refugees and asylees.

- Family member/parents with protected status who are temporarily living in the country due to dangerous circumstances in their home countries.

People with unofficial or unauthorized entry status:

- Individuals who entered unofficially into the nation. These may include adults, a parent, or a family member.
- Families and children who entered unofficially.

A mosaic of diversity

Immigrants represent a myriad of different realities that drove families and their children to become immigrants. The nature of their entry also defines the reasons for becoming immigrants. Immigrant families and children are an extremely diverse group. Trying to identify the primary characteristics of immigrant families and children begins by pointing to their shared dreams for a better life. Diversity is another characteristic they shared in common. Figure 2.1 lists some of the distinctive traits characterizing immigrant children. Overall, they embody a diversity of ethnic backgrounds, cultures, faiths, and languages. Rich cultural roots and traditions clearly characterize immigrant families and their children. They are also distinguished by a diversity of primary languages. Many are speakers of English and others bring different levels of English proficiency. They also come from a variety of environments, some from cities and others from rural communities. Families also bring different educational levels and skills.

Children's wellbeing as a common goal for families

No single profile would fit the reality of immigrant children or that of their families. They are characterized by their unique family and personal experiences, which calls for individualized understanding of their needs and circumstances. Most of all, their families are best characterized by their desire to build a future and search for a place where there is hope, stability, and opportunities. They are defined by their goal to maintain a supportive and positive environment for their children. Most immigrant children live with both parents and many include extended family members, which has added a stronger circle of support to their young (Fortuny et al. 2009). These same characteristics have defined immigrants in the past and today. Common to all families and their children is their commitment to do their best for their children. This high sense of compromise for children is one of the main factors characterizing families of immigration. Other factors in common include

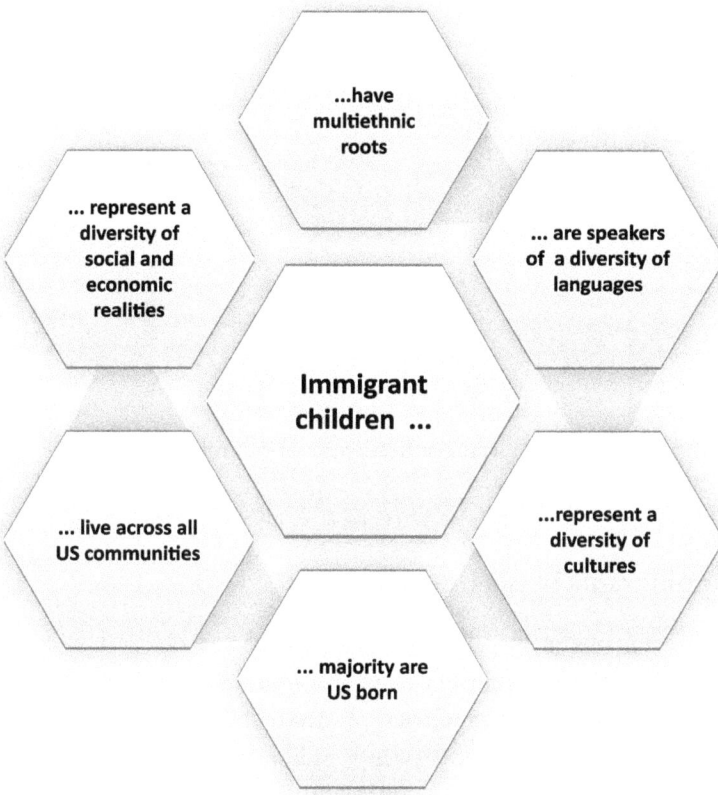

Figure 2.1 Key traits of immigrant children in the United States.

their resilience and determination to overcome challenges to provide for their children. Though very culturally diverse, strong family ties defines immigrant families. Their determined mind-set is another trait contributing to ensure their children's well-being.

Time to reflect ... *Families seeking a future of hope*

Countless families continue to leave their homelands together with their children. Consider the immigrant families that live in your community or whose children are in our classrooms. If you were an immigrant family, what would you want people to know about your reasons to immigrate? What would you like them to do to support your aspirations for children?

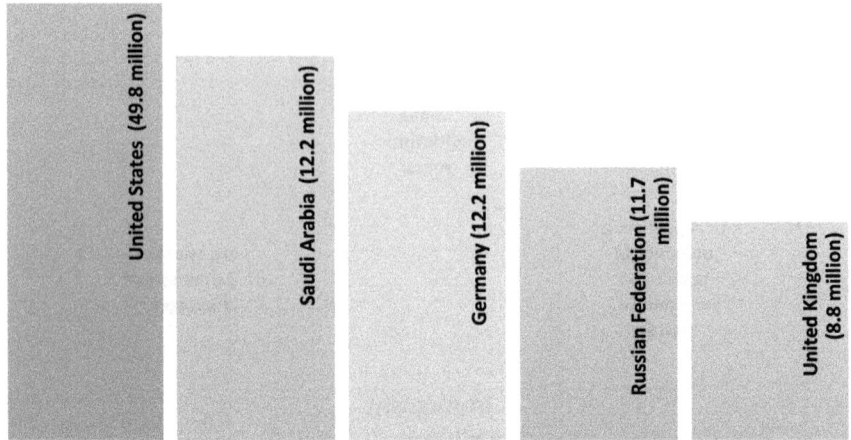

Figure 2.2 Main countries serving as destination for immigrants (2017).
Source: United Nations (2017a).

Child immigrants in the United States

A large portion of the world's child immigrants live in the United States, a country that is in the top of the five main destinations for the world's immigrants (Figure 2.2). Leading the countries of destination for global immigrants, United States is home to almost twenty million child immigrants under age 18, representing 26.5 percent of children in the nation (Child Trends 2018b). Evidencing its continuing immigrant heritage, today in the United States, one in four children are members of an immigrant family, where the majority are second generation. The fact is that the large majority of child immigrants are children citizens (Child Trends 2018a). Population estimates are projecting these numbers to maintain a steady rise in the decades ahead.

The mosaic of languages, ethnicities, and cultures that children and families bring to our communities adds to the continuing immigrant ancestry of the country. Young immigrant children are present in classrooms and communities throughout the nation. School enrollment reports show that 23 percent of students in the nation's schools are immigrants (Camarota, Griffith, and Zeigler 2017; Dinan 2017), a percentage that is expected to continue growing. In some school districts, immigrant children already represent the majority of the student enrollment. Such is the case in many districts in Florida, Texas, Nevada, and California. The indelible presence of immigrant children across the PreK-12 student community accentuates the nation's unique, diverse, and multicultural essence.

Table 2.1 Key terms about child immigrants in the United States

Foreign born	Any individual who is not a US citizen at birth. The term "alien" is also used to designate the foreign born
Child immigrant	Child who has at least one parent who is foreign born
First generation	Individuals born outside the United States
Second generation	Individuals born in the United States with at least one foreign-born parent

Source: U.S. Census Bureau (2019c).

Many of the nation's child immigrants are offspring of those who themselves at one time came with their families during their childhood. In the United States, child immigrants are those born in other countries or who are US born and have at least one foreign-born parent. Definitions of the official terms used in the United States referencing the immigrant population are provided in Table 2.1.

The rising child immigrant population

Population reports indicate that child immigrants are expected to continue increasing their presence in years to come. Based on projections, the increase will significantly impact the nation's population gain levels. Overall, immigrant children together with their native-born peers represent a growing segment of the nation's seventy-three million child population, projected to continue increasing to almost 80 million by 2050 (Child Trends 2018a). For many demographers and sociologists, the anticipated growth of the child immigrants is considered to be a major factor influencing the overall character of the country and of the population of its children. Undoubtedly, this fact evidences the enduring and continuing impact of immigrants in the nation. Projections indicate that the resulting population increase will be mostly from second-generation child immigrants along with children born in other countries. In 2018, the large majority of child immigrants in the country, 88 percent, were US citizens and who were themselves second-generation immigrants (Zong, Batalova, and Burrows 2019). This fact also confirms that child immigrants represent a vital factor in the overall population growth of the nation. Furthermore, the majority of the US child population increase during 1994–2014 was driven by the growth of child immigrants in the nation (Lu, He, and Brooks-Gunn 2020). In numerous communities, immigrants have also become the main factor responsible for their population growth. Early childhood classrooms in most parts of the nation already, urban and rural, evidence the rising immigrant presence. For early childhood professionals, getting to learn about immigrant children is relevant to ensure ways to respond and meet their learning and overall developmental well-being.

Diversity: A trait of the child immigrant

Diversity is the predominant characteristic of child immigrants. We cannot emphasize enough how their presence contributes to the diversity character of communities and classrooms around the country. Today it is not uncommon for early childhood classroom enrollment to be distinctively culturally and ethnically diverse and of immigrant origin. They are a vibrant population milestone for the nation where the nation is witnessing how "American-born children and grandchildren of immigrants … are leading this change in our demographics (Hernández and Napierala 2013, 1). In many of the classrooms that the authors visited, a majority of young preschoolers were from a variety of ethnic, linguistic, and cultural backgrounds. Some recently arrived seated alongside peers whose parents came to the country during their childhood. Similar images repeat themselves in classrooms across the nation.

Ethnically, child immigrants represent a varied and diverse group. So are the traits that also distinguish them, including their experiences. Some come from urban and metropolitan areas while others lived in rural and remote communities. Culturally, they represent the multiplicity of cultures from the global community. Some of the traits characterizing child immigrants are also their languages, race, and ethnic backgrounds. Coming from all parts of the globe, they are speakers of many different languages. In some cases, besides their heritage language, they are proficient in English. For others, English is their primary language. Given that a large number of child immigrants are of Hispanic or Latino descent, Spanish is one of the main languages spoken by young immigrants. Socioeconomically, child immigrants and their families represent all the socioeconomic spectrum including many child immigrants living in poverty (Annie Casey Foundation 2017). Despite the challenges faced by many including an upsurge in discriminatory views toward immigrants, they are also characterized by their resilient and optimistic attitude (Gándara 2018), two traits contributing to their ability to cope with challenges. Both the social and linguistic diversity of immigrant children are relevant factors in understanding and appropriately responding to their needs. They also are relevant to clarify and erase stereotypes that blur views defining who is an immigrant child.

Of the different characteristics describing immigrant children and their families, three in particular demand our attention: socioeconomic reality, language, and ethnic diversity. These are further discussed in the next section.

Social diversity of immigrant children

Immigrants are an important contributing factor in the social and economic life of the country. Their presence and participation place them across the socioeconomic spectrum. This is also reflected by the broad and wide social and economic status of immigrant children and families. Economic success has indeed characterized countless immigrants. The arrival of immigrant families with higher levels of education has influenced the social and economic profile of immigrants in the nation. Attracted by educational and professional opportunities, they are changing the image of immigration in many communities. This is contributing to more and better social and economic opportunities and resources among immigrant ethnic groups. In some groups, as in the case of Asians, it is more likely to have more secure employment and family income levels (Hernandez and Napierala 2013). Reports show that immigrants from India and the Philippines had the lowest poverty rate (Zong and Batalova 2019).

Educational backgrounds and immigration status continue as a main factor impacting the socioeconomic opportunities for immigrant families and their children. Many immigrant families with lower educational levels and skills and those confronting difficulties due to immigration status face struggling circumstances Lower employment opportunities place many immigrant families and children to live in low-income households where "one in four is poor" (Annie Casey Foundation 2017). Poverty rates are higher among Hispanic families and children. Factors such as education, language barriers, immigration status, and discrimination continue to impact immigrants' probabilities to live in poverty (Hoynes, Page, and Stevens 2006).

Linguistic diversity

Bringing their rich and diverse ethnic and cultural heritage, immigrant children are also characterized by their linguistic diversity. The variety of languages spoken by child immigrants and their families throughout communities is a sample of many of those spoken around the world. At the national level, most child immigrants speak Spanish, the language spoken by a large majority of the immigrant student population. Besides Spanish, , in some states other languages such as Portuguese, Haitian Creole, Somali, and Vietnamese denote the linguistic diversity of families in their communities.

Immigration has been a main source responsible for the diversity of languages spoken in the United States, which is particularly present in metropolitan and urban areas (Rumbaut and Massey 2013). Immigrant influence continues today

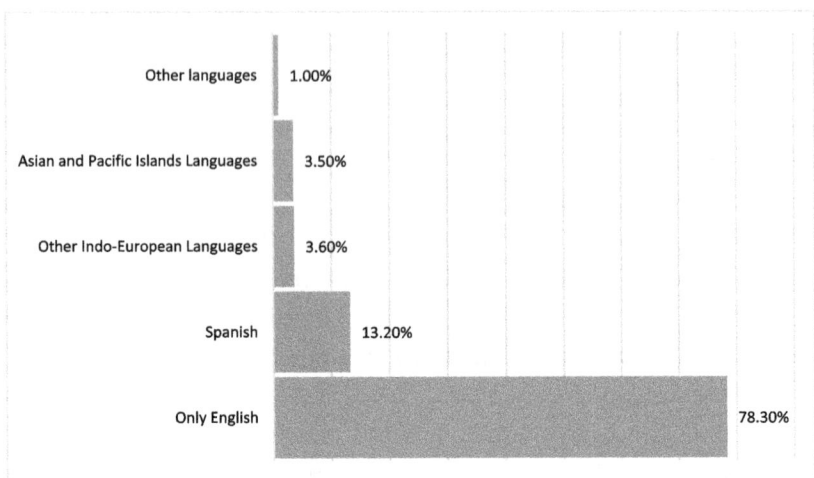

Figure 2.3 Languages spoken in the United States (2017).
Source: U.S. Census Bureau (2019b).

with an increasing number of people speaking languages other than English at home, which has "doubled since 1990" (Zeigler and Camarota 2019, 1). Over 20 percent of people living in the United States speak a language other than English (see Figure 2.3). Among those ages 5–17, reports show that 21 percent speak Spanish at home (U.S. Census Bureau 2017). Increasing numbers of immigrant children from Asia and the Middle East have added Chinese, Arabic, and Vietnamese as languages now spoken in the nation's schools (National Center for Education Statistics 2019). Almost 400 different languages characterize the multilingual character of PreK-12 US students (U.S. Department of Education 2017). Support for the preservation of students' primary languages has gained greater attention in recent years. Evidence about the developmental benefits for children who are dual language learners has particularly encouraged supportive practices. This has also been influenced by immigrant advocates whose efforts for recognition and respectful treatment are unceasing.

Increasing language diversity among immigrant children

Recent years have seen an increase in the variety of languages spoken, with the presence of many other primary and indigenous languages beyond those traditionally spoken in US classrooms and communities. This has become evident mainly since the arrival of families from countries particularly from Asia, Africa, and Central America. In some cases, presence of languages such as

Somali and Nepalese indicates the influence of refugees now living in the nation. Over 300,000 of the child population enrolled in Head Start and Early Head Start programs are dual language learners who are speakers of over 140 different languages (Office of Head Start 2019). In some states, like Florida, more than 300 primary languages are spoken by children in their school classrooms. Overall, the arrival of a more linguistically diverse immigrant group has influenced communities across the nation. They are also reflective of the rising multiethnic character of immigration.

Time to reflect ... *A diversity of languages*

Today, language diversity is another main characteristic describing the immigrant influence in our communities. How linguistically diverse is your community? How are these reflected in your school, in your community?

Ethnic and racial diversity of immigrant children and families

Another factor that cannot be ignored is the increasing ethnic diversity of the immigrant children and family population. Faces of children with a diversity of ethnic origins are common across classrooms everywhere, including urban and rural areas. Since the latter part of the twentieth century, the United States has seen a gradual growth in the diversity of ethnic groups of immigrants coming to the nation. With fewer immigration from European nations, the ethnic nature of immigrants has grown increasingly diverse. Families and children from all parts of the Americas, Africa, the Middle East, and the Pacific now call the United States their home. They also represent a marked range of ethnic and racial groups. Numerous emerging ethnic groups are now integral to the demographics in many classrooms and communities.

The presence of multiethnic immigrant groups has brought forward the issue of race. Racialization of immigrants (Silverstein 2005; Suárez-Orozco, Yoshikawa, and Tseng 2015), underlines race as another paradigm in the discourse about immigration. We cannot emphasize enough that race is a misleading construct to distinguish people's diversity. It is well known how racially biased conceptualizations have led to prejudiced views and discriminatory practices in society. Those continue in current times in arguments targeting immigration. They are also covertly present in many environments (American Psychological Association [APA] 2012). With a greater ethnic diversity—languages, physical features, beliefs, cultural practices—many immigrant groups have become more "visible" (Sáenz and Douglas 2015) and easily identifiable than those "who pass as white" (Suárez-Orozco, Yoshikawa, and Tseng 2015, 5).

Some scholars have cautioned that greater immigrant visibility of immigrants is also contributing to perpetuating views about them as "outsiders" (Lee, Park, and Wong 2016), which, when seen " as belonging to an 'outgroup' can lead to prejudice and discrimination" (APA 2012, 22). Such views continue to unfairly hinder their integration as contributing members of the communities where they live. At the same time, with new anti-immigrant sentiments emerging around the nation, recent years have witnessed a rise in cases of discrimination and prejudiced views across many communities. These, regrettably, have not skipped our schools and classrooms.

Experiencing biases

The impact of racist views on children has been pointed out by many educators (Abo-Zena 2018; Adair 2015; Derman-Sparks and Edwards 2010; Suárez-Orozco, Yoshikawa, and Tseng 2015). Numerous educators have recognized bigoted attitudes and discriminatory practices as an experience commonplace to children of immigrants (Adair 2015). Frequently, these experiences transpire through subtle comments and behaviors. Incidents of microaggressions cannot be ignored. These subtle discriminatory and prejudicial behaviors have comparable effects on all children. Awareness of the existence of prejudice and hurtful experiences is vital to counteract them and to effectively understand their impact on the young child. The fact is that negative views and behaviors about people are socially and emotionally damaging for everyone, those who receive them as well as those who discriminate against others and those witnessing such actions.

Time to reflect … *Counteracting damaging views*

Welcoming environments promote inclusion and counteract misleading attitudes. In the children's story *I walk with Vanessa* (Kerascoët 2018), the main character stands for the young child who is rejected and shows that everyone belongs. Consider the courageous actions of the character in the story and reflect on ways to prevent any discriminatory actions in the classroom.

The growing Hispanic/Latino child immigrants

A large majority of immigrant children are of Hispanic or Latino roots, already comprising 25 percent of the population and expected to continue increasing in the coming decades (Federal Interagency Forum on Child and Family Statistics 2018). Previously pointed out in Chapter 1, Hispanics are a very heterogeneous and diverse ethnic group with distinctive cultures, religions, and indigenous languages. Racially, they are also very diverse. Already the largest immigrant ethnic group in the United States, it is projected that by 2060, Hispanics or Latinos will constitute about 32 percent of the country's child immigrant population (Vespa, Armstrong, and Medina 2018). Fifty-three percent of Hispanic children born in the United States have a foreign-born parent (Murphey, Guzman, and Torres 2014). Representing an estimated 68 percent of the child immigrant population, most Hispanic children living in the country are of Mexican descent (Child Trends 2018a). They are followed by children from the Spanish-speaking Caribbean and Central America.

The rising Asian immigrant population

Presence of Asian immigrants in the United States dates to the nineteenth century. In recent times, census data have revealed that children of Asian roots are a rising immigrant group, already representing 22 percent of the population in 2017 (U.S. Census Bureau 2019a). At present, Asians comprise 5 percent of the country's child population. Similar to Hispanics, Asians are another highly diverse cultural and ethnic group. Our nation is the main destination of choice for Asians (Zong and Batalova 2016). Most Asian children living in the United States are from India, China, Korea, and the Philippines (Child Trends 2018a). Because of the growing influx of immigrants from Asia, it is estimated that by 2060, 8 percent of the nation's child population under age 18 will be of Asian descent (Vespa, Armstrong, and Medina 2018).

Emerging immigrant populations

In recent years, US communities have experienced an increase in the number of children from the Middle East, some Asian nations, and African countries. Many of these children are refugees and immigrants from emerging populations in the United States. Emerging populations is the term used to designate groups that are becoming more visible among the population. Data from the Migrant Head Start program, an early intervention federally funded program that also provides services to immigrant children from low-income families, showed that since 2013, a rising number of children enrolled in their program were from emerging populations representing more than seventy different countries (Office of Head Start 2017). Reports from the Census Bureau further confirm the increasingly diverse child immigrant population from other countries now attending early childhood programs. During 2010–17 immigration from new countries of origin reflected an increase with immigrants from Nepal. In fact, Nepalese immigrants have become one of the fastest-growing immigrant group followed by people from Burma, Afghanistan, Saudi Arabia, and Syria (Zong and Batalova 2019). This may help explain the rise in children enrolled in early childhood programs who are from emerging population groups in the United States.

Time to reflect … *Impact of child immigrants on the child population growth*

In a report from the Foundation for Child Development it was pointed out that children of immigrants accounted "for nearly the entire growth in the US child population between 1990 and 2008" (Hernández and Cervantes 2011, 3). As you consider this statement, reflect on its societal and educational implications. How evident are these implications already in your community? As educators, what considerations should be taken in order to ensure the well-being of the projected increasing child immigrant population?

The long-time presence of immigrants in the nation's classrooms

Immigrant children, whether they are born in other countries or born to immigrant parents, have long been part of the student population in the country. Many of us, immigrants ourselves, were part of the immigrant student population. Countless early childhood educators continue to work with immigrant children or had them as students in the past. The many strengths they bring along with their rich cultures, traditions, and languages contribute to the continuing growth in our communities. In many cases, as immigrants ourselves, we continue to see in our classrooms the future of the nation growing stronger through the wealth of ideas, views, and knowledge emerging from its diverse population.

Many early childhood educators have been witnessing the realities of immigrant children through the years. Working with children and their families, early childhood professionals have come to understand the intricate diversity of experiences and socioeconomic realities they represent. Many are recent arrivals into the nation while others have been long-time residents, offspring of generations past who like many today came seeking opportunities; others came escaping from conditions of poverty and insecurity. Their stories are a reflection of the same aspirations and needs of those trying to come into the country in recent and current times. This is perhaps what also helps in understanding the rising numbers of families arriving through the borders of the country during 2018–19. In the first half of 2019, 53 percent of people apprehended at the borders were families trying to find a safer place for themselves and their children (Gramlich and Noe-Bustamante 2019). Similar aspirations for safer places and opportunities for children motivated families in the past who came to live in the United States. Considerations to some of their realities experienced by children who came as immigrants are explored in the section that follows. Stepping into the past will further help us in constructing our views about children's experiences as participants in immigration.

Child immigrants in the United States yesterday and today

Throughout the history of the nation, child immigrants have been a contributing factor in shaping US society. As we ponder the realities of immigrant children, we briefly look at the past to help us focus our understanding of today. Times may be different but aspirations of families, as we will explore, continue to be the same: seeking a better life for their children. Many adults who came during their childhood today remember their days growing up in our communities as immigrants. One of those we met arrived with his mother as a toddler from Puerto Rico during the 1960s. He still remembers the small apartment where they lived and the many times they moved. So many moves that he lost count, with his mother always saying, "Vamos a estar bien," we are going to be fine. That optimism indeed has been and continues today guiding many immigrants working and doing their best for a better life.

Time to reflect ... *Children and families*

Many of our stories about our own childhood and family roots are kept alive in the family photos. They are treasured as a living document of who we are and where we come from. Take time to review your own family photos. Reflect on what they reveal about your own roots and the journeys of your family that brought you to where you are now.

As in the present, socioeconomic realities of child immigrants in the past were wide ranging. Most records and studies have targeted the journeys of adults, and little has been examined about children and their immigration experiences (Zayas et al. 2017). Their presence as protagonists is not as clear as that of our days. Yet, while many of the historical accounts focused mostly on the adults, their presence is recorded in the documents about their arrival as well as of the children born from immigrant parents. Klapper (2007), in her study of child immigrants in the United States during 1880–1925, noted that children were mostly overlooked and not considered as part of the immigration journey into the country. In her consideration, she contends that the history and trajectory of immigration belonged, too, to children that came or were born to immigrant parents. Both of us, as authors, agree with Klapper in affirming the role of children as protagonists in the story of immigration in the United States and throughout society. Though the focus was not on children before, today we are urged to recognize their participation and experiences. This is especially pertinent if we are to effectively provide children with what is socially just and fair to support and address their development.

Coming to America

Understanding the present cannot be fully done without a look at the past. This is what allows us to grasp a more comprehensive view about the circumstances and events of the present. Immigration, which has and continues to influence education decisions and practices, demands deepening into its realities deeply rooted in the past. Examining some of the events of the past will provide insights to educators about the challenges faced by children and families arriving and growing up as immigrants in the United States.

Rising immigration of families and children: A look at the past

Like today, in the early part of the twenty-first century, a boom of immigration experienced over a hundred and fifty years earlier denoted and influenced the character of US society. During the nineteenth and early part of the twentieth centuries, large groups of immigrants arrived in the country. The wave of immigrants during these periods contributed to the changing landscape of the country's population. The evolving industrialization and economic progress observed in the nation was one of the pull factors for the mostly European immigrants that came to the United States. The possibilities of a better life attracted thousands who ventured across the Atlantic to settle in the United States. Poor living conditions and limited employment options in their countries attracted many of those who decided to migrate seeking the promise of new opportunities in the United States. Many of the immigrants were families that came together with their children. Others began raising their families in their new homeland. Coming from other parts of the European continent, the second immigration wave (1880–1925) was particularly characterized by the arrival of immigrant family groups. Hundreds of children came along during this time.

Journeying to other countries has always been a challenging decision. It is today the same even though technology has eased and shortened distances. Traveling in the past was especially difficult given the available transportation of the times. New technological advances during the mid-1800s reduced the length of travel and ships with larger capacity made travel less costly, enticing entire groups of families who crossed the Atlantic during this time (McLemore and Romo 2005). As to the reasons that attracted many families to come, many "migrated for the explicit purpose of offering their children better lives" (Klapper 2007, 16). Despite the challenges of starting their lives over in a new place, hopeful families and children with their multitude of cultures and languages built their future in the United States. With a large influx of immigrants, cities and communities reflected their special diverse character. Many of those that arrived during the early decades of the twentieth century remembered the diversity encountered in the neighborhoods where they came to live. One of those that arrived during this time was a 16-year-old from Hungary who came in 1920. Reflecting on his experience years later, he commented, "All of a sudden I started life new, among people whose language I didn't understand ... everything was different ... but I never despaired, I was optimistic" (Lawlor 1995, 32).

Time to reflect ... *Motivations guiding people to migrate yesterday and today*

Many of the reasons pushing people to immigrate in the past were due to the social and economic conditions in their communities. For them, the United States represented a shining light of hope.

Reflect on the reasons attracting individuals to leave their homelands. Consider any parallels between those in the past and those in current times.

Photo 2.1 Immigrant children at Ellis Island.

Source: Photograph 90-G-125-29; Immigrant Children, Ellis Island, New York; ca. 1908; Public Health Service Historical Photograph File, 1880–1943; Records from the Public Health Service; National Archives at College Park, College Park, MD. [Online Version, https://www.docsteach.org/documents/document/children-ellis-island, June 22, 2020]

Ellis Island: A gateway for child immigrants

The presence of children as immigrants is also evident in the records of Ellis Island (Photo 2.1). Countless immigrants arrived in the country through the nation's East Coast ports of New York, Boston, Philadelphia, and Baltimore. The annals from Ellis Island, the main immigration entry port along the East Coast, recorded the arrival of hundreds of children among the twelve million people who came through its doors from 1892 to 1954 (National Park Service 2018). Most of the child immigrants arriving in the United States came with adults, whether parents or relatives. Others also came unaccompanied. Records show groups of children coming alone or together with older siblings, many of whom were children themselves. These young travelers came to meet with relatives and family members already living in the country. It has been said that the first person to enter through Ellis Island in 1892 as an immigrant was a 15-year-old girl from Ireland, coming to be with her parents who had previously migrated (Lawlor 1995; Roberts 2006). While details of her story are unclear, it is said that like many others at the time, she represents those who came as children to this country.

Accounts in the archives of local newspapers reported "thousands of children" arriving through Ellis Island. A story that appeared in the *New York Tribune* in 1904 captures their presence and records efforts to ameliorate their stay while at the Ellis Island facility. At the time, all immigrants, including children, were required to pass physical exams to officially enter the country. Those failing the exams were housed in the Ellis Island hospital facility until considered healthy. Many children remained at the Island while recovering. According to the story,

> The grounds did not furnish an appropriate place for a playground, but diligent examination revealed an ideal place on the large, flat roof of the main building. There, with the erection of awnings and the raising of parapets, the children could play to their heart's content. There they could enjoy the sea breezes of the New York Harbor, precisely the sort of tonic needed after their passage ... the result is an amply equipped play space, where the future Americans recover from the effects of their voyage and learn their first lessons In (sic) liberty. (*New York Tribune* 1904, n.p.)

Lawlor (1995), in her oral history project about Ellis Island, captured the voices of some children and youth that came through those doors. Some of the comments gathered through her interviews revealed the emotions and impressions people had when, as children, they embarked on the immigration journey. One of those interviews captures the sentiments of a young child coming from Armenia in 1922 as he entered the immigration port: "Coming to America had meaning. I was a kid of seven and in contrast to what I had gone through, Ellis Island was like not haven but a heaven" (20). Another interview conveys the memories of a 6-year-old arriving in 1924 who remembered her mother's shoes "resoled and stitched and mended in Sweden to hold them together till she could get to America" (18).

Voices for immigrant children

Images of immigrants arriving during the second immigration wave, the 1880s and early part of the 1900s, are a testimony to the optimism and aspirations of thousands of families and children who came to the United States. Coming in hopes of better circumstances, many incoming families and their children settled in urban communities where work was available. Several of these urban communities became mostly known as immigrant neighborhoods, with numerous still retaining their immigrant essence. Life in the tenements presented multiple challenges and many faced severe living conditions. The harshness of the realities experienced by many immigrant families and their children elicited the attention of individuals and organizations. Aware of the unfair living conditions for children, concerned individuals and organizations publicly denounced their difficult situations. Among those who advocated for socially just conditions during the early days of the twentieth century was Mary McDowell. A graduate from the then National Kindergarten College (Social Welfare History Project 2019), she was known as an activist protecting children of immigrants and who advocated for the rights of young children. Aware of the unsuitable living conditions for children, she condemned their condition in her talk titled *What Has Settlement Work Done for Social Justice?* (*Day Book* 1913). In her talk, she stated, "Immigration children are cooped up in small rooms, with no sunlight, bad air and poor food. Young boys and girls are forced to go to work before they have developed their minds and their bodies" (n.p.).

Mary's voice was one of the many whose efforts gave way to programs and services that continue to support children and people in need today. Activist Jane Addams was another voice whose work in Chicago supported the needs of immigrants and who dedicated her life to social justice actions. Highlights of the work of Jane Addams, whose dedication and efforts on behalf of children of immigrants and the poor earned her national and international recognition, are found in Box 2.1. The opening of Hull House in Chicago, where thousands received support and guidance for decades, is remembered as one of the landmark contributions of her humanitarian work.

Box 2.1 Connecting ideas: *Responding to the needs of immigrants: Early social justice efforts*

For many immigrants, living conditions in the United States during the latter part of the nineteenth century and early decades of the twentieth proved very difficult. As high numbers of families continue to arrive and settle in the urban areas of many of the receiving cities like New York, Boston, and Chicago, they encounter many grim realities. With most immigrants choosing to live where work was available, it resulted in crowded communities, with city services failing to meet the demands of the neighborhoods. The difficult living conditions for families and children prompted responses from many individuals and organizations who provided hope and alleviated many of their needs. One of them was Jane Addams, who dedicated her life to help the needy and to promote peace and civil rights. She was a social activist and one of the founding members of the National Association for the Advancement of Colored People.

In 1889, efforts of Jane Addams and her friend, Ellen Starr, led to the establishment of Hull House, a settlement home in an immigrant neighborhood in Chicago that provided services to needy immigrants and the poor. A nursery, a kindergarten, classes for adults, and a dispensary were later added to the services available. Hull House soon became a harbor of hope for the many immigrants in the Chicago area. Addams continued her advocacy for children, expanding her work to support children throughout the world. In 1931, Addams's humanitarian work earned her the Nobel Peace Prize, becoming the first American woman to receive the high honor (Fradin and Fradin 2006).

The continuing reality of immigrant children coming to the United States

Children have always been part of the immigration reality in the nation. In fact, this is not an isolated occurrence but a continuing reality. For decades, families have left with their children aiming at finding opportunities where their children can thrive and grow without fear but with hope. Recently, their journeys and struggles have garnered everyone's attention. In a conversation with a parent from Central America, he shared the reasons for leaving behind his community saying, "*Venimos porque ya no habia esperanza* [we are coming because there was no hope]."

Increased interest in immigrant children

Attention to children as immigrants grew strongly with the unaccompanied children crisis experienced in 2014. During the period of 2013–14, the number of children and adolescents unaccompanied crossing the nation's southern borders raised the attention of everyone. Though incidents of unaccompanied children have occurred before, it had never reached such record levels, with an increase by as much as 90 percent (Department of Homeland Security 2018). Entering undocumented and yearning for a welcome receptive to their needs, children faced then and now a system that, in the opinion of advocates, was not equipped to receive a wave of children immigrants. Four years later, the wave of immigrant caravans in 2018 brought again the presence of a childhood turned into immigrants, this time with many coming unaccompanied and others arriving with their families. The nature of their entry as undocumented individuals brought them to face treatment that in numerous cases challenged the essence of the compassionate and humanitarian approach of the United States to those in need. At present, thousands of children, unaccompanied and others with their families, entering unofficially continues, though at a lesser level given the impact of new immigration policies enacted in 2019.

The images of arriving parents and children have refocused attention on immigration, while shifting the conversation and placing attention on the young child. It has also reignited interest in the experiences of children as immigrants in the country. At the same time, they shed light on the integral societal presence of immigrants defining the nation. More than ever before, people are becoming aware of immigration as a topic of relevance to our society. Modern communication technologies are alerting everyone about the numerous children and families who are arriving today in Europe as well as in the United States. Presently, multiple social and political circumstances remain as challenges to families in many parts of the world. Countless families find themselves pressured to leave in search of a safe and stable living.

Time to reflect ... *Children coming to a new land*

Just as in the past, many children continue to arrive in the country. Imagine their impressions as they enter a new country after a long and arduous journey. Reflect on some of their thoughts and needs. How could you make them feel welcome? How could you meet their immediate social and emotional needs?

Immigration patterns of children and families today

The nature of immigration decisions made by families is another element characterizing them and their children. Whether immigration was voluntarily planned or involuntarily forced, it adds an important factor to their individual realities. In both cases, issues about the legality of their entry describe and impact their lives.

Planned immigration responds to pull factors as families consider opportunities and follow official channels to enter with proper documentation and authorization into the country. Thousands continue to arrive officially or authorized through the country's ports of entry. Records show that over one million authorized immigrants entered in 2017 (Department of Homeland Security 2018). In the nation's schools, enrollment of immigrant students has doubled over the past decades (Dinan 2017), continuing to demarcate their growing presence.

Integral to the social reality of the United States are also immigrant families that, confronted with difficult and life-threatening situations, come through unofficial or undocumented routes. It is unquestionable why they come. The severity of their circumstances, ranging from poor social conditions to complex emergencies and armed conflicts, remains as the primary factor prompting many of them to leave their homes. Some of those families that the authors met shared their difficult journeys and trying times once they entered the country. Despite language barriers and constant concern about their unofficial status, each one agreed that seeing their children in safer communities reaffirmed the efforts made. Though numbers are lower now, accounts show that in 2018 nearly half a million undocumented immigrants were apprehended at the US–Mexico border, where one-third of them were families (Bialik 2019).

Today, many of the images of children and families that flash on our TV screens are cases of forced migration. An understanding about the realities that confront families is essential to fairly judge and determine ways to assist them. A social justice issue, at stake remains the inherent responsibility that society has for children. Beyond cultural, ethnic, or political lines, every child is entitled to protection and to experience the necessary conditions essential to safeguard their future (UNICEF 2016). The need for attention and effective response to the needs of immigrants entering and living in the nation is an issue of social justice and of ethical responsibility.

Forced immigration of children and families: Asylees and refugees

It would be inaccurate to say that all immigrants share the same circumstances or motivations. Political circumstances, armed conflicts, and difficult situations remain today, leading many to seek asylum or refuge as they are forced to leave their countries. Compassionate attention to their needs has brought many to be relocated in other countries or to be given entry as a humanitarian response to their difficulties. The United States has traditionally opened its doors to those in need, continuing to respond to families and children experiencing humanitarian crises.

Talking with those who entered as refugees during their childhood allowed the authors to sample through their words the anxiety and challenges faced. Though today as adults they understand the urgency of what led to their escape, back then it was difficult to comprehend. For many of them, leaving behind their home was a remote idea or never even considered. Countless people have been left with little options but to leave. Many of them have entered as *refugees* given the humanitarian concerns and dangerous circumstances forcing them to leave their homes (U.S. Citizenship and Immigration 2019). Others proceeded to request asylum upon entering the United States seeking protection due to persecution or fear of becoming its victims. *Asylum* is given in the United States to people who are experiencing persecution or who may be its victims given their political views, religious beliefs, race, nationality, or membership in a particular social group (U.S. Citizenship and Immigration 2019).

Box 2.2 Voices of immigration: *An experience of a lifetime*

For an experienced educator, immigration became a major life event. Born in Cuba, she and her family were forced to seek asylum in the United States following the rise of the Castro regime. Even though she left the Cuban island at age 12, the motivation to leave was a decision made by her parents when she was 8 years old. In her mind, she was already an immigrant, not knowing when it would be the day to leave behind what she had known. The four-year wait finally ended when one day the family flew to the United States and later to Puerto Rico. Today an early childhood teacher educator, reflecting on her experiences, we listen to her voice in what she described as her story as an immigrant. Through her experiences, we learned about the difficult time trying to leave and then adjusting to a new setting and culture. Many children share similar experiences today. Recently, children and families who crossed the US border expressed their anxiety and struggle adapting to a new reality, including that of schools. They also shared about the support received from advocates, without whom "*todo sería mucho mas difícil,*" everything would be even harder.

This story started when I was 12 years old ... I think that at that moment, I was too young to be an immigrant ... I remember that day and all the emotions that arise with this experience; being separated from my cousins, my aunts, my grandmother, my friends, my school, my house, my dog ... which was a sad feeling. But at the same time, there was the excitement of traveling on a plane for the first time, to have the opportunity to go to a different country. But much more than this, it was a happy feeling of being reunited with my brother again as a family. He left Cuba when he was 15 years old and what was supposed to be a two weeks separation turned into a four years period. The reason for this was a conflict between two governments—Cuba and the United States—that caused the Cuban government to decide that no Cuban citizen could travel out of Cuba, something too complicated for a young girl to understand.

At that time, I have to live in a country where food was scarce; where I have to sing songs at school praising socialism—that for me was the reason why my family were apart, where we cannot celebrate Christmas. Finally, we were able to leave Cuba when a "door" to leave the country was opened for Cuban families who had minor children living in the United States. We were able to travel when the government approved this according to their rules and on the date that they decided … . I remember that the people that came to let us know that we had the permission to travel to the United States came one day before and at that moment, we had to leave our house and our belongings. The front door of our apartment was sealed and everything that we had inside was now a government property.

It was the month of April when I left my country; we came to Miami where we were for two days, and then, we flew to Puerto Rico. It was on a Holy Thursday-when we arrived in San Juan to start a new life … Finally, the four of us could be together, with part of our family that were living there … I loved the feeling of being together, I liked that I could speak Spanish and learn some new Puerto Rican words; a few months after, I started my school in a Catholic school-which was forbidden in my country. In a more negative part of this adaptation process, I knew what it was to be called a foreigner. Then, things changed … Cubans were integrated into the Puerto Rican society and I was part of this process. Now, Puerto Rico is my second country- where I lived for 38 years, where I got married, the place where my two sons were born, were my parents died and were buried, and where I had the opportunity of being an educator for many years and to leave a legacy to that country that somehow adopted me.

Now, I have been living in the mainland United States for the last fifteen years and even though I became an American citizen since I was 18 years old, I'm proud to be an immigrant; I'm proud to be a Latina. I can say that my story as an immigrant is a positive and successful story and the reason for this is that even in the most difficult times, I always had the support and company of my parents-, which is so important for a child. Our history and all the sacrifices they made for my brother and I to have a better life in a free country, has always been an example for me to be, first, the best daughter for them, and later in my life, a good wife, mother, grandmother, and professional. The girl that became an immigrant when she was 12 years old became a citizen that with the blessing of God has contributed to this American society in a positive way.

Refugees: An increased reality throughout the global community

According to the UNHCR, a refugee is "a person forced to flee their country because of violence, or persecution" (2019, n.p.). They cross an international border to find safety. Many times, the urgent nature of their circumstances leads them to leave their country with just what they are wearing and able to carry. Globally, in 2018, almost 30 million people including children were refugees (UNHCR 2019a). All refugees are protected under the international law in accordance with the 1951 Convention relating to the status of refugees. Central to the Convention are the principles of nondiscrimination, nonpenalization, and non-refoulement (no expulsion of refugees without their consent) (UNHCR 2010). Continuing conflicts in the global community remain, forcing the relocation of thousands including children. Almost half of the refugees are children under age 18.

Time to reflect ... *Forced to leave*

In the story *My Two Blankets* (Kobald 2015), the author conveys the challenge experienced by children leaving behind what was known and coming to live in a different place. Mindful about the well-being of young children, what considerations should be kept to ease the challenges faced by young children who are forced to leave their home countries?

Given the severity of conditions and situations experienced in their homelands, recently both Europe and the United States have seen a dramatic increase in forced migration, with thousands of families and children desperately crossing borders seeking refuge in other countries. Multifaceted situations and crises particularly in Africa, Asia, Middle East, and Central America can be cited as being responsible for driving families and their children to seek safer places, thus forcing their migration. Over 22,000 refugees were resettled in the United States during 2018.

Forced immigration occurs when circumstances reach a high severity level endangering the lives of people. Sadly, at the time that we write, various critical global situations and conflicts continue to be experienced in areas from where thousands of child and family immigrants have been forced to leave since 2014. Violence, civil insecurity, and poverty in Central America continue to force thousands to leave their countries, entering through the southwestern borders

Top Ten Countries of Origin of Refugees Arriving in 2017

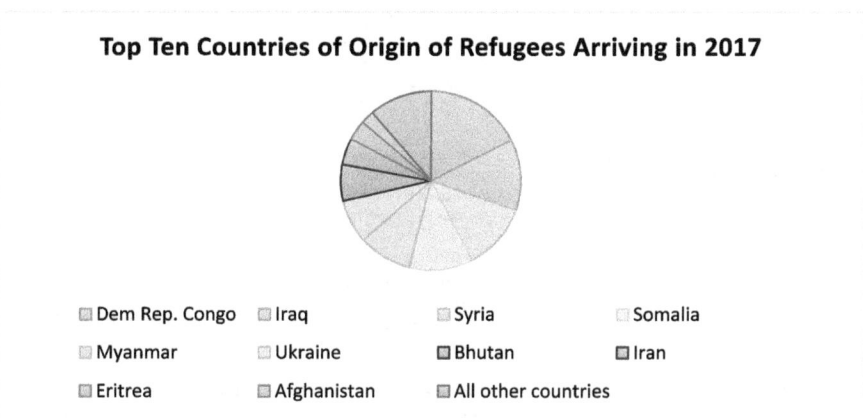

Dem Rep. Congo	Iraq	Syria	Somalia
Myanmar	Ukraine	Bhutan	Iran
Eritrea	Afghanistan	All other countries	

Figure 2.4 Top ten countries of origin of refugees (2017).
Source: Nadwa (2019).

of the United States and requesting asylum (Bialik 2019). Civil conflicts in Africa paired with succeeding loss of economic and social supports continue forcing many others to leave their countries. People from Syria, Ethiopia, Congo, and Eritrea were among the ten top countries of origin for refugees coming to the United States in 2017 (see Figure 2.4).

Seeking refuge in the United States

For decades, the United States has responded to the needs of people living in other countries and who are facing special humanitarian concerns (Figure 2.5). Those entering as refugees in the United States are those who "were persecuted or fear persecution due to race, religion, nationality political opinion, or membership in a particular social group" (U.S. Citizenship and Immigration Services 2019, n.p.). Every year, priorities for admission and admission levels are revised and determined. In 2019, the admission level was 30,000 for people applying to enter as refugees. The majority of those who entered that year were refugees from the African continent followed by people from East Asia (U.S. Department of State 2019).

Refugees receive resettlement assistance including social and educational services and programs from the moment they arrive into the country. These services and resources are intended to assist families and individuals with their incorporation into the United States (U.S. Department of Health and Human Services, Administration for Children and Families, Office of Refugee Resettlement 2019).

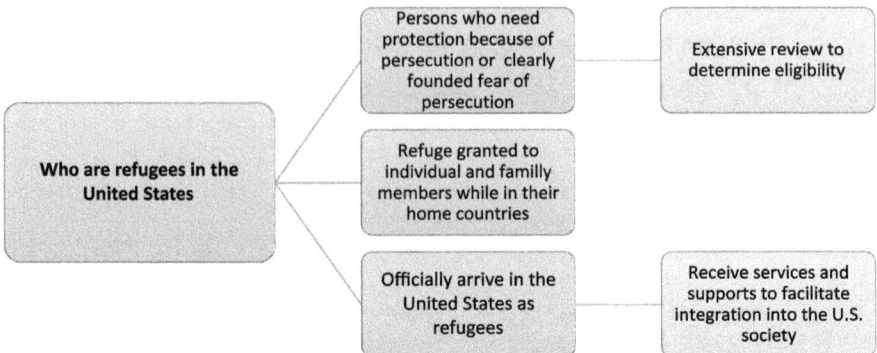

Figure 2.5 Main characteristics of refugees in the United States.
Source: U.S. Department of Health and Human Services, Administration for Children and Families, Office of Refugee Resettlement (2019).

Asylum: Another reality of people seeking safety

According to UNHCR, annually, close to one million people make an attempt to find asylum in other countries (UNHCR 2019a). Data from the UNHCR revealed that in 2018, three-and-a-half million asylum seekers were still awaiting decisions about their applications. Almost two million were new applications, with the majority applying for asylum in the United States (UNHCR 2019b). Reasons forcing people to seek a safer place are multiple. The common shared fact was that they faced life-threatening circumstances, leaving individuals with no other option but to leave and find protection. Those seeking asylum are individuals "whose request for sanctuary has yet to be processed" (UNHCR 2019a). Many asylees include families and their children. During 2018, the largest number of new asylum applicants came from Venezuela where unrest and life-endangering conditions have pushed numerous families to seek safety in other countries. Many have settled in the United States where they are a thriving community.

In the United States, asylum is granted to individuals who are escaping from persecution and dangerous situations preventing their safe stay in their communities (ORR 2012). Unlike refugees, asylees "on their own, travel to the United States" (ORR 2019) where they request protection. The Office of Refugee Resettlement (ORR) provides resources and support for asylees. Some asylees arrive as students, tourists, businesspeople, and others enter unauthorized. A review of their specific cases determines if they are granted asylum in the United States. Figure 2.6 lists some of the main characteristics of asylees.

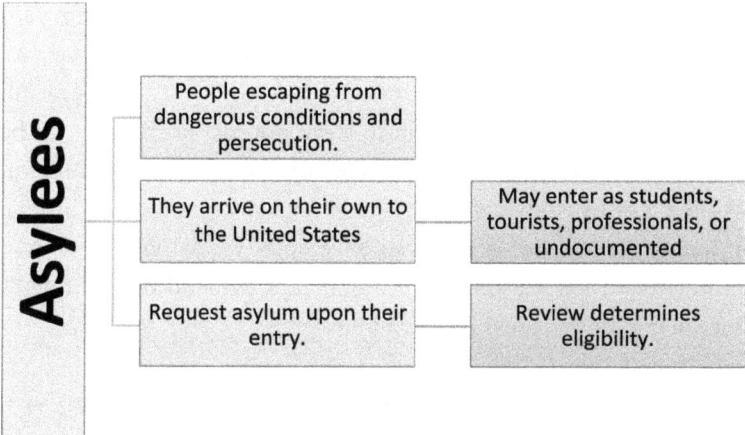

Figure 2.6 Main characteristics of asylees in the United States.
Source: U.S. Department of Health and Human Services, Administration for Children and Families, Office of Refugee Resettlement (2019).

In common: Searching for a safe place

Many of the arriving asylees and refugees are children similar to the thousands who arrived in the past. Coming from a multiplicity of settings, they share the need for a place where they can safely live, grow, and develop. The saga of their journeys is reflected by authors of recent stories drawn from ongoing events, where attention is called to the experiences continuing to challenge children and families. In *The Journey* (Sanna 2016), the child character reflects the emotions of leaving what is known for the unknown as the family departs from their home seeking refuge in a safe place where they can start again. A similar message is conveyed by Ruurs in her story *Stepping Stones: A Refugee Family's Journey* (2016), where the characters echo their dream for a place where they can freely and safely be a family. This same story continues to repeat itself today with children and their families escaping difficult and life-threatening conditions. It is as well what was heard from families that shared their stories with the authors while gathering information about their experiences (see Box 2.2 *Voices of immigration*).

Families seeking a safe place

Since the beginning of the 2010s, the rise in the arrival of immigrant children and families has multiplied in the United States. For some families with whom we spoke like Josefina (pseudonym), a single parent from Guatemala, it was their only hope to live, "la única esperanza para poder vivir." Similarly, a young Honduran parent told us that she became too fearful, "tenía mucho miedo," with all the threats and made the decision to leave not just for her but for her two children. Some of the controversies surrounding issues about immigrants are rooted in the legality of their arrival. While regular or authorized immigration has continued, many other immigrants have opted for arriving undocumented or unauthorized. Their reasons are multiple and demand consideration given the nature of conditions pressing them to leave.

Crossing borders: The debate over unauthorized immigration

Recent years have reignited the debate about immigration in the country. While many attempts have been made or proposed to amend the immigration legislation, these have been unsuccessful, resulting in still maintaining the same immigration legal umbrella. Meanwhile, the discourse on immigration has grown more intense. As you recall from the discussion in Chapter 1, the 1960s immigration law opened doors to a more diverse immigration flow. The 1965 immigration law gave an impetus to a larger immigration, changing the geographical scope of the nationalities of people coming into the nation. Subsequent immigration policies continued to dramatically change the ethnic profile of people entering into the United States. Different from the past when Europeans essentially characterized immigration, most of the arriving immigrants in recent years have been from Asia and Latin America (Schaefer 2016). In fact, the pronounced diversity of immigrants has intensively led to the cultural transformation of the nation in recent decades. At the same time, the more marked presence and diversity of immigrants has also brought to light the reality of individuals arriving unauthorized or undocumented into the nation. Some of the facts describing individuals and families that entered unauthorized are included in Table 2.2.

Undocumented entries into the nation have continued as a reality for decades. Estimates show that in 2015, twelve million unauthorized individuals lived in the country (Department of Homeland Security 2018b). Nine percent of undocumented individuals were young immigrants under age 18. At present, a large percentage of US-born children with unauthorized immigrant parents are students in schools throughout the nation. It is estimated that, overall, five-and-a-half million children holding US citizenship under the age of 18 live with unauthorized immigrant parents (Chaudry et al. 2010; Passel and Cohn 2018).

Table 2.2 Undocumented immigrants living in the United States: Key facts

Undocumented population	It is estimated that nearly twelve million immigrants with unauthorized entry live in the United States. Most have been living in the country for more than ten years. Many entered legally and overstayed their visas. Largest states with undocumented immigrants are California, Texas, and Florida. Undocumented immigrants an active part of the US workforce.
Cultures and ethnicities	Most undocumented immigrants are Hispanics. Majority of unauthorized immigrants are Mexicans, followed by immigrants from Central America and Asia. Recent years have also seen immigrants from African nations entering through the US southern borders.. Many undocumented immigrants are speakers of languages other than English. Spanish is spoken by most undocumented immigrants and their families.
Children and families	Most undocumented immigrants are parents. The large majority of their children are US citizens. Close to six million children live in families where a parent or both are undocumented. Despite their challenges, families have strong commitment and dedication to their children.

Source: Baker (2018).

They are long-time residents

A large number of unauthorized immigrants have been long-time residents in the nation's communities. Almost seventeen million people are estimated to reside with at least one family member who is undocumented (American Immigration Council 2019). In fact, two-thirds of parents with undocumented status have been residents for more than a decade in communities across the country. The majority of their children, in turn, are US born, most of whom are young children under age 6 (Yoshikawa and Kholoptseva 2013). However, contrary to what the media may show, since 2007, undocumented population particularly Hispanics has been declining. Demographers consider that this may be due to a decrease in the number of unauthorized Mexican immigrants arriving into the United States. Reports show that many have been returning to their country, adding to the decreasing presence of the undocumented population (Krogstad, Passel, and Cohn 2019; Radford 2019). On the other hand, since 2010, it has become evident that presently, many undocumented immigrants actually entered legally and overstayed their visas (Passel and Cohn 2019). Their reasons continue to be similar, aspirations for a better life.

Immigration enforcement and children's well-being

Delving into the legality and political angles of the immigration debate is not the aim of this book. However, it is relevant for educators to become aware of some of its characteristics and implications on the well-being of children. Awareness about these circumstances is especially pertinent as we work to ensure equitable responses to the needs of child immigrants and their families. Equity is owed to each and every child and mindful considerations to circumstances that inhibit their development and future are paramount. This, simply stated, is another way to inform practices for young immigrant children.

Stricter immigration enforcement has been a topic impacting the well-being of children and families with unauthorized status. Thousands of families with members with undocumented status have experienced deportation or live in fear of being deported. The end result has led to countless children to live without a parent or to experience the fear of losing them. Reports showed that immigration enforcement resulted in the deportation of over 100,000 parents of children who are US-born citizens (Chaudry et al. 2010). Since the beginning of this century, recent changes in immigration have given rise to greater scrutiny and enforcement. They are also the result of legislation passed in response to attention to undocumented immigration and of national security concerns after the events of 9/11. Elevated immigration enforcement has made the path to legal residence a more difficult one (Lovato et al. 2018). The outcome of the legislative actions has been an increase in the number of deportations of undocumented individuals, many of whom are parents. Fear of deportation already looms large in many communities and households, with children growing up under the threat of losing a parent. For many families, deportation has separated countless children from their parents (Philbin and Ayón 2016). Many now live without a parent or in the care of relatives. Consequences on children are multiple, ranging from loss of economic support to housing and food insecurity, and influencing behavioral changes on the impacted children (Chaudry et al. 2010). Living with uncertainty and fear further leaves emotional marks on children.

Box 2.3 Connecting ideas: *Implications of a family's immigration status on children*

Implications emerging from the parents' immigration status are relevant to early childhood practices. The fact is that the immigration status of parents has been identified as one of the factors influencing the well-being of families and children. While many children find supportive environments, there are several critical implications impacting the family and child's well-being. The following are relevant to be considered:

- Lower opportunities for employment, poverty, and lesser access to health care are not uncommon among many families where a parent may have an undocumented status (Chaudry et al. 2010).
- Limitations to access services and programs due to misinformation or fear to request these due to their unauthorized immigration status. Ironically, most of the time children of undocumented immigrant parents are entitled to receive services, something sometimes unknown to families or avoided due to concerns with "la migra," immigration.
- Fear of deportation due to renewed enforcement of immigration, which poses additional social, economic, and emotional stress to children and their families. It has also resulted in declining enrollment of children in early childhood programs (Greenberg, Rosenboon, and Adams 2019).
- Struggling circumstances due to parents' deportation. Many children have also been left without support or live under struggling circumstances (Yoshikawa and Kholoptseva 2013).

Work of advocates remains critical to ensure children receive the needed supports they are legally eligible to receive.

Reading the story *From North to South* (Colato Lainez 2013), images of children separated from parents come forward. In the story, the author brings to life the reality of losing a parent to deportation. Today, this is not an uncommon story. As authors, we have personally heard the accounts from children and their teachers. One of the authors remembers when one of her graduate students called her shocked after the mother of two of her young students was deported. The truth is that no child during the most vulnerable years or family should experience the fear of losing a parent. Like a parent in a study by Philbin and Ayón (2016) stated, *"fear should not be present in the [lives of] children"* (emphasis added) (130).

Crisis in Central America

Words cannot express enough the difficult circumstances happening in Central America. Crises in Central America have driven thousands of families to escape serious and dangerous circumstances (see Figure 2.7). An ongoing challenge emerging in a more pronounced way since 2014 with the arrival of unaccompanied children, it has evidenced the high levels of social violence and poverty forcing people to leave. During the months of October 2018 to May 2019, over 300,000 family units were reported as crossing undocumented the borders into the United States. Family unit is the term used by the U.S. Border Patrol to designate "individuals (either children under age 18, parent, or legal guardian) apprehended with a family member" as they cross the border (U.S. Customs and Border Protection 2019). Though numbers declined at the end of 2019, due to new immigration practices haltering their entry, unquestionably, the continuing arrival of families evidences the difficult circumstances faced in the Central American region prompting families to migrate.

A serious reality of today: The plight of unaccompanied children

The flow of unaccompanied children and the attempted entries into the United States of children and their families from Central America and Mexico exposed the harshness of inequalities and circumstances experienced by so many. Demanding and dangerous conditions remain, threatening the well-being and stability of families and children who see no other option and in desperation are leaving their homelands. Though unauthorized, the thousands of families entering through the border are coming in hopes of safety for their children and themselves. As Colleen Kraft, president of the American Academy of Pediatrics, posited, "*We must remember that children do not immigrate, they flee. Parents will continue to flee violence to protect their children and seek haven in our country*" (emphasis added) (2018).

During FY 2018, the federal government reported over 50,000 unaccompanied children entering through the southwest border of the country. Fifteen percent of children arriving in 2018 were ages 0–12 (Department of Health and Human Services 2019). According to federal law, unaccompanied child immigrants entering without documentation are referred to as *unaccompanied alien children*. Under federal custody, unaccompanied alien children are considered as:

> A child who has no lawful immigration status in the United States; has not attained 18 years of age; and with respect to whom: 1) there is no parent or legal guardian in the United States; or, 2) no parent or legal guardian in the

United States available to provide care and physical custody. (Office of Refugee Resettlement 2016)

For thousands of unaccompanied children, their entry into the country begins as they are taken into custody by border patrol. Their first experience is the detention centers where their cases are reviewed and processed. Coming under the custody of the ORR, the designated agency to respond to the needs of unaccompanied children who enter into the nation without authorization, children are placed in temporary care provider facilities. A network of shelters located across the nation house unaccompanied immigrant children (ORR 2019).

Detention: An issue and concern

Children and families entering unauthorized face the reality of their detention as they crossed the US borders. While their cases are reviewed, thousands of children have ended trapped in the detention centers. Their cases have been in the news headlines on too many occasions. Conditions reported in 2019 alerted the public about what young children, including toddlers, have experienced. More than once, the news has also reported the loss of a minor held in custody (Joung 2019). Time spent at the detention centers has also raised concerns among children and migrant advocates. In particular, concerns emerge about the overall physical and mental health of children when their detention is prolonged (Chatterjee 2019). Statements from the American Academy of Pediatrics have

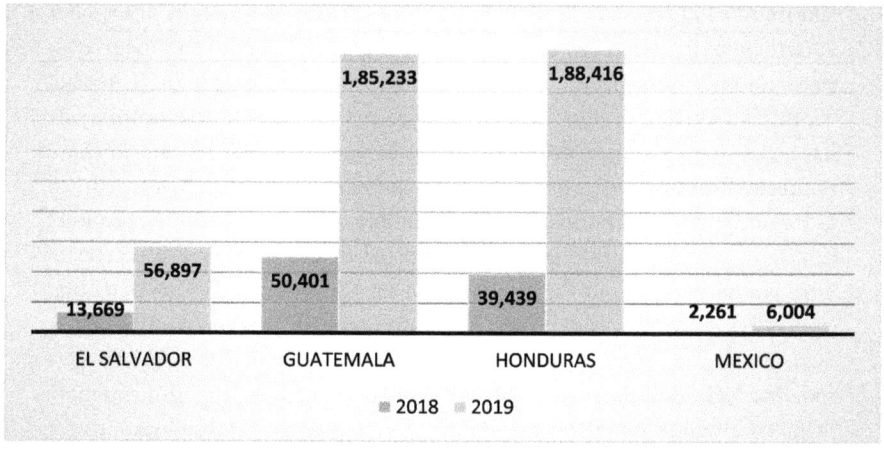

Figure 2.7 Countries of origin of families arriving from Central America through the US southwest border (FY 2018–19).
Source: U.S. Customs and Border Protection (2019).

warned about the adverse effects of the resulting stress and trauma caused to children who are detained (Linton et al. 2017). The fact is that the obligations of immigration authorities toward children in custody were determined in 1997 by the Flores settlement, defining rigorous standards for their care. Based on the Flores settlement, children cannot be kept more than twenty days in detention. It is relevant to mention that with the unexpected increase in the number of children arriving during FY 2019, many children ended staying longer that what the law established. Haughloner and Sacchetti (2019) reported that the unexpected high number of child arrivals overwhelmed the immigration system procedures to effectively relocate children in shelters.

Meanwhile, according to the Flores settlement, authorities are required to provide the least restrictive environment for children. They are also mandated to follow strict standards to deliver care and attention to children (Sussis 2019). Based on the Homeland Security Act of 2002, care and custody of unaccompanied children was transferred from immigration to the ORR. According to ORR, "By law, the U.S. Department of Health and Human Services (HHS) has custody and must provide care for each UAC [unaccompanied alien child]" (ORR 2019).

Box 2.4 Connecting ideas: *Children and families at the borders*

Continuing arrivals of immigrants through the southwest borders particularly since 2018 has caught everyone's attention. Reaching unprecedented numbers, almost 700,000 crossed into the United States during the months of October 2018 to June 2019 (U.S. Customs and Border Protection 2019). This time arrivals were not only from Central America but also included people from African countries (Averbusch and Sieff 2019) and, reportedly, Chinese immigrants have also joined those seeking to enter into the United States. The high number of immigrants arriving through the borders in 2019, "overwhelmed U.S. immigration infrastructure" (Haughlohner and Sacchetti 2019), resulting in overcrowded detention centers as reported by the press and advocates of immigrants. News about the overcrowded situation in many of the detention centers raised the voices of protest from immigrant advocates (Acevedo 2019; Silva 2019). The urgency to resolve the status of children crossing the borders remains high, especially given the adverse effects of their stressful situation. Steps continue to be taken to improve the conditions in these locations for children and adults.

Under the law, children are entitled to receive services and educational experiences. While in custody, they are provided with education services at the facility until their appropriate placement is determined. Those with relatives living in the United States are placed under their sponsorship (ORR 2019). Today, many unaccompanied children continue to wait in shelters for a resolution to their cases and a placement suitable to address their needs. Circumstances at some of these shelters were denounced, causing an uproar among children advocates. While their cases are reviewed, cases of children who lost their lives while in custody (Acevedo 2019; Van Sant 2019) have elevated the severity of the situation and have called for further action to safeguard the well-being of child immigrants.

Time to reflect ... *For your family*

The incessant flow of families forced to leave behind their homes is a shocking reality of today. Many families already live in our communities and their children are in our classrooms. Considering what has driven them to leave everything behind, think how you would respond if found in their situation. What would you hope to find for your own family in the community and schools?

The migrant caravans at the border

News in 2018 about caravans of immigrants forming in Central America and headed to the United States drove the attention of the nation. Hundreds of families with their children left their communities driven by serious levels of insecurity, social violence, and poverty in Central America. They were following the same road taken in past years by families trying to escape from serious and challenging realities (Chishti and Hipsman 2016). Along with adults, the caravans included hundreds of unaccompanied children under the age of 18. According to Semple (2016) reporting on the border subject, "Gang violence in El Salvador, Honduras and Guatemala has conspired with economic desperation to drive an unrelenting exodus of migrants including entire families, seeking safety in other countries, mainly the United States" (A6). Despite the many immigrants that attempted to cross the borders and ended been apprehended, hundreds have continued to enter through the southwest border.

Table 2.3 Number of family units and unaccompanied children arriving through the southwest border (2017–19)

Year	Unaccompanied children	Family units
2017	41,435	75,622
2018	50,036	107,212
2019	76,020	473,682

Source: U.S. Customs and Border Protection (2019).

Official reports show that in 2018, the number of family units and unaccompanied children taken into custody at the southwest border increased, setting a high record (Miroff 2019; U.S. Customs and Border Protection 2019). The numbers of families and children crossing the borders were staggering, a fact stressing the severity of their realities. This became even more evident when reports in 2019 showed a rise in arrivals of children and families. Most of the families crossing into the country were from Central America, with the majority coming from Honduras followed by Guatemala and El Salvador, respectively (U.S. Customs and Border Protection 2019).

Many immigrants who opted to join the caravans thought that traveling in large groups was a safer way to reach the US border. While large caravans "fizzled out" (Alvarez 2019), some people still continue to travel in groups. New policies about immigrants trying to cross the US border issued in 2019 have further decreased the number of arrivals. Meanwhile, smaller groups of migrants continue to persist in their efforts to reach the US border. Ongoing reports from the border patrol confirm the migrants' efforts. Overall, and beyond the numbers, the evidence loudly speaks about the critical crises taking place in other countries. Through it all, one cannot forget children who have been experiencing these conditions and who are in so many ways victims of these continuing situations.

Box 2.5 Connecting ideas: *Immigration enforcement at the borders: Children separated from families*

The separation of children from their families has been one of the most challenging episodes emerging from the experience of immigrants crossing undocumented through the US borders. In 2018, images were broadcasted documenting the journey of hundreds of families with young children traveling from Honduras, El Salvador, Guatemala, and Mexico. News of the approaching caravans in April and October 2018 added to the long-time issue about immigration, particularly concerning irregular or unauthorized arrivals. Those who attempted to enter were detained following immigration and border enforcement policy. Others, immigrants requesting asylum, remained on the border waiting for answers to their petitions (Burnett 2018). Following immigration enforcement rules, with their families detained, children ended up being separated from their parents. The result was that over 2,500 children were separated from their families. They were housed in shelters located mostly in Texas and Florida (Administration of Children and Families 2018; Haigh 2018). Their apprehensions came as a result of the zero-tolerance immigration policy regarding families issued in summer 2018 (Department of Homeland Security 2018a). Among the children sent to shelters, 103 were under age 5, who despite their young ages were still separated from their families. The policy was later revoked following the controversy and furor of advocates and the public.

News about separation of children from their families and reported conditions where they were housed led to a public outrage. Advocates' efforts and the public voice led to a halt in the separation of children from families. National organizations like the NAEYC joined their voices calling for the protection and well-being of young children (Evans Allvin 2018). Reunification of the youngest ones, children under age 5, was court ordered in 2018 while others waited to be reunited with families or relatives. Based on media and official government reports, hundreds of children have continued to be housed in shelters, where the majority are age 14 or older. At the time of writing this chapter, the separation issue continues to spark controversy given the implications of this experience for children and the integrity of the family. Thousands of advocates and the public have raised their voices concerned about the well-being of children.

Continuing immigration of families and children

Many different circumstances continue, leading families to leave behind their home countries. (Anonymous)

The steady increase in the number of children and families leaving their home countries has clearly defined the first two decades of this century. Motivations vary, with many continuing to officially arrive through the nation's borders. Yet, urgent and challenging situations in many places push others to enter through other routes. Globally, the media and the pleas from advocates have made society well aware of the presence of children and particularly about the perils experienced. Actions in their support continue to be debated particularly in Europe and in the United States where the numbers of arrivals have been in the thousands. How long will it take decisions to be made? With growing concern about the future of children placed in this serious situation, we ask how long they will have to wait. Children cannot wait, as Nobel laureate poet Gabriela Mistral so powerfully said. Response to the needs of children is what also remains as guiding humanitarian efforts today, similar to those that took place in the past.

Support for children: Humanitarian efforts

The gardens of kindness never fade. (Greek proverb)

Someone will always hear the voice of a child. The needs of children have always captured the attention of those who recognize the inherent responsibility toward children. The kindness of those who advocate and believe in children, as the Greek proverb says, will always be ample to help those in need. They will find ways to come to their aid. Over the years, humanitarian efforts from advocates, government, and nongovernmental agencies have made it possible for thousands of children to find hope relocating into our nation. During the twentieth century, hundreds of children, victims of First World War, came into the United States following the efforts of advocates and the government that welcomed their arrival. Similarly, children displaced by the crisis of the Hungarian Revolution in 1956 found the doors open to receive them as refugees in the United States. Thousands of children and families fled their homes after the Vietnam War, finding a home in the United States. Some came with their families while many others came unaccompanied.

A reality of the past and today: Unaccompanied children

Over the years, hundreds of children forced to leave their realities have also arrived unaccompanied into the country. The case of unaccompanied children in recent years is another somber episode underlining critical situations facing children and their families. One of these cases was the Cuban children who arrived in the Pedro Pan flights during the early 1960s. It was the efforts of many advocates who joined their energies to make possible the arrival of thousands of Cuban children. Accounts about the flights and the circumstances leading to the airlifts from Havana to Miami that brought over 14,000 children appears in Box 2.6.

Box 2.6 Connecting ideas: *Operation Pedro Pan, the children's flights*

The rise of the Castro regime in Cuba in January of 1959 brought dramatic political and social changes to the Caribbean island lasting to the present. With Castro embracing Marxism, soon the government announced its plans for indoctrination of children into the ideology. For families in Cuba, the fear of indoctrination was immeasurable. Even more was the idea of losing their parental rights as announced by the government. With parents not allowed to leave the island, families secretly began to consider how to prevent their children from becoming indoctrinated. During the fall of 1960, a family was able to send their son Pedro, unaccompanied, on one of the flights to Miami to stay with relatives. Living under very difficult conditions, his relatives went to the Catholic Welfare Bureau for assistance. A priest from Miami, Father Brian Walsh, soon realized that many other "Pedros" could also come aboard the flights from Havana. Through his efforts he was able to make a deal with the US State Department that allowed him to sign visa waivers for children age 16 and under. Secretly recruiting throughout the island and with the visas accepted by the Cuban government, children began to travel out of Havana aboard the flights to Miami.

Relatives already living in Miami welcomed about half of the group of children, while arrangements were made for others without relatives to stay in camps and foster homes. From there, many whose parents were unable to leave the island were sent to orphanages throughout the country. During the 1960–62 period, over 14,000 unaccompanied children were flown out of Havana. Today a successful executive, for one of the children who came together with his sister in one of the flights, the experience remains vividly present. He still remembers being at the airport trying to see his father through a glass wall and the inability to reach him. It would take him and his sister over a year to finally be with their parents again who were now in Miami. Thoughts about the experience continue to be vivid in his mind.

The flights ended in October 1962 when the Cuban missile crisis ended the commercial flights into the island. Today, the Pedro Pan flights remain an example of concerted efforts that allowed thousands of children to escape a difficult reality.

Source: Allen (2011); Personal communication, November 2018.

Immigration is a human rights issue

Everyone has the right to life, liberty and security of person, reads article 3 of the Universal Declaration of Human Rights (United Nations 1948). This statement asserts human rights and stresses that these are inalienable to every individual. They remain as defining traits of individuals across social, cultural, and political lines. Intrinsic to the declaration of human rights is the affirmation of people's integrity and dignity. With the circumstances and challenges facing thousands of immigrants today, respect for their rights is paramount. Immigration has become a human rights issue. Far from political lines, images of the youngest migrants alone or with their families and of the thousands already living in the nation continue to flash on our screens. They are a reminder to society that everyone has a right to a better life.

Implications for early childhood educators clearly point to the need to ensure that attention and responses to their needs are equitably provided. Whether they are recent arrivals or are already part of the thousands of immigrant children living in the country, they are deserving of attention and actions that are socially just and developmentally appropriate for their well-being. Far beyond reasons and labels, immigrants remain as an integral element to the nation. Many immigrants earlier just as today experienced challenging situations that motivated thousands to seek other lands. This time we see the rising flow of families and children more than ever. The call is for an empathetic and compassionate response with consideration to their needs and to the fact that while some come voluntarily, many others are driven away from their homelands to ensure a future for their children and themselves. The issues faced are many: hunger, poverty, fear due to civil instability, and violence among others.

Giving a voice to the child immigrant

The steep increase in child immigrants and refugees that multiplied between 2010 and 2015 (UNICEF 2016) and the hundreds coming from Mexico and Central America underline the urgency and the reality experienced by thousands of immigrant children and families. It also clearly brings attention to immigrant children already living in our communities who many of us teach, support, and care for every day. While the United States is a nation anchored in immigration history, recent experiences with the increased arrival of people through the southern borders have elevated immigration to be a heatedly contentious topic.

Throughout the conversation and discussions, the voice of the child is indelibly present, though obscured by the tone of some of the arguments. Their needs and circumstances loudly call for early educators to hear them and to respond to their needs as children, not to the status or legality of their arrivals. We need to be their voice!

A child is a child

Beyond adjectives and labels, immigrant children are simply children. Many of them are growing up in places foreign to them where circumstances may have taken them to live. Others are children citizens, born to immigrant parents and beginning to develop in communities across the nation. As the discussion unfolded earlier, reasons explaining the motives that may lead so many families and children to immigrate vary as much as their life circumstances are as well. Irrespective of the reasons that bring a child to live in another land or that brought their parents to build their families' future in our country, we must first remember that they are children. They have a right to their childhood and to have their voices heard. More importantly, they have a right to a bright future. This is at the heart of social justice for the child. This is also what defines what is ethically relevant. It is essential that every community responsibly recognize the potential in each child and what each child represents for the future of society.

Ethically, for early childhood educators, supporting and addressing the needs of the young immigrant child entails a responsibility inherent to the profession (NAEYC 2019). How does that translate to social justice actions on behalf of child immigrants? Championing the cause of the child is a humanitarian response in our society and is a moral responsibility for educators. The beginning starts by listening to their voices and becoming mindful of their needs. What is critical to support their needs? How could early educators ensure they receive fair and equitable opportunities? How could we best secure their success? This and many other questions are critical as we consider, plan, and take actions that are fair and socially responsive to the child. With the world and the nation's community increasing awareness on child immigrants, their circumstances and difficulties are coming to the forefront. As we focus our attention on their realities, throughout the coming chapters, we will continue to center on the experiences of child immigrants in the United States through the lenses of culture, ethics, educational practices, and social justice.

Key ideas

- Although not directly reflected in the literature, children have always been participants in the immigration experience. Emphasis has been on the events and experiences of adults and families, which has overshadowed the presence of children. Interest in the impact and happenings they experience has gained national and global attention in recent years. Immigration is a life experience for everyone and a major event for a child. It directly influences their development and future as they grow up as child immigrants.
- Historical records help us trace the experiences of children through time as immigrants in the United States. Many child immigrants came to the nation as part of humanitarian efforts by advocates and with the support of the government.
- Child immigrants constitute a large percentage of the country's child population. Their presence is projected to increase and to become a significant factor in the overall population growth.
- Multiple crisis in current times are forcing the migration of thousands of families and children. Their situation has become a humanitarian crisis.
- Attention to the needs of children and their families is an ethical responsibility of early childhood educators.

To think, do, and reflect …

1. Reflect on the implicit responsibilities early educators have to ensure child immigrant's needs are met. Which needs would you say are the three main challenges still to be addressed?
2. Consider the main traits characterizing immigrant children and their families. Identify implications for delivering early childhood services and programs.
3. What are some of the factors responsible for the increase in childhood immigration levels?
4. What socially just actions would you suggest needs to address the immigration situation of unaccompanied children?
5. In view of the needs of citizen children living with unauthorized status parents, what additional steps should be considered to ensure their rights?

References

Acevedo, Nicole. 2019. "Why are migrant children dying in U.S. custody?"
   NBC News. May 29. Retrieved from https://www.nbcnews.com/news/latino/
   why-are-migrant-children-dying-u-s-custody-n1010316.

Administration of Children and Families. 2018. *Unaccompanied Alien Children
   Program. Fact Sheet—December.* Retrieved from https://www.hhs.gov/sites/default/
   files/Unaccompanied-Alien-Children-Program-Fact-Sheet.pdf.

Allen, G. 2011. "Children of Cuba remember their flight to America." *Weekend
   Edition Saturday. NPR.* November 19. Retrieved from https://www.npr.
   org/2011/11/19/142534943/pedro-pan-childrens-life-altering-flight-from-cuba.

Alvarez, Priscilla. 2019. "What happened to the migrant caravans?" *CNN Politics.*
   Retrieved from https://www.cnn.com/2019/03/04/politics/migrant-caravans-trump-
   immigration/index.html.

American Immigration Council. 2019. *U.S. Children Impacted by Immigration
   Enforcement.* Retrieved from https://www.americanimmigrationcouncil.org/sites/
   default/files/research/us_citizen_children_impacted_by_immigration_enforcement.
   pdf.

American Immigration Council. 2020. *Immigrants in the United States.* April 21. Fact
   Sheet. Retrieved from https://www.americanimmigrationcouncil.org/research/
   immigrants-in-the-united-states.

American Psychological Association, Presidential Task Force on Immigration. 2012.
   Crossroads: The psychology of immigration in the new century. Retrieved from http://
   www.apa.org/topics/immigration/report.aspx.

Annie Casey Foundation. 2017. *Race for Results. 2017 Policy Report. Kids Count.*
   Retrieved from https://www.aecf.org/m/resourcedoc/aecf-2017raceforresults-2017.
   pdf#page=34.

Averbusch, Maya, and Kevin Sieff. 2019. "Hundreds of Africans tried to reach he United
   States. Now they're stuck in Mexico." April 16. *Washington Post.* Retrieved from
   https://www.washingtonpost.com/world/the_americas/hundreds-of-africans-tried-
   to-reach-the-united-states-now-theyre-stuck-in-mexico/2019/04/16/6ebb7b48-5fa4-
   11e9-bf24-db4b9fb62aa2_story.html.

Baker, B. 2018. "Estimates of the illegal alien population residing in the United
   States: January 2015." In *Population Estimates. Illegal Alien Population Residing in the
   United States: January 2015.* Washington, DC: Department of Homeland Security,
   Office of Immigration Statistics. Retrieved from https://www.dhs.gov/sites/default/
   files/publications/18_1214_PLCY_pops-est-report.pdf.

Bankston III, Carl. 2010. "Social justice: Cultural origins of a perspective and a theory."
   Independent Review 15(2): 165–78.

Bialik, Kristen. 2019. "Border apprehensions increased in 2018—especially
   migrant families." *Fact Tank. News in Numbers.* Pew Research Center. January

10. Retrieved from https://www.pewresearch.org/fact-tank/2019/01/16/border-apprehensions-of-migrant-families-have-risen-substantially-so-far-in-2018/.

Breiseth, Lydia. 2018. *How to support immigrant students and families. Strategies for schools and early childhood programs.* ¡Colorín, Colorado! Retrieved from https://www.colorincolorado.org/sites/default/files/Immigration-Guide-FINAL_4-26-19.pdf.

Burnett, John. 2018. "After traveling 2,000 miles for asylum, this family's journey halts at the bridge." June 15. *National Public Radio.* Retrieved from https://www.npr.org/2018/06/15/620310589/after-a-2-000-mile-asylum-journey-family-is-turned-away-before-reaching-u-s-soil.

Burrone, Sara, Bina D'Costa, and Goran Holmqvist, G. 2019. *Children's Wellbeing Linked to Migration Desire, Plans.* Gallup Topics. Retrieved from https://news.gallup.com/opinion/gallup/246578/children-wellbeing-linked-migration-desire-plans.aspx.

Camarota, Steven, Bryan Griffith, and Karen Zeigler. 2017. *Mapping Immigration's Impact on Public Schools.* Center for Immigration Studies. Retrieved from https://cis.org/sites/cis.org/files/camarota-pumas_2.pdf.

Chatterjee, Rhitu. 2019. "Lengthy detention of migrant children may create lasting trauma, say researchers." *NPR. Public Health.* August 23. Retrieved from https://www.npr.org/sections/health-shots/2019/08/23/753757475/lengthy-detention-of-migrant-children-may-create-lasting-trauma-say-researchers.

Chaudry, Ajay, Randy Capps, Juan Manuel Pedroza, Rosa María Castañeda, Robert Santos, and Molly Scott. 2010. *Facing Our Future: Children in the Aftermath of Immigration Enforcement.* The Urban Institute. Retrieved from https://www.urban.org/research/publication/facing-our-future/view/full_report.

Child Trends. 2018a. *Immigrant Children.* Retrieved from https://www.childtrends.org/indicators/immigrant-children.

Child Trends. 2018b. *Racial and Ethnic Composition of the Child Population.* Retrieved from https://www.childtrends.org/indicators/racial-and-ethnic-composition-of-the-child-population.

Chishti, Muzaffar, and Faye Hipsman. 2016. "Increased Central American migration to the United States may prove an enduring phenomenon." *Policy Beat.* Washington, DC: Migration Policy Institute.

Chishti, Muzaffar, Faye Hipsman, and Isabel Ball. 2015. *Fifty Years on, the 1965 Immigration and Nationality Act Continues to Reshape the United States. Policy Beat.* Washington, DC: Migration Policy Institute.

Colato Lainez, Rene. 2013. *From North to South/Del norte al sur.* San Francisco, CA: Children's Book Press.

Copple, Carol, and Susan Bredekamp. 2009. *Developmentally Appropriate Practice In Early Childhood Programs Serving Children from Birth through Age 8* (3rd ed.). Washington, DC: NAEYC.

Department of Homeland Security. 2018a. *Fact Sheet: Zero Tolerance Immigration Prosecution—Families. Press Releases.* Washington, DC. Retrieved from https://www.dhs.gov/news/2018/06/15/fact-sheet-zero-tolerance-immigration-prosecutions-families.

Department of Homeland Security. 2018b. *Population Estimates: Illegal Alien Population Residing in the Unites States: January 2015*. Washington, DC: Office of Immigration Statistics.

Dinan, S. 2017. Assimilation under threat as children of immigrants flood U.S. public schools. March 15. *The Washington Times*. Retrieved from: https://www.washingtontimes.com/news/2017/mar/15/immigrants-children-numbers-growing-us-public-scho/

Evans Allvin, Rhian. 2018. "Early childhood educators #Protect families." Blog (originally sent as a letter to NAEYC members). October 26. National Association for the Education of Young Children [NAEYC]. Retrieved from https://www.naeyc.org/resources/blog/early-childhood-educators-protectfamilies.

Federal Interagency Forum on Child and Family Statistics. 2018. *America's Children in Brief: Key National Indicators of Well-Being, 2018*. Washington, DC: U.S. Government Printing Office.

Fortuny, Karina, Randy Capps, Margaret Simms, and Ajay Chaudry. 2009. *Children of Immigrants: National and State Characteristics. Brief 9*. The Urban Institute. Retrieved from https://www.urban.org/sites/default/files/publication/32986/411939-Children-of-Immigrants-National-and-State-Characteristics.PDF.

Fox, Mem. 2006. *Whoever You Are*. New York: HMH Books for Young Readers.

Fradin, Judith, and Dennis Fradin. 2006. *Jane Addams: Champions of Democracy*. New York: Clarion Books.

Gándara, Patricia. 2018. *Immigrant Students, Our Kids, Our Future*. Retrieved from https://learningpolicyinstitute.org/blog/immigrant-students-our-kids-our-future.

Gramlich, John, and Luis Noe-Bustamante. 2019. "What's happening at the U.S.-Mexico border in 6 charts." *Fact Tank. News in Numbers*. Pew Research Center. April 10. Retrieved from https://www.pewresearch.org/fact-tank/2019/04/10/whats-happening-at-the-u-s-mexico-border-in-6-charts/.

Greenberg, Erica, Victoria Rosenboom, and Gina Adams. 2019. *Preparing the Future Workforce: Early Care and Education Participation among Children of Immigrants*. Washington, DC: Urban Institute.

Haigh, Marilyn. 2018. "What's happening at the border? Here's what we know about immigrant children and family separations." *TEXplainer*. June 29: *The Texas Tribune*. Retrieved from https://www.texastribune.org/2018/06/18/separated-immigrant-children-families-border-mexico/.

Hauslohner, Abigail, and Maria Sacchetti. 2019. "Hundreds of minors held at U.S. border facilities are there beyond legal time limits." *Washington Post*. May 30. Accessed July 13, 2019. Retrieved from https://www.washingtonpost.com/immigration/hundreds-of-minors-held-at-us-border-facilities-are-there-beyond-legal.

Hernández, Donald, and Cervantes, Wendy. 2011. *Children in Immigrant Families: Ensuring Opportunities for Every Child in America.* New York: First Focus. Foundation for Child Development.

Hernández, Donald, and Jeffrey Napierala. 2013. *Diverse children: Race, ethnicity, and immigration in America's new non-majority generation.* July. Foundation for Child Development. Retrieved from https://www.fcd-us.org/assets/2016/04/Diverse-Children-Full-Report.pdf.

Hoynes, Hilary, Marianne Page, and Ann Stevens. 2006. "Poverty in America: Trends and explanations." *Journal of Economic Perspectives* 20(1): 47–68.

International Organization for Migration. 2017. *World Migration Report 2018.* Geneva, Switzerland: Author. https://publications.iom.int/system/files/pdf/wmr_2020_en_ch_8.pdf.

International Organization for Migration. 2020. *World Migration Report 2020.* Geneva, Switzerland: Author. https://publications.iom.int/system/files/pdf/wmr_2020.pdf.

Joung, Madeleine. 2019. "What is happening at migrant detention centers? Here's what to know." *Time.* July 12. Retrieved from https://time.com/5623148/migrant-detention-centers-conditions/.

Klapper, Melissa. 2007. *Small Strangers: The Experiences of Immigrant Children in America, 1880–1925.* New York: Ivan R. Dee.

Kobald, Irena. 2015. *My Two Blankets.* Australia: Houghton Mifflin.

Lawlor, Veronica. 1995. *I Was Dreaming to Come to America: Memories from the Ellis Island Oral History Project.* New York: Puffin Books.

Lee, Stacey, Eujin Park, and Jia-Hui Stefanie Wong. 2017. "Racialization, schooling, and becoming American: Asian American experiences." *Educational Studies* 53(5): 492–510.

Levitin, Sonia. 1996. *A Piece from Home.* New York: Dial Books for Young Readers.

Linton, Julie, Marsha Griffin, Alan Shapiro, and Council on Community Pediatrics. 2017. "Detention of immigrant children." *Pediatrics* 139(5): e20170483.

Lovato, Kristina, Corina Lopez, Leyla Karimli, and Laura Abrams. 2018. "The impact of deportation-related family separations on the wellbeing of Latinx children and youth: A review of the literature." *Children and Youth Services Review* 95: 110–16.

Lu, Yao, Quian He, and Jeanne Brooks-Gunn. 2020. "Diverse experience of immigrant children: How do separation and reunification shape their development?" *Child Development,* 91(1): e146–e163. Retrieved from https://srcd.onlinelibrary.wiley.com/doi/epdf/10.1111/cdev.13171.

"Mary McDowell blames the rich for the rank conditions among the poor." 1913. *The Day Book,* November 17, 1913. Image 30. Library of Congress.

McLemore, S. Dale, and Romo, Harriet. 2005. *Racial and Ethnic Relations in America* (7th ed.). Boston, MA: Pearson.

Migration Policy Institute. 2018. *Children in U.S. Immigrant Families.* Retrieved from https://www.migrationpolicy.org/programs/data-hub/charts/children-immigrant-families.

Miroff, Nick. 2019. "Record numbers of families arrested in December while crossing U.S. border." January 10. *National Post.* Retrieved from https://nationalpost.com/news/world/record-number-of-migrant-families-arrested-in-december-while-crossing-u-s-border.

Murphey, David, Lina Guzman, and Alicia Torres. 2014. *America's Hispanic Children: Gaining Ground, Looking Forward.* Child Trends. Hispanic Institute. Retrieved from https://www.childtrends.org/wp-content/uploads/2014/09/2014-38AmericaHispanicChildren.pdf.

Nadwa, M. 2019. *Annual Flow Report. Refugees and Asylees: 2017.* Table 3. Washington, DC: Department of Homeland Security, Office of Immigration Statistics.

National Association for the Education of Young Children. 2019. *Advancing equity in early childhood education. Position Statement.* Washington, DC: Author.

National Center for Education Statistics. 2019. *English language learners. Fast Facts.* Retrieved from https://nces.ed.gov/FastFacts/display.asp?id=96.

National Park Service. 2018. *Ellis Island: History and Culture.* Retrieved from https://www.nps.gov/elis/learn/historyculture/index.htm.

New York Tribune. 1904. "Immigrant children on the roof playground at Ellis Island." Image 28. August 28. Washington, DC: Library of Congress.

Office of Head Start. 2017. *Services Snapshot: Migrant Seasonal Program (2016–2017).* Retrieved from https://eclkc.ohs.acf.hhs.gov/sites/default/files/pdf/service-snapshot-mshs-2016–2017.pdf.

Office of Head Start. 2019. *Dual Language Learners.* Retrieved from https://eclkc.ohs.acf.hhs.gov/culture-language/guide-dual-language-learners-program-assessment-dllpa/dual-language-learners.

Office of Refugee Resettlement [ORR]. 2012. *Who We Serve-Asylees.* Retrieved from https://www.acf.hhs.gov/orr/resource/who-we-serve-asylees.

Office of Refugee Resettlement [ORR]. 2016. *Children Entering the United States Unaccompanied: Guide to Terms.* Retrieved from https://www.acf.hhs.gov/orr/resource/children-entering-the-united-states-unaccompanied-guide-to-terms.

Office of Refugee Resettlement [ORR]. 2019. *Unaccompanied Alien Children Program. Fact Sheet.* Retrieved from https://www.hhs.gov/sites/default/files/Unaccompanied-Alien-Children-Program-Fact-Sheet.pdf.

Passel, Jeffrey, and D'Vera Cohn. 2018. *U.S. Unauthorized Immigrant Total Dips to Lowest Level in a Decade.* Pew Research Center. Retrieved from http://www.pewhispanic.org/2018/11/27/u-s-unauthorized-immigrant-total-dips-to-lowest-level-in-a-decade/.

Passel, Jeffrey, and D'Vera Cohn. 2019. *Mexicans Decline to Less Than Half the U.S. Unauthorized Immigrant Population for the First Time.* Pew Research Center. Retrieved from https://www.pewresearch.org/fact-tank/2019/06/12/us-unauthorized-immigrant-population-2017/.

Pew Hispanic Research Center. 2013. *A Nation of Immigrants: A Portrait of the 40 Million, Including 11 Million Unauthorized.* Pew Research Center. Retrieved from https://www.pewhispanic.org/2013/01/29/a-nation-of-immigrants/.

Philbin, Sandy, and Cecilia Ayón. 2016. "Luchamos por nuestros hijos: Latino immigrant parents strive to protect their children from the deleterious effects of anti-immigration policies." *Children and Youth Review* 63: 128–35. Retrieved from http://dx.doi.org/10.1016/j.childyouth.2016.02.019.

Radford, Jynnah. 2019. Key findings about U.S. immigrants. June 17. *FactTank*. Pew Research Center. Retrieved from https://www.pewresearch.org/fact-tank/2019/06/17/key-findings-about-u-s-immigrants/.

Roberts, S. 2006. "First through gates of Ellis I., she was lost. Now she's found." *New York Times*, A1.

Robles-Meléndez, Wilma, and Wayne Driscoll. 2018. "Poverty and immigrant children: Moving ahead with *esperanza*, with hope." *Dimensions of Early Childhood* 46(2): 21–4.

Rumbaut, Rubén, and Douglas Massey. 2013. "Immigration and language diversity in the United States." *Daedalus* 142(3): 141–54.

Ruurs, Margriet. 2016. *Stepping Stones: A Refugee Family's Journey*. Olympia, WA: Orca Book.

Sáenz, Rogelio, and Karen Mages Douglas. 2015. A call for the racialization of immigration studies: On the transition of ethnic immigrants to racialized immigrants. *Sociology of Race and Ethnicity* 1(1): 166–80.

Sanna, Francesca. 2016. *The Journey*. London: Flying Eye.

Schaefer, R. 2016. *Race and Ethnicity in the United States* (8th ed.). Boston, MA: Pearson.

Semple, Kirk. 2016. "A surge of families moves northward, away from gangs." *New York Times*, November 13, A6.

Silva, Daniella. 2019. "Almost 300 children removed from Texas facility described as "appalling." *NBC News*. June 25. Accessed July 13, 2019. Retrieved from https://www.nbcnews.com/news/latino/nearly-300-migrant-children-removed-texas-facility-described-appaling-n1021151.

Social Welfare History Project. 2019. *Mary McDowell*. Retrieved from https://socialwelfare.library.vcu.edu/people/mcdowell-mary/.

Suárez-Orozco, Marcelo, and Carola Suárez-Orozco. 2001. Children of Immigration. Cambridge, MA: Harvard University Press.

Suárez-Orozco, Carola, Hirokazu Yoshikawa, and Vivian Tseng. 2015. *Intersecting inequalities: Research to reduce inequality for immigrant-origin children and youth.* February. William T. Grant Foundation.

Sussis, Matt. 2019. *The History of the Flores Settlement: How a 1997 Agreement Cracked Open Our Detention Laws.* Center for Immigration Studies. February. Retrieved from https://cis.org/sites/default/files/2019-02/sussis-flores-history.pdf.

Turney, Kristin, and Grace Kao. 2009. Barriers to school involvement: Are immigrant parents disadvantaged? *Journal of Educational Research*, 102(4): 257–70.

United Nations. 2017a. *Population Facts.* No. 2017/5. Retrieved from http://www. un.org/en/development/desa/population/migration/publications/populationfacts/ docs/MigrationPopFacts20175.pdf.

United Nations. 2017b. *International Migrant Stock 2017: Age Distributions of Total Population and International Migrants by Major Area of Destination.* Retrieved from http://www.un.org/en/development/desa/population/migration/data/estimates2/ estimatesgraphs.shtml?6g6from.

United Nations High Commissioner for Refugees. 2010. *Convention and Protocol Relating to the Status of Refugees.* Retrieved from https://www.unhcr.org/3b66c2aa10. html.

United Nations High Commissioner for Refugees. 2019a. *Refugees.* Retrieved from https://www.unrefugees.org/refugee-facts/what-is-a-refugee/.

United Nations High Commissioner for Refugees. 2019b. *Figures at a Glance.* Retrieved from https://www.unhcr.org/en-us/figures-at-a-glance.html.

United Nations. 1948. *Universal Declaration of Human Rights.* Retrieved from https:// www.un.org/en/universal-declaration-human-rights/index.html.

UNICEF. 2016. *Uprooted. The Growing Crisis for Refugee and Migrant Children: Executive Summary and Key Findings.* New York: Author.

U.S. Census Bureau. 2017. *Characteristics of People by Language Spoken at Home. 2013–2017. American Community Survey 5-Year Estimates.* Table S1603. Retrieved from https://factfinder.census.gov/faces/tableservices/jsf/pages/productview. xhtml?pid=ACS_17_5YR_S1603&prodType=table.

U.S. Census Bureau. 2019a. "Asian-American and Pacific Islander heritage month: May 2019." *Facts for Features.* Retrieved from https://www.census.gov/newsroom/facts- for-features/2019/asian-american-pacific-islander.html.

U.S. Census Bureau. 2019b. *Language Spoken at Home: American Community Survey 5-Year Estimates 2013–2017.* Table 1601. Retrieved from https:// factfinder.census.gov/faces/tableservices/jsf/pages/productview. xhtml?pid=ACS_17_5YR_S1601&prodType=table.

U.S. Census Bureau. 2019c. *Foreign Born.* Retrieved from https://www.census.gov/ topics/population/foreign-born/about.html.

U.S. Citizenship and Immigration Services. 2019a. *Refugees.* Retrieved from https:// www.uscis.gov/humanitarian/refugees-asylum/refugees.

U.S. Citizenship and Immigration Services. 2019b. *Asylum.* Retrieved from https:// www.uscis.gov/humanitarian/refugees-asylum/asylum.

U.S. Customs and Border Protection. 2019. *Southwest Border Migration FY 2019.* Retrieved from https://www.cbp.gov/newsroom/stats/sw-border-migration/fy-2019.

U.S. Department of Education. 2017. *Our nation's English learners.* Department of Education. Retrieved from https://www2.ed.gov/datastory/el-characteristics/index. html#three.

U.S. Department of Health and Human services. 2019. *Unaccompanied Alien Children Program. Fact Sheet May.* Retrieved from https://www.hhs.gov/sites/default/files/Unaccompanied-Alien-Children-Program-Fact-Sheet.pdf.

U.S. Department of State. 2019. *Arrivals by Region.* Bureau of Population, Refugees, and Migration. Office of Admissions-Refugee Processing Center. Retrieved from https://www.wrapsnet.org/admissions-and-arrivals/.

U.S. Office of Refugee and Resettlement. 2019. "Age breakdown of unaccompanied children." *Facts and Data.* Retrieved from https://www.acf.hhs.gov/orr/about/ucs/facts-and-data.

Van Sant, Shannon. 2019. Teenager is latest child to die in custody. *NPR.* May 20. Retrieved from https://www.npr.org/2019/05/20/725117838/teenager-is-latest-migrant-child-to-die-in-u-s-custody.

Vespa, Jonathan, David M. Armstrong, and Lauren Medina. 2018. "Demographic turning points for the United States: Population projections for 2020 to 2060." *Current Population Reports*, P25-1144, Washington, DC: U.S. Census Bureau.

Waslin, Michele. 2011. *The Secure Communities Program: Unanswered and Continuing Concerns.* Immigration Policy Center. Retrieved from https://www.americanimmigrationcouncil.org/sites/default/files/research/SComm_Exec_Summary_112911.pdf.

Yoshikawa, Hirokazu, and Jenya Kholoptseva. 2013. *Unauthorized Immigrant Parents and Their Children's Development. A Summary of the Evidence.* Washington, DC: Migration Policy Institute.

Zayas, Luis, Kalina Brabeck, Laurie Cook Heffron, Joanna Dreby, Esther Calzada, J. Ruben Parra-Cardona, Ala Dettlaff, Lauren Heidbrink, Krista Perreira, and Hirokazu Yoshikawa. 2017. "Charting directions for research on immigrant children affected by undocumented status." *Hispanic Journal of Behavioral Science* 39(4): 412–35.

Zeigler, Karen, and Steven Camarota. 2019. *67.3 million in the United States spoke a foreign language at home in 2018.* October. Center for Immigration Studies. Retrieved from https://cis.org/sites/default/files/2019-10/camarota-language-19_0.pdf.

Zong, Jie, and Jeanne Batalova. 2016. *Asian Immigrants in the United States.* Migration Policy Institute. Retrieved from https://www.migrationpolicy.org/article/asian-immigrants-united-states.

Zong, Jie, Jeanne Batalova, and Mycayla Burrows. 2019. *Frequently Requested Statistics on Immigrants and Immigration in the United States. Spotlight.* Retrieved from https://www.migrationpolicy.org/article/frequently-requested-statistics-immigrants-and-immigration-united-states#Children.

3

In Search of Socially Just Practices for Immigrant Children

Through this chapter, we will

- Define social justice
- Discuss key expectations for socially just responses to the equity issues and educational needs of young immigrant children
- Present a multifocal, four lenses approach to examine the needs of young immigrant children

Key concepts

- Social justice
- Multifocal four lenses approach
- Equity and diversity

NAEYC standards

- NAEYC #1 Child Development
- NAEYC #6 Becoming a Professional

Sharing stories: Seeking opportunities

Stuart's family immigrated from apartheid South Africa as a reaction to his sisters' kidnapping and the need for educational opportunities. They were seeking social justice. His parents enrolled him in a parochial preschool program where school personnel expressed to his parents that he had "some problems." They placed him in the back of the room because according to what his teacher told his parents he was "difficult." He spent his time in the back of the room drawing. At recess, he remembered always spending his time alone. His classmates would tease him because of his accent and called him names. He cried every day in preschool and was heard saying he disliked people. At the end of the school year, his performance showed little progress and his teachers, consequently, retained him for another year. Later years were not very different. Finding strength from those who along the way believe in him, today, an adult, his memories from childhood still resound as vividly as when he was a child. His hopes are for other children to find what every child justly deserves.

The imperative need of equity for young immigrant children

In the United States and globally, media outlets frequently report about the experiences and the challenges of individuals, families, and children as they navigate and make sense of life as immigrants. This is the continuing reality in a country built on immigration. The same aspirations that drove thousands of individuals in the past remain today as the driving force for so many recently arrived immigrant families. At the core of their hopes is the yearning for fair and equal opportunities for employment, education, freedom, stability, and safety. They are especially in search of the promise of a better life for their children as pointed out before. Today is not any different. Hundreds of immigrants continue to arrive every day through the nation's airports, ports, and borders, officially entering with high hopes for their children and themselves. Over a million arrive every year and settle in communities across the country. Others, living in desperate circumstances and fearful for their families, arrive unauthorized through the nation's borders. A pattern increasingly followed since the 2014 crisis that brought thousands of unaccompanied children into the country, it continues today as thousands of children and family groups arrive unauthorized through the nation's borders. During the early summer days of June and July 2019, the country experienced an unprecedented number of families, many with young children, who came through the southwest borders. Most were from Central America and others from continents as distant as Africa (Baynes 2019; Owens 2019). What they had in common was their hope of a new beginning for their children.

Time to reflect ... *Considering the dreams of parents and families*

Statistics continue to show the increasing number of families with children arriving as immigrants into the United States. Beyond the data, scholars agree children's future is one of their motivations to leave everything behind. As early childhood educators, reflect on the implications of their aspirations. What should anchor practices for children? What should be considered to ensure their aspirations are addressed?

Parents everywhere care and consider all the options to ensure a future for their children, even if that means leaving behind their homelands. Keels and Raver (2009) note that the family's choice to immigrate to a new and unfamiliar environment itself is likely to represent "a bold act of protective parenting." Personally knowing the stories of so many families, the authors agree. Leaving behind everything one has known to start again compels us to understand the dedication and caring responsibility of parents who in the past, as today, come to live in our country. This is precisely what has guided families to leave their country seeking safety and a future for their child, something that all children are entitled to enjoy. It is the same, too, that immigrant families long-established in US communities aspire for their children. Finding the support needed for their children is the aspiration for every immigrant family and children. They are in search of equity, equity that would pave the way to success for their children.

We owe it to children

Ascertaining the right to opportunities to safely and appropriately grow and develop is something that society owes to its children, that is, to all children irrespective of whether they are born in the United States or in another country. Sadly, some stories reveal the struggles endured by many as they adjust to life in a different context, with expectations and practices sometimes unfamiliar to arriving families and their children. No less true is the fact that systemic and structural factors in society also leave many unprepared to respond to the needs of immigrants (Goodwin 2017; Suárez-Orozco and Suárez-Orozco 2001). This is what is reflected in Stuart's experience. For us as educators, we have also learned it through our own experiences working with students and families. Some of these challenges, imbedded in the system, continue to maintain unfair circumstances despite concerted efforts to establish equitable experiences and services for immigrant children.

Time to reflect ... *Prepared to respond to immigrant children*

Immigration is not new but a constant reality in society. Children of immigrants, both newly arrived and US born, call for attention and responsive practices. How ready do you consider yourself to equitably respond to their needs? What may be hindering their responsible attention?

Over two thousand years ago, Greek philosopher Plato posited that, "The direction in which education starts a child will determine the child's future." Nowadays, his observations resonate echoing the concerns of those calling for social justice for our immigrants. Their demands are for equal and equitable educational experiences leading the path to their future success. Imperative today is to consider the multiple implications emerging from what thousands of children of immigrants, whether born in the United States or recently arrived, experienced in the past and what so many others are experiencing today in classrooms across the nation. We must remember that children are the seed of society's future; therefore, fair and same opportunities for their success are paramount to society. The matter is not of who they are but rather of what they need to develop and thrive. Because of their young age, their vulnerability is evident, placing them at risk if equal access and attention are not provided. The issue is one of social justice and a challenge facing everyone in our society.

Educator John Dewey once wisely stated that, "What the best and wisest parent wants for his own child, that must the community want for all its children" (1990, 3). The message is clear, reminding everyone about the shared responsibility every community has to ensure the future of children. This is also what defines aspirations to center opportunities in equity, a core goal for early childhood education voiced by national and international organizations (NAEYC 2019; UNICEF 2015).

Children's future: A social justice issue

In the opening scenario we learned about Stuart who was a preschooler when he came to live in the United States. Stuart's family arrived hopeful to find a place where their child would grow without fear. They wanted an environment that would nurture his development and where he would be welcomed. Though today he is a successful adult, his experiences from those years attending school in a country where he came as a child are memories he has tried to forget. He still wonders why they never saw that he was just a child fearful and anxiously waiting to find support and understanding. The dream of justice and equitable experiences eluded him like it has other children of immigration. They are happening now. The reality is that existing inequalities continuing to threaten children must be addressed. Reports show that educational equality still escapes children of diverse backgrounds and realities including those who are immigrant (Adair 2015; Oleinik 2018). No reasons exist preventing the country to eliminate and stop unequal experiences. The fact is, according to Priscilla Idele, director of the United Nations' research center, "Countries can offer their children the best of both world: They can achieve standards of excellence and have relatively low inequality" (Oleinik 2018, n.p.). Conscious awareness about this reality challenges everyone to action. The call is to provide children what is socially just and fair for their well-being. That is, in fact, the ultimate goal of education.

Time to reflect ... *Stuart's experience*

When Stuart shared his story, he punctuated that what brought his parents was their hopes for justice and educational opportunities. Instead, his story was a disappointing reality. Reflect on his story and consider the implications of his experience from the perspective of fairness.

Today, we recognize how the resurgence of the immigrant issue has shifted the topic to the center of significant debates. Governments, in our nation and globally, communicate and debate how immigration and immigrants affect their economic resources, goods, and educational programs. Urgency for attention to the realities of immigrant children is indisputably critical and challenges aspirations for social and individual equity. As denoted by UNICEF, "Achieving equity means that societies have to address the underlying drivers of inequity that often appear even before a child is born" (2015, n.p.). Noted by various scholars, some have pointedly stated that "current circumstances and future prospects of children in immigrant families are important not only to these children themselves but to all Americans" (Hernandez, Denton, and Macartney 2008, 1). Clearly, the need is for efforts directed at establishing policies and practices for immigrant children that equitably address and respond to their needs, opportunities, and promise for a successful future.

Meanwhile, there is a human dimension to immigration deserving attention. More specifically, the very future of thousands of children is at stake. Their ongoing stories have been part of the immigration process, yet what they have experienced has not come as clearly to the forefront as it has today. The faces of children on the different media avenues call for compassion and alert us to understand the urgent call for action. In many communities, the conditions, practices, and opportunities in programs and services for US-born immigrant children instill the same level of urgency. In a nation born out of immigration, they are, as well, a reminder about the generations of children of immigration growing up and that grew up in the United States. By way of example, an educator whose family came in from an Eastern European country escaping communism reflected on her personal immigration experience. She stayed with her grandparents while her mother came to the United States in search of better conditions, working hard to later bring her daughter and start a new life. Her efforts, as she pointed out, were not in vain. They gave her the opportunities that changed her life. She reminded us that everyone hopes to find an opportunity to do their best for their family, even if that means leaving your home country to start again. Generations later, this same aspiration drives families to, voluntarily or forced by circumstances, become immigrants. Today, similar to the past, countless families are in search of a better life in another place that welcomes them as their own. They follow their dreams hoping for freedom, stability, employment opportunities, quality education, and, above all, socially just treatment for their families and children. At the heart of what they yearn is the search for equity for their children (Philbin and Ayón 2016).

They want what is best for their children

Simply stated, thousands of families and children of immigrants aspire for what is socially just. They are just people seeking what is best for themselves, their families, and their children. We are compelled to understand the experiences as well as needs and rights of immigrant families and their children. Their stories may be similar or familiar to some of you who may have experienced it. The call is for minimizing the nature of the arguments and distorted views about immigrants while seeing immigration through the lens of social justice as an essential focal point. Only then will we be able to clearly see the nature of their experiences and of their hopes and dreams. Sadly, unfounded ideas and xenophobic views have blurred the ongoing conversation about families and children with immigrant roots (Adair 2015; APA 2012). Erasing these is a priority for everyone.

Time to reflect ... *Immigration as a healthy debate or a distorted argument*

Immigration is a highly debatable issue calling for our deeper reflection. Thoughtfully reflect on your own biases and assumptions about immigration. Do you view immigration with a lens of disdain or compassion? Explain your reasoning and basis for your view.

Seeking social justice

The search for social justice is unending. It has always been a goal for society as it is today. Social justice remains as one of the main factors integral to a society anchored in equality and equity. As a characteristic of society, a social justice perspective is a vital community component fostering fairness and conscious awareness about inequalities (Torres-Harding and Meyers 2013). These are fundamental parameters in a democratic society where social justice denotes the right for equitable, fair experiences, and opportunities for what is essential to individual success. Moreover, social justice embodies human equality in the broadest sense. As an umbrella concept, efforts guided by what is socially just evoke the essence of the common good and of what is right for everyone irrespective of their diversity. At its core is the search and aspiration for equity, which simply stated implies parity of opportunities and experiences (UNICEF 2015; Robles-Meléndez and Beck 2019).

Elusive as a concept, equity is implicitly embedded in experiences and actions anchored in social justice. Much has been debated in recent years about the core meaning of social justice. Overall, it is the search for what is fair and essential to people's welfare. We must remember that, particularly for children, their rights to a promising future and to finding supportive conditions for their well-being are universal.

The echoes of voices for social justice have been raised high across society in recent times. The call for equity is a main aspiration today guiding efforts of individuals and organizations across the nation and throughout the global society. Increased awareness about unbalanced and unequal circumstances is acknowledged by many who have denounced the need for changes. They are raising their voices demanding elimination of barriers to level access and opportunities for everyone. A similar calling is present in early childhood education where efforts for inclusivity and equality remain a priority in its educational agenda. In its recent position statement on equity, the U.S. National Association for the Education of Young Children (NAEYC 2019) urged the early childhood community to stand against unfairness in all its forms. The clamor is for every child to experience quality and support conducive to his/her successful development during the foundational years and beyond (Crosnoe 2013; Philbin and Ayón 2016; Takanishi 2004). We hold the same aspiration for all immigrant children.

Time to reflect … *What is right for children*

A child's well-being centers efforts in early childhood education. Take a moment to consider what would be right to ensure and promote children's development and well-being. How can you contribute to achieving it?

What is social justice?

As a concept, social justice is a critical idea centered on the rights of individuals to equality and fairness in a democratic society. Efforts to define social justice in education confirm its complex nature and interrelationships with diversity and multicultural education (Cho 2017) and with attention on inclusivity (Herbert 2013; Mevawalla 2013). Given the complexity of the concept, there is no single definition for social justice. Rather, it is characterized by the pursuit of the collective well-being of individuals in response to the existence of unfair conditions inhibiting equitable realities to everyone. Figure 3.1 identifies some of the key elements implicitly present in social justice perspectives. In education, conceptualizations on social justice imply an awareness about existing inequities and to efforts made to eliminate unequal circumstances, which frame the need for practices that are inclusive of every child. Furthermore, social justice raises concerns about our own knowledge of existing dichotomies in educational realities and to the need to build and increase awareness. This is what was indicated by Luke (cited by Herbert 2013) who stated, "It's imperative that we understand who is exactly left out and left behind, educationally and economically" (302). We must add that awareness implies a call for action.

Figure 3.1 Main elements in social justice.
Source: Herbert (2013); Mevawalla (2013); Robles-Mélendez and Beck (2019).

Social justice: Focusing on the individual

Delivering the promise of social justice happens every day in our classrooms, while teaching and working with children and with their families. Still, it is not a parameter commonly defining experiences and practices in every classroom or educational setting. The need for equitably establishing social justice as a defining education experience of every child remains waiting for action. To effectively make this happen, practices call for mindful attention to the individual stories and experiences of children. This is precisely what McDonald (2005) posited when she stated that teaching with a focus on social justice is responsively meeting the needs of students according to their individual circumstances. Essential to her views is the attention to what is particularly defining and critical to the student as an individual. The nature of the child's own experiences, realities, and needs becomes the focus for actions and decisions. McDonald's emphasis on the individuality of children strongly highlights a position common to early childhood education, anchoring it as a social justice perspective. A focus

Figure 3.2 Key elements: Responding to individual needs through social justice.
Source: Robles-Meléndez (2017); Robles-Meléndez and Driscoll (2017).

on the individual culture and experiences of a child is one of the core elements in developmentally based educational practice (Copple and Bredekamp 2009). Its emphasis brings attention to the distinct and influential circumstances a child and family may experience and to the need for consideration to these in the planning and delivery of practices.

While diversity continues to be a defining characteristic of immigrants, language, culture, and the specific immigration trajectory of the child and family pose consideration for actions required to appropriately support educational needs. Becoming mindfully aware about the individual stories, traits, and needs of a child necessary for their well-being anchors an educator's responsibilities toward children (Figure 3.2). Ethically, this delineates a social justice dimension to all the efforts and actions for children. This is a position emphasizing attention to circumstances, needs, and existing disparities preventing equitable opportunities for every child. The call is for decisions, actions, and practices essential to achieve equity in all experiences, services, and programs. This is what all children deserve.

Early childhood as social justice in action

Overall, in education, views on social justice tacitly posit the critical role early childhood educators play to ensure equity of experiences for every child. Strongly rooted in the aspiration to support and promote children's development and opportunities, early childhood education typifies social justice. Its belief on the child and the pursuit to optimize individual development and opportunities for every child echo the aspirations of social justice (Hart, Press, and Gibson 2013).

This is what guides practices centered on defeating obstacles and affirming what children are equitably entitled to receive.

Social justice takes place in classrooms, programs, and services as professionals engage in actively responding to end inequities and counteract unfairness. As an expectation, this is also inherent to early childhood education efforts. From the parameter of early childhood education, social justice demands efforts anchored in fairness through responsive attention to children's needs and circumstances. Fairness implies erasing any damaging actions limiting others from participating, receiving, and enjoying what is owed to them. The spectrum of fairness in practices is wide-ranging. Some of these include attention to the parity of opportunities provided, freeing oneself from biases to impartially attend to needs. It also means to respond and stop prejudiced comments and stereotyped views about children and families. Responding with fairness also entails actively addressing microaggressions happening every day that are painful to children and families.

Teaching in early childhood with a social justice orientation recognizes the existence of inequities and the calling to address these through targeted actions and advocacy. It further places attention to responding with fairness to individual circumstances and experiences, such as diversity and immigration, with consideration to the whole child (NAEYC 2019; Robles-Meléndez, Valdés, and Robles 2018). Social justice is also exhibited through equitable teaching and learning experiences, and opportunities in the context of classrooms, programs, and services. It is also demonstrated through respectful attention to the child and families' individual cultures, needs, and experiences. Such position implies attention to prevent and defy inequitable practices and actions. What is more, we must reiterate, expectations of social justice are inherent to what is ethically defined for early childhood educators teaching and working with children and their families (NAEYC 2011).

Time to reflect … *Social justice and children's individual needs*

According to McDonald (2005), social justice entails addressing and meeting the needs of individual students. Reflect on what she suggests and share your own views on what social justice implies for children and their families who are immigrants.

Conscious actions addressing fairness

Social justice calls for conscious actions and practices. This position, rooted in what Freire ([1974] 2013) described as critical consciousness, underlines the need for educators to be mindful about circumstances, either existing or emerging, that may influence children's success or opportunities. Such stance calls for early educators working with young immigrant children to responsively address inequities and pursue actions to eliminate or deter their impact. Addressing inequities begins by an understanding that disparities exist in services and in experiences and on how these may influence children's future. Some of the current inequities such as persisting stereotypes, language barriers, and discriminatory practices in programs and schools serving immigrant children have existed for years (Adair 2015; Tamer 2014). Practices that consciously target eradication of inequalities are what the authors deem central to responsive education in early childhood. All efforts count and bring equality closer to a reality for every child.

Searching for equality

Juan was a young child when he came to the United States with his mother and two brothers escaping his country after his father and older brothers became political prisoners. His memories from elementary school are those of a child struggling to fit in in an environment where he felt isolated (see *Voices of immigration*). Though time has passed, still today as an adult, recollections of his first years living in the United States are not happy ones. Equality in experiences and responses escaped those days deeply carved in his memories.

Equality is at the core of social justice. Implications of parity in experiences and opportunities open to everyone are paramount to efforts socially just guided. For immigrants, the image of the United States as a destination where equality is at the heart of society remains as attractive today as in the past. For decades equality and justice attracted families escaping from serious realities. Recent influx in immigration has also brought to attention the conditions and experiences of immigrant families and children in many parts of the world. It must be reiterated again: the improvement of their situation is what continues motivating families to journey into immigration bringing many to our country. The dream of giving their children an education that can fulfil their visions of successful futures continues as one of the major factors driving parents and families to risk their lives, to embark on the journey of immigration. Holistic attention to their needs is dramatically compelling, particularly when considering the increase in the number of families with young children arriving in current times (Stanton 2019). Responses to the needs of immigrant children, as Stanton points out, must correspond to the promise of equality and liberty defining the core values of the United States.

Voices of immigration: *Feeling welcome in a new place*

Juan left Cuba with his mother and two older siblings. They came as political exiles escaping the trauma of life in a place of political unrest and national uncertainty. They had no plans to stay in the United States permanently. They always thought they would be back. Upon arrival, they obtained temporary status and were provided with a safe haven in a rented house with other people. Eventually, the family saved enough money to purchase their own home. His mother, who could only complete four years of primary school, dedicated herself to work and to ease their lives in a place unfamiliar to her. She focused on survival, managing her fears, and worrying about her husband and two sons imprisoned in Cuba. Those were hard times as his mother tried to adjust to their new reality. Looking back, he cannot remember any stories read or shared during those times when every day brought new challenges, with his mother always doing the impossible to safeguard them. Via word of mouth, friends urged her to enroll Juan in an elementary school. He remembers the school and that it was not prepared for a non-English-speaking shy child who could not communicate with his classmates or teacher. In school, he felt alone, ignored, and lonesome. He spent school time unaware of what was going on around him and daydreaming that all would be the same way he had lived before. He never remembered any experiences during those first years when he was trying to see if he really belonged. It was not until the beginning of sixth grade when Juan felt comfortable and productive in a place he would now feel as his own, too.

Years passed, but he still vividly described the struggling times at a school, a system still beginning to learn how to respond to children just like him.

Immigrants and their advocates primarily view the concept of social justice as a matter of obtaining similar opportunities everyone else enjoys (Bankston 2010). Anchoring the concept of social justice is the acknowledgment of existing social disparities and the active search for equity (Freire 1970). For immigrants, the opportunity to live in a place where their hopes and dreams of equality and social justice are a possible reality is what continues motivating their efforts.

In early childhood education, we must reiterate, the meanings of social justice implicitly denote a stance defining actions rooted in what is rightfully owed to all children. It is a posture geared to ensure that inequities hindering equal and high-quality experiences for children are eliminated. This is also how the authors view social justice for the families of child immigrants. The search for what is indispensable to successfully grow and develop remains at the heart of early childhood education efforts, efforts that are directed at the holistic needs of children. Irrefutably, education is a significant tool essential to achieve social justice in society for every child (Box 3.1).

Box 3.1 Connecting ideas: *An unending quest for educational equality, a social justice challenge*

Generally, people take for granted that children and youth everywhere are receiving a free and appropriate education that meets and responds to their individual realities. Arguments about immigration sometimes overlook the humanitarian reality. This reality includes the quest for access to education and to enjoy the opportunities to build a future, which continues to motivate others to move to other nations. As educators, we sadly know that this is not the case in other parts of the world. The World Health Organization (WHO), the United Nations Educational, Scientific, Cultural Organization (UNESCO), and the NAEYC all define early childhood as a period of growth and development from birth to age 8. Developmental expectations of young children remain the same after migration (Roopnarine and Jin 2012), demanding continued attention and responsive practices. The early childhood years is a time during which young children learn the basic intellectual skills needed in formal schooling (Leo-Rhynie et al. 2009; Roopnarine, Bynoe, and Singh 2004). Given that preschool benefits immigrant children and significantly increases their readiness for future schooling, findings strongly suggest that enrolling children in preschool would help to reduce inequality in skills at formal school entry (Magnuson, Lahaie, and Waldfogel 2006).

Unfortunately, not all children are experiencing equally available opportunities. Many young immigrant children may be receiving minimal quality early childhood educational experiences. The consequences are obvious. Unequal experiences will not prepare them adequately to acquire the knowledge and skills needed for their future to become successful adults and citizens. Members of a promising generation of productive and informed citizens in the land of opportunity and dreams, their realities weigh heavily on everyone.

Socially just actions in early childhood: A long tradition

In early childhood education, the search for social justice has been ongoing. Many milestones have been accomplished for children. Today, it continues with vigor, working to ensure children's opportunities for successful development and their inherent rights to quality and equitable educational experiences and conditions. From the work of early childhood pioneers, efforts to support children recognized the dignity of childhood and the ensuing needs of the child (Roopnarine and Johnson 2013).

Many of the pioneering efforts centered on addressing inequalities, which remains today as examples driving actions, particularly cognizant of current children's vulnerabilities. One of these milestone efforts is Maria Montessori's work, which exemplified socially just efforts addressing diversity of children's needs, which highlighted their equal rights to education. Equally relevant was the kindergarten movement that led to the opening of programs for young children in the United States. Many of these early kindergartens were established in immigrant neighborhoods serving hundreds of young immigrant children during the nineteenth century. Among these were those opened by Jane Addams in Chicago's Hull's House that welcomed countless immigrant families and children. The launch of the Head Start program during the 1960s War on Poverty was another important example of social justice in action for the most vulnerable children. Head Start's comprehensive program addressing children's needs essential for successful development continues today serving thousands of immigrant children. Recognition of the rights of immigrant children, including those with unauthorized entries, to receive education, which is discussed in Chapter 5, is another milestone effort continuing today to benefit children across the nation. Today seekers of socially just efforts pursue equitable practices and demand these in recognition of the rights of children. They also consider that recognizing what every child is entitled to enjoy is a major step leading to experiences and programs essential to support their cultural heritage and optimize their development (Copple and Bredekamp 2009; NAEYC 2019; Robles-Meléndez and Beck 2019). This is the same vision that continues to guide efforts of early childhood professionals and advocates for all children. It is this same vision that is aimed for child immigrants. Engaging in social justice is preparing and setting the course for children's successful development and achievement. Conscious and determined decisions guide the activities and work taking place already in so many classrooms and communities. The committed and determined work of early childhood educators bring social justice into action, with practices firmly anchored and guided by principles of equity and developmentally oriented efforts. Sadly, this is not a reality, yet common to every immigrant child with many still experiencing ill-fitting realities. The calling is for every child to find equitably grounded experiences that recognize and promote their development and future success (Abo-Zena 2018).

Social justice is about expectations for equity

Every time we talk with a parent, their voices echo what we heard from an immigrant mother from South America: "*Quiero que ellos [mis hijos] tengan éxito como los demás y aqui no pueden.*" [I want them to be successful like the others and here they can't.] Similar comments continue to be heard from thousands coming to live as immigrants. Their words reiterate their hopes hindered by a multitude of social, economic, and political circumstances that threaten their dreams for their children.

Social justice is more than just an ideal pursued by those who believe in the equal rights of children. It is a call for success and for making it accessible to every child. Translated into action, principles of social justice are aimed at what is essential for all children to fully reach their successful development. This position considers what is relevant to erase any disparities hindering equity in early childhood, particularly due to existing systemic and structural factors. Lack of information about services, unavailability of programs, biased attitudes, and barriers due to cultural and linguistic differences are but some of the prevailing obstacles hindering fairness. Discrimination remains as one of the barriers continuing preventing a sense of integration and belongingness for many immigrants, particularly evident when there is fewer representation of similar ethnic groups in the community (Salami et al. 2018).

Time to reflect ... *Systemic and structural obstacles*

Systemic or institutional challenges continue as obstacles preventing many immigrant children from receiving equal opportunities and benefiting from services. Consider which ones are still prevailing in your state or community. How could these be overcome?

Table 3.1 Key indicators of fairness in practices for children of immigrants

---

- Availability and equitable access to quality programs and services irrespective of the child's immigration status.
- Environments that are safe and welcoming for children and families
- High expectations for all children denote classroom experiences irrespective of the child's diverse background
- Experiences that are rich, developmentally and culturally based addressing individual children's needs
- Acknowledgment and recognition of children's diverse cultures and experiences
- Effective support for children's dual-language development in environments free of biases and prejudiced notions
- Well-prepared early educators who consciously center practices on what is vital for children's development
- Supportive programs and services for children addressing individual developmental and cultural needs
- Collaborative and participatory practices that engage all families
- Respectful interactions with children and their families or guardians

---

Source: Adair (2015); Copple and Bredekamp (2009); Crosnoe (2013); García (2005); González et al. (2005); NAEYC (2019); Takanishi (2004).

Envisioning equitable and fair practices demands clear indicators defining expectations for practices oriented to support fairness for children of immigrants and their families. Some of those deemed as key to establishing expectations for socially just responses are outlined in Table 3.1. Gleaned from the experience of educators seeking fairness in educational practices, they are a working draft to set directions in addressing and erasing obstacles preventing the promise of equity. Consideration to social justice for children is embedded as an ethical expectation in early childhood education. In professional practice, equity is paramount and integral to pursuing and achieving the well-being of every child (NAEYC 2011).

Action is the key

Expectations for children's success imply action. This is especially relevant and necessary to eliminate existing disparities, some of which will be discussed in the next chapters. They continue preventing children of immigrants from what is equitable and from what they are entitled to receive. Diversity, in its broad sense as a reality of child immigrants, is already mostly acknowledged, but more is needed beyond acknowledgment. The need is for more comprehensive and targeted actions favorable to support children's development and equitable experiences. Need for concerted efforts from early childhood educators and advocates is central to effecting changes that can lead to what is socially just and owed to the youngest immigrants. From a Freirean perspective, this implies bringing conscientious awareness into effective acts conducive to overcoming challenges preventing a child from receiving what is justly fair (Freire 1970).

Equitable educational opportunities: A right of all children

When Lizabeth's parents came to the United States from Trinidad, their hope was to give their young daughter and son an opportunity to be their best. They envisioned them as professionals and cheered when she graduated from college. Lizabeth, now a parent herself, could never forget all her parents had done for her. Working different jobs and sacrificing time and effort, she is grateful for what they did for her and her brother to have a future. She remembers the long hours that his father worked to make sure they would have everything they needed. Her only hope now is to do the same for her own children. Just as her immigrant parents dreamed for her, aspirations for educational opportunities that can make a better life possible continues as one of the most relevant goals driving individuals and families to migrate. The thousands of families and children recently arrived into the country, some officially and others unauthorized, share in common similar dreams.

Like Lizabeth, countless accounts of successful stories about immigrants who came as children evidence how despite challenges, they were able to overcome some of the obstacles and succeed. That is, after all, the American dream. How they will make their dreams come true takes us to question conditions and circumstances facing not only those arriving into the nation but also immigrants already living in our communities. In times when immigration continues as one of the factors defining the future of the nation's population, attention is needed to establish greater connectedness with the realities, cultures, and needs of the thousands of immigrant children growing up in our classrooms. We need to be mindfully cognizant of what children are experiencing and how it contributes to fostering and to making possible their aspirations.

Box 3.2 Connecting ideas: *Seeking the American dream*

The search for the American dream remains today as one of the motivations leading families to come to the United States. It is a dream for opportunities, safety, and stability. Reaching the dream, however, for some immigrants is a journey filled with memories of indifference and preconceived views. Fortunately, there are those who also remember how caring individuals they met were the light that made the difference in their lives. This is what one of the authors gathered from Constanza when she shared her memories of immigration.

Constanza came to the United States as a 6-year-old from a hostile and dangerous environment in Colombia. Accompanying her on her journey was her mother and younger brother and sister. They were joining her father, sponsored by his brother-in-law who had obtained his citizenship. After a couple of months, she and her siblings enrolled in the local school. Still today, she recollects placement in a classroom together with her brother and sister, something she could not understand. The school personnel expressed to her uncle that they did not know what to do with three children who spoke only Spanish. During recess, she remembers how the other children would call them names, staring and glaring at them. Strong for her younger siblings, she learned to ignore them. But most of all, she felt alone and confused. Her father's insistence that she and her siblings were Americans only increased her confusion. "He made us memorize the Pledge of Allegiance. This was the first English we learned," she remarked. Her experiences at school also gave her the motivation to succeed. It came from some of her teachers who caringly helped her to move forward. Today, she only hopes that others understand why they came.

Ogden, Sorlie, and Hagen (2007) contend that the immigrant status of children becomes a risk factor for their future schooling. Similar position has been echoed by other researchers concerned about the challenges that immigration status poses for children (Gelatt 2016; Rojas-Flores and Medina-Vaughn 2019; Sidhu and Song 2019). Even when their arrivals are official and even for those whose families have long been established in our communities, many children are still confronted with serious challenges, placing their future at risk. This is evident from the memories shared by Constanza who arrived when she was only 6 years old. As immigrants in a new and often hostile environment, children are at a point where their development is still unfolding and necessitates the nurturing support of a caring and understanding early childhood educators. Only then will they be able to build the developmental skills needed to overcome and thrive despite the challenges that may await them in the future. It becomes relevant to reaffirm what the director-general of UNESCO, Audrey Azoulay, said stating that *"Education is a human right, a public good, and a public responsibility. Let us prioritize education as a public good"* (emphasis added) (United Nations 2019, n.p.).

With an increasing immigrant population, UNICEF (2016) advises the need for improving the overall accessibility to early childhood programs that can more responsively meet the needs of young immigrant children. This advisory has implicit considerations related to the diverse needs and experiences of children and their families. Attention to this recommendation follows in the next chapters.

Time to reflect ... *Educational opportunities realized or denied*

Revisit Costanza's story of her first experiences as a young immigrant child in the local school district classroom. Her father's dream and goal were for his family to become US citizens. He insisted that his children be Americans and live the American dream. Why was Costanza so confused and alone?

Public and private education has long struggled to meet the needs of children from diverse immigrant cultures (Bradley and McKelvey 2007). The reasons are many, with some attributing this to social and cultural views on immigration. At stake is the fact that the well-being and educational progress of young migrant students depend to a major degree on their school experiences (Nilsson and Bunnar 2016). Reports show that immigrant children are less likely to participate in early childhood education opportunities. This is in light of research findings strongly suggesting that increasing their enrollment in preschool would help to reduce inequality in skills at elementary school entry (Magnuson, Lahaie, and Woldfogel 2006). Attendance and participation in an appropriate, quality early childhood education program by young immigrant children continue to be identified as key to the child's later schooling success. Yet, it remains both complicated and challenging for many children of immigrants. The immigration status of families remains as a major factor in determining the ease or difficulty by which immigrant children are enrolled and attend educational programs (Berestein-Rojas 2013). Language barriers, differing views about parent involvement, and unfamiliarity with the US education system have been pointed out as deterrents to participation in early childhood programs (Crosnoe 2013; García Coll et al. 2002; Takanishi 2004). Yet, these barriers can be overcome with determined efforts consciously aware of the circumstances hindering families from accessing services. Needed are intentional actions to address known obstacles. An issue of fairness and equity, efforts begin with consideration to families and to their aspirations for children, steps fundamental to their engagement and involvement.

Equitable educational experiences and opportunities

Equitable opportunities for child immigrants are more than just a dream. Their rights have been recognized by the United Nations' Universal Declaration of Human Rights, signed in 1948, which serves as a foundational document on human rights law (United Nations 2019). Further recognition comes from human rights provisions pertaining to migrants' rights and protection (see Box 3.3). In the United States, access and participation in educational services and programs are lawfully recognized for all immigrant children entering and living in the country (U.S. Department of Education 2014). Education constitutes one of the nation's core societal elements of equality. Aspirations to make equitable access to educational experiences happen are what guides the determined efforts and advocacy of educators whose support is vital to children's success. What is needed is to bring socially just actions to responsively address the needs and dignity of children. Equitable integration of immigrants into the social fabric of the United States demands such actions. It begins during the early years and centers on an equitable and responsive education. As Wrigley, Lingard, and Thomson (2012) state, what is required from education is highly multifaceted, demanding concerted and targeted efforts, yet essential. Mirroring the goals for social justice, they further characterize the need for a respectful educational response centered on recognition of the students' experiences, realities, and voices. This is as well what we aspire for young children of immigrants.

With a position on equity for children, it is undeniable that stories of experiences and practices contrary to what is envisioned demand attention and action. Impressions and feelings from experiences during childhood are powerful life episodes that remain with us. We learn about Constanza's experiences, who shared some of her memories from her childhood (Box 3.2), vividly remembering the feelings of confusion and loneliness experienced at school. Her account not only reveals the unfairness of what she experienced but also the lack of knowledge of educational practices appropriate to address her and her siblings' needs. One also recognizes the disappointing and uncompassionate response that Constanza experienced. Actions to avoid similar experiences are vital if equity is to become a reality for each and every child.

Equity is intrinsically embedded as an aspiration for every child (UNESCO 2016). While even one child fails to equitably receive what her or she is entitled to experience, efforts must continue to ensure their rights. At present, in the context of derogatory and misleading views about immigration, prejudiced positions and discriminatory actions demand rigorous attention to experiences confronting children and their families. They pose additional challenges adding to vulnerabilities already faced by children of immigrants. Studies have clearly identified that present intensification of immigration policies have led to "new barriers and increase levels of fear, uncertainty, and isolation for many immigrant children and families" (Chavez et al. 2012, 11). The climate of current policies and attitudes toward immigrants continues to demand everyone to be more mindfully aware and consider how these may impact children and their families (Rubio-Hernández and Ayón 2016; Zayas et al. 2015).

Box 3.3 Connecting ideas: *Equity in education, a global right*

The right to education is recognized universally for all individuals. It is intrinsic to the core of equal and common rights of people. In 1948, the United Nations (UN) General Assembly in its Declaration of Human Rights proclaimed education as a fundamental human right and a necessary element of individual development. Article 26 of the declaration further stated that "Education shall be directed to the full development of the human personality and to the strengthening of respect for human rights and fundamental freedoms. It shall promote understanding, tolerance and friendship among all nations, racial or religious groups, and shall further the activities of the United Nations for the maintenance of peace" (United Nations [1948] 2018, n.p.).

The right to education and its primordial need for everyone has since been reaffirmed through many of the UN initiatives. In 1989, the milestone Convention on the Rights of the Child reasserted education as a right of all children. It specifically affirmed the right to receive quality educational experiences, constituting it as a socially just expectation for all children. The UN 2030 Sustainable Developmental Goals (2015) further confirmed education as a matter of equity, indicating that "we commit to providing inclusive and equitable education at all levels; especially those in vulnerable situations; and, should have access to life-long learning opportunities that help them acquire knowledge and skills" (United Nations, n.p.). The recent surge in immigration has created greater concern about the well-being of children. In particular, it has brought attention to the vulnerability of children and to the need to protect their rights. The most vulnerable migrant population are the young children who accompany their parents and families seeking access to equitable and equal educational opportunities that for many are not accessible in their countries or regions. Advocates, such as UNICEF, nongovernmental organizations, and many other international programs, continue their watch to ensure services and programs are made available for children and responsibly provide for their well-being.

A multifocal approach to immigration and children

Everyone has opinions about life events and circumstances. The same applies to current views on immigration where everybody seems to have their own ideas about this ongoing reality. Unfortunately, some views have made the reality of children and their families cloudy. It has also made the conversation harder and convoluted. Efforts to objectively view immigration and its impact on children are what has guided us as authors to examine immigration as a factor experienced and influencing young children and their families. This is what motivated us as authors to select a multifocal approach consisting of four lenses guiding views to more fully understand its implications on children (Robles-Meléndez and Driscoll 2016).

While not a unique approach, a lens framework can more effectively help in gathering the diverse aspects in the continuing story of immigration. For instance, Bolman and Deal (2008) in their work about leadership and organizations identified four distinctive frames or lenses from which people view the world around them. Lenses are filters used to order our experiences, information, and perceptions. Lenses filter some things in and allow other things to pass through. No one utilizes one single lens all the time. However, each one of us uses a preferred lens based upon present and prior life experiences. Nevertheless, together, they provide a broader sense about reality while viewing situations from different angles.

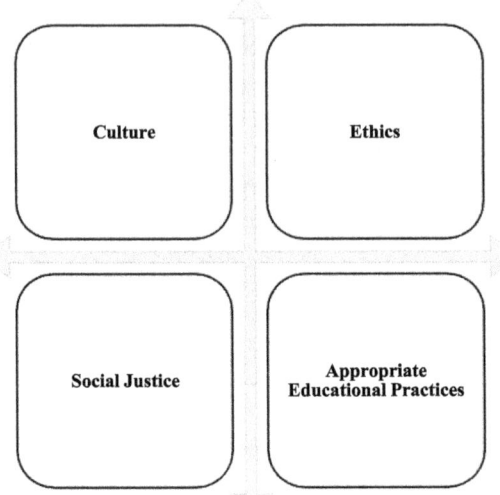

Figure 3.3 Four lenses multifocal immigrant experience approach: Children and immigration.
Source: Robles-Meléndez and Driscoll (2016, 2017).

Four lenses approach

Every issue possesses multiple angles revealed as different perspectives are considered. Such is the case of immigration and children where a four lenses approach was chosen to delve into its different realities. Four lenses were identified to examine issues of immigration and early childhood (Figure 3.3). Each of the lenses chosen helps in sharpening views on a reality that is multidimensional. Far from politics, in selecting them, our vision centered on what is essentially relevant in seeing children as immigrants. The multifocal model allows one to see the truth of immigrants through the eyes of inherent tenets represented by each lens where each serves as an unbiased way to become aware of one's blind knowledge spots and to consciously focus our thoughts. Lenses are interrelated and help in focusing circumstances from more than one perspective, thus expanding the outlook on issues that may impact the child.

The *lens of culture* encompasses the values, language, experiences, perceptions, and thoughts. Through this perspective, culture is viewed as a strength brought by immigrants. It also compels us to consider the implications of the socialization process children experience, growing up and building knowledge about their own heritage culture while immersed in the cultural environment of the United States. Through the *lens of ethics*, we ponder the professional responsibility and commitment of early childhood educators toward children and their families.

Using NAEYC's ethical principles (2011) and the best interest principle, this lens provides us with ways to view the holistic needs of child immigrants and determine what is pertinent to the child and the concomitant responses from early educators. Furthermore, it focuses attention on what is ethically needed as a moral responsibility to the child.

We added the *lens of appropriate educational practice* to underline the demand for educational experiences centered on programs, services, and classroom practices, all viewed from the perspective of what is best for children based on their individual needs and circumstances critical to support and foster positive development. This lens further places attention on quality as a paradigm for practices in the teaching and educational experience of immigrant children and their families. The *lens of social justice* focuses on equity as the overarching archetype defining responses, attention, and inclusivity of practices for young immigrant children and their families. Through this lens, issues of prejudice, discrimination, and unfairness are focused on the discussion of immigration as existing factors demanding attention and action. Viewing the immigrant situations through the social justice lens provides an ever-changing picture based on established laws and policies, as well as governmental responses to what has been labeled as the "immigrant crisis."

In the chapters ahead, the reader is encouraged to view and consider concepts, information, experiences, and the voices of immigrant children and parents seen through the four lenses. Discussions will allow you to reflect on your views and positions as an early childhood educator while you consider the immigrant experience of children in communities across the nation. We urge you to remember that, similar to other children, they are children too.

Key ideas

- Yearning for fair and equal opportunities, education, freedom, stability, and safety serve as the core of the dreams and hopes that continue to motivate immigrant families.
- Social justice focuses attention on current inequities in the experience of immigrant children and their families. Viewing immigration through social justice minimizes arguments and distorted views about the immigrant crisis. Education is a significant tool needed to achieve social justice for immigrant families and children. Ethically, social justice efforts and practices in early childhood education are aimed at eliminating barriers inhibiting children from enjoying equitable services and experiences.

- Multifocal lenses consciously filter our experiences, information, and perceptions about the immigrant situation. Many individuals continue to have prejudiced views, lack of information, or knowledge about immigration. Blind spots negatively affect judgments, reasoning, and perceptions about immigrants and immigration. Use of a multifocal lens allows individuals to see the truth of immigrants through the eyes of inherent principles. Four lenses helping to examine immigration and its impact on children and families are culture, ethical practice, educational practice, and social justice.

Things to do and reflect on

1. Revisit the stories of Stuart, Constanza, and Juan. What school experiences do the three immigrant children have in common during their initial experiences in early schooling? As an early childhood teacher, what would you do to flip the script on their common experiences?
2. Based on the discussion of social justice and from the perspective of ethical practice, what responsibilities does it ascribe to early childhood education professionals?
3. International law and US legislation recognize the educational rights of immigrant students. Given this recognition, what implications does this have for early childhood program practices?
4. Review the multifocal immigrant experience model. Based on your experiences and wealth of knowledge, define the cultural, social justice, ethical, and developmental practice lenses.
5. Considering the four lenses described in this chapter, which lens do you use to filter the immigrant situation based on your experiences, information, and perceptions? Are you mindful of your knowledge blind spots as you organize your thoughts about the immigrant experience? How do you plan to deal with your conscious blind spots?

References

Abo-Zena, Mona. 2018. "Supporting immigrant-origin children: Grounding teacher education in critical developmental perspectives and practices." *Teacher Educator* 53(3): 263–76.

Adair, Jennifer. 2015. *The Impact of Discrimination on the Early Schooling Experiences of Children from Immigrant Families*. Washington, DC: Migration Policy Institute.

American Immigration Council. 2016. *Public Education for Immigrant Students: Understanding* Plyler vs. Doe. Retrieved from https://www.americanimmigrationcouncil.org/sites/default/files/research/public_education_for_immigrant_students_understanding_plyer_v_doe.pdf.

American Psychological Association, Presidential Task Force on Immigration. 2012. *Crossroads: The Psychology of Immigration in the New Century*. Retrieved from http://www.apa.org/topics/immigration/report.aspx.

Bankston, Carl. 2010. "Social justice: Cultural origins of a perspective and a theory." *The Independent Review* 15(2): 165–78.

Baynes, Chris. 2019. "US detaining hundreds of African migrants at border after 'dramatic rise' in arrivals." *The Independent*. June 7. Retrieved from https://news.yahoo.com/us-detaining-hundreds-african-migrants-083330444.html.

Berestein-Rojas, Leslie. 2013. "How parents' immigration status affects their children's education." *Multi-American*. May 30. Retrieved from https://www.scpr.org/blogs/multiamerican/2013/05/30/13829/how-parents-immigration-status-affects-their-child/.

Blizzard, Brittany and Jean Batalova. 2020. *Cuban Immigrants in the United States*. Migration Policy Institute. Retrieved from https://www.migrationpolicy.org/article/cuban-immigrants-united-states.

Bolman, Lee, and Terrence Deal. 2008. *Reframing Organizations: Artistry, Choice, and Leadership*. New York: Jossey-Bass.

Bradley, Robert H., and McKelvey, Lorraine. 2007. "Parenting stress of low-income parents of toddlers and preschoolers: Psychometric properties of a short-term form of the Parenting Stress Index." *Parenting: Science and Practice* 1(1): 25–56.

Chavez, Jorge, Anayeli Lopez, Christine M. Englebrecht, and Ruben P. Viramontez Anguiano. 2012. "*Sufren los niños*. Exploring the impact of unauthorized status on immigrant children's wellbeing." *Family Court Review* 50(4): doi:10.1111/j.1744-1617.2012.01482.x.

Cho, Hyunhee. 2017. "Navigating the meanings of social justice, teaching for social justice, and multicultural education." *International Journal of Multicultural Education* 19(2). Retrieved from https://files.eric.ed.gov/fulltext/EJ1148050.pdf.

Copple, Carol, and Sue Bredekamp. 2009. *Developmentally Appropriate Practice in Early Childhood Programs Serving Children Birth through Age 8* (3rd ed.). Washington, DC: National Association for the Education of Young Children.

Crosnoe, Robert. 2013. *Preparing the Children of Immigrant for Early Academic Success*. Migration Policy Institute. Retrieved from https://www.migrationpolicy.org/research/preparing-children-immigrants-early-academic-success.

Dewey, John. 1990. *The School and Society*. Chicago, IL: University of Chicago Press.

Freire, Paulo. 1970. *Pedagogy of the Oppressed*. NY: Bloomsbury Academic.

Friere, Paulo. [1974] 2013. *Education for Critical Consciousness*. London: Bloomsbury.

García, Eugene. 2005. *Teaching and Learning in Two Languages. Bilingualism and Schooling in the United States.* New York: Teachers College Press.

García Coll, Cynthia, Daisuke Akiba, Natalia Palacios, Benjamin Bailey, Rebecca Silver, Lisa DiMartino, and Cindy Chin. 2002. "Parental involvement in children's education: Lessons from three immigrant groups." *Parenting Science and Practice* 2(3): 303–24. Retrieved from https://doi.org/10.1207/S15327922PAR0203_05.

Gelatt, Julia. 2016. "Immigration status and the healthcare access and health of children of immigrants." *Social Science Quarterly* 97(3): 540–54.

González, Norma, Luis Moll, and Cathy Amanti. 2005. *Funds of Knowledge: Theorizing Practices in Households, Communities, and Classrooms.* New Jersey: Lawrence Erlbaum.

Goodwin, Lin. 2017. "Who is in the classroom now? Teacher preparation and the education of immigrant children." *Educational Studies* 53(5): 433–49.

Hart, Louise, Frances Press, and Megan Gibson. 2013. "'Doing' social justice in early childhood: The potential for leadership." *Contemporary Issues in Early Childhood Education* 14(4): 324–34.

Herbert, Jeannie. 2013. "Interrogating social justice in the early years education: How effectively do contemporary policies and practices create equitable learning environments for indigenous Australian children?" *Contemporary Issues in Early Childhood* 14(4): 300–10.

Hernandez, Donald, Nancy Denton, and Susan McCartney. 2008. "Children in immigrant families: Looking to America's future." *Social Policy Report* 22(3): 1–12.

Keels, Mycere, and C. Cybele Raver. 2009. "Early learning experiences and outcomes for children of U.S. immigrant families: Introduction to the special issue." *Early Childhood Research Quarterly* 24(4): 363–6. Retrieved from https://doi.org/10.1016/j.ecresq.2009.09.002.

Leo-Rhynie, Elsa, C. Minott, S. Gift, M. McBean, A. Scott, and Wilson. 2009. *Competency of Children in Guyana, Rural Jamaica, and St. Vincent and the Grenadines: Making the Transition from Pre-Primary School with Special Emphasis on Gender Difference.* Kingston: Dudley Memorial Fund.

Magnuson, Katherine, Claudia Lahaie, and Jane Waldfogel. 2006. "Preschool and school readiness of children of immigrants." *Social Science Quarterly* 5: 1241–62.

McDonald, Mona. 2005. "The integration of social justice in teacher education." *Journal of Teacher Education* 56(5): 418–35.

Mevawalla, Zinnia. 2013. "The Crucible: Adding complexity to the question of social justice in early childhood development." *Contemporary Issues in Early Childhood* 14(4): 290–9.

National Association for the Education of Young Children [NAEYC]. 2011. *Code of Ethical Practice and Statement of Commitment: A Position Statement of the National Association for the Education of Young Children.* Washington, DC: Author.

National Association for the Education of Young Children [NAEYC]. 2019. *Responding to Equity in Early Childhood Education: Position Statement.* Washington, DC: Author.

Nilsson, Jenny, and Nihad Bunar. 2016. "Educational responses to newly arrived students in Sweden: Understanding the structure and influence of post-migration ecology." *Scandinavian Journal of Educational Research* 60(4): 399–416.

Ogden, Terje, Marianne Sorlie, and Kristine Hagen. 2007. "Building strength through enhancing social competence in immigrant students in primary: A pilot study." *Emotional and Behavioral Difficulties* 2(2): 105–17.

Oleinik, Irina. 2018. Rich economies not a promise of education equality, new report finds. *UN News.* October 29. Retrieved from https://news.un.org/en/story/2018/10/1024392.

Owens, Quinn. 2019. "New surge of African migrants arriving at US southern border." *ABC News.* June 17. Retrieved from https://abcnews.go.com/Politics/surge-african-migrants-arriving-us-southern-border/story?id=63764050.

Philbin, Sandy, and Cecilia Ayón. 2016. "Luchamos por nuestros hijos: Latino immigrant parents strive to protect their children from the deleterious effects of anti-immigration policies." *Children and Youth Services Review* 63: 128–35. Retrieved from https://doi.org/10.1016/j.childyouth.2016.02.019.

Robles-Meléndez, Wilma. 2017. "Integrating social justice in the early childhood curriculum." Paper presented at the Annual Conference of the Florida Association for the Education of Young Children, Orlando, Florida, December 4, 2017.

Robles-Meléndez, Wilma, and Vesna Beck. 2019. *Teaching Young Children in Multicultural Classrooms: Issues, Perspectives, and Strategies* (5th ed.). CA: Cengage.

Robles-Meléndez, Wilma, Mabel Valdés, and Eric Robles. 2018. "Explorando conceptos de justicia social y equidad en el nivel preescolar" [Exploring social justice and equity concepts in the preschool level]. Paper presented at the Annual Conference of the National Association for the Education of Young Children, Washington, DC, November 16.

Robles-Meléndez, Wilma, and Wayne Driscoll. 2016. "Working with immigrant families. A primer of experiences." Paper presented at the Annual Conference of the European Early Childhood Research Association, Dublin, Ireland, August 31–September 3.

Robles-Meléndez, Wilma, and Wayne Driscoll. 2017. "Here I am! Listening to the voices of immigrant children and their families. An analysis of socially just practices supporting children's sociocultural development." Paper presented at the Annual Conference of the European Early Childhood Research Association, Bologna, Italy, August 31–September 3.

Rojas-Flores, Lisseth, and Jennifer Medina-Vaughn. 2019. *Determinants of Health and Well-Being for Children of Immigrants: Moving from Evidence to Action.* Foundation for Child Development. Retrieved from https://www.fcd-us.org.

Roopnarine, Jaipaul and James Johnson. 2013. *Approaches to Early Childhood Education* (6th ed.). Boston, MA: Pearson.

Roopnarine, Jaipaul, and Bora Jin. 2012. "Indo Caribbean immigrant beliefs about play and its impact on early academic performance." *American Journal of Play* 4(4): 441–63.

Roopnarine, Jaipaul, Pauline Bynoe, and Ronald Singh. 2004. "Factors tied to the schooling of children of English-speaking Caribbean immigrants in the United States." In Une Gielen and Jaipaul Roopnarine (eds.), *Childhood and Adolescence: Cross-Cultural Perspectives and Applications*, 319–49. New York: Praeger.

Rubio-Hernández, Sandy, and Cecilia Ayón. 2016. "*Pobrecitos los niños*: The emotional impact of anti-immigration policies on Latino children." *Children and Youth Review* 60: 20–6.

Salami, Bukola, Jordana Salma, Kathleen Hegadoren, Salima Meherali, T. Kolawole, and Esperanza Díaz. 2018. "Sense of community belonging among immigrants: Perspective of immigrant service providers." *Public Health* 167 (February): 28–33.

Sidhu, Shawn, and Susan Song. 2019. "Growing up with an undocumented parent in America: Psychosocial adversity in domestically residing immigrant children." *Journal of the American Academy of Child & Adolescent Psychiatry* 58(10): 933–5.

Stanton, Bonita. 2019. "Foreword: Delivering on the promise of the Statue of Liberty." *Pediatrics Clinics of North America* 66(3): xv–xvi.

Suárez-Orozco, Carola, and Marcelo Suárez-Orozco. 2001. *Children of Immigration*. Cambridge, MA: Harvard University Press.

Takanishi, Ruby. 2004. "Leveling the playing field: Supporting immigrant children from birth to eight." *Future of Children* 14(2): 61–79.

Tamer, Mary. 2014. "The education of immigrant children." *Research Stories: Usable Knowledge*. December 11. Accessed July 5, 2019. Retrieved from https://www.gse.harvard.edu/news/uk/14/12/education-immigrant-children.

Torres-Harding, Sarah, and Steven Meyers. 2013. "Teaching for social justice and social action." *Journal of Prevention &Intervention Community* 41(2): 213–19.

UNESCO. 2016. *Education for People and Planet: Creating Sustainable Futures for All.*" Retrieved from https://en.unesco.org/gem-report/2016/education-people-and-planet-creatingsustainable-futures-all.

UNICEF. 2015. *Equity: A Fair Chance for Every Child. What Is Equity*. Retrieved from https://www.unicef.org/equity/.

United Nations. [1948] 2018. *Universal Declaration of Human Rights*. United Nations. Retrieved from https://www.un.org/en/universal-declaration-human-rights/index.html.

United Nations. 2015. *Transforming Our World: The 2030 Agenda for Sustainable Development*. Retrieved from https://sustainabledevelopment.un.org/post2015/transformingourworld.

United Nations. 2019. "Education transforms lives' says UN chief on first ever international day." *UN News.* January 24. Retrieved from https://news.un.org/en/story/2019/01/1031202.

U.S. Department of Education. 2014. *Educational Services for Immigrant Children and Those Recently Arrived to the United States.* Retrieved from https://www2.ed.gov/policy/rights/guid/unaccompanied-children.pdf.

Wrigley, Terry, Bob Lingard, and Pat Thomson. 2012. "Pedagogies of transformation: Keeping hope alive in troubled times." *Critical Studies in Education* 53(1): 95–108.

Zayas, Luis, Sergio Aguilar-Gaxiola, Hyunwoo Yoon, and Guillermina Natera Rey. 2015. "The distress of citizen-children with detained or deported parents." *Journal of Child and Family Studies* 24(11): 3213–23. doi:10.1007/s10826-015-0124-8.

4

Caring and Understanding the Immigrant Child: Developmental and Cultural Considerations

Children are the hope of a new tomorrow. It was yesterday and will always be. (Anonymous)

Through this chapter, we will

- Define culture and its influence on the immigrant child's development
- Identify the factors influencing the immigration experience for young children
- Explore some of the factors supporting the cultural identity development of children with immigrant roots

Key terms

- Culture lens
- Immigrant families
- Cultural identity
- Funds of knowledge
- Consciously centered practices

NAEYC standards

- NAEYC #1 Promoting Child Development and Learning
- NAEYC #2 Families and Communities
- NAEYC #6 Professionalism

Sharing experiences: Dreams come true

During so many nights, I dreamt of the day when my children would be grown up and with a career of their own. They were in my dreams when I came here from my country. It was a long way from la sierra and don't even want to remember what it took me to get here. Coming on foot, my life started again that night when we finally crossed into what is now my home. I have worked so hard and continue today but would never regret it for a moment about coming to live here. My life started again here when our children were born. I still remember that evening when my first child was born and how all that I had struggled suddenly went away. It has not been easy. But there are no regrets. Today I can smile. Every time I share what they are, I smile and the slightest thought about how tired I may be slips away. My eldest was the first one to graduate from college and he is already working. I'm so proud of him. Soon my youngest son will be a doctor, a doctor! What else could I wish? (A Peruvian mother)

For our children

"Every time we learn that a child is born the future opens up"—this is what one of our authors once heard from parents in one of our communities. They were proudly sharing anecdotes and photos about their children. "*Son mi orgullo*," they are my pride, one of the parents said showing the photo of her children. Undeniably, this is the image so many of us continue to see as we work with young children and their families. Children will always bring hope of a new tomorrow. Regardless of where they come from, their ethnic or cultural roots, children are always the essence of a new generation and society.

Just like in the past, thousands of children and their families continue to arrive from near and distant places and so many others are born to immigrant parents—our neighbors, our friends, our colleagues, our relatives, or our own. For their parents, they are one of the reasons motivating their efforts and struggles to continue to do everything possible for their success. This is what the mother in the opening vignette expressed when we asked her about her children, today already adults. She dreamt of them even before they were born and worked hard for them. Her story reflects that of countless other parents across the nation's communities. Their children are now in our classrooms. The mission of ensuring their future and well-being remains as the impetus driving equitable and just educational experiences for all.

Time to reflect ... *All for children*

In every culture and country, children always bring a smile to people's faces. Behind their smiles lies their feelings and dreams for what a child represents for their families and communities. Take a moment and remember what the news about a child being born evokes in people, families, and in you. Reflect on what a child means to you as a member of society and as an early childhood educator. What words would best describe your sentiments?

Knowing the immigrant children we teach

Someone once asked what they would need to work with immigrant children. Indeed, the answer is both a simple one and one that calls for ongoing conversations. The simple answer is that they are children with their eyes and hopes on us. Simply children. They are our country's children. Efforts to know them personally are critical, particularly in ensuring what must be equitably afforded to all children. It all starts by asking ourselves, how well do we know children? What do we know about their own experiences? How well do we know their culture? Beyond what one reads in the press and hears from the media or from people, the experience of immigration is a many-faceted event, where all aspects are relevant as one tries to address the essential and individual needs of the child immigrant.

Time to reflect ... *Valuing diversity*

Appreciating and understanding children and families of immigration begin with acknowledging their multiple diversities. Bateson's statement echoes this aspiration when she stated, "What would it be like to have not only color vision but culture vision, the ability to see the multiple worlds of others?" (1995, 3). Consider her statement and reflect on its message for early childhood educators working with immigrant families and their children.

Children are, first and foremost, children. Their experiences as well as the circumstances of their families and their lives vary (Greenberg, Rosenboom, and Adams 2019). They cannot be fitted into one set of characteristics. While there are many trying situations that some may face, over the years, countless immigrants have and continue to successfully address and navigate the challenges of life, becoming part of the nation's society. We know so many of them who have been and are our students. Some have described this as the immigrant paradox, referring to the accounts of thousands of immigrants who have overcome what for some would have been unsurmountable challenges (García Coll and Marks 2012; Suárez-Orozco and Suárez-Orozco 2001). Similar to the mother in the opening vignette to the chapter, proud of their sons who are now professionals, many others have been able to turn the American dream into a reality. Their achievements continue every day as a testimonial of the promise children of immigrants bring to the US society.

Rather than listing generalized traits of immigrant children, it is imperative to consider their individuality and the circumstances that may surround the young life experiences of child immigrants. Meeting their needs and supporting their development demand an understanding of who they are, their culture, and their experiences now and before coming to the country, especially in the case of recently arrived immigrant children. As we take time to learn about their unique experiences and circumstances, we will be better informed to make decisions and provide children with our support. Only then will we be able to deliver the promise of what is socially just and fair for children who are immigrants.

Time to reflect ... *Child immigrants in our classrooms*

Our country is home to over five million children from birth to age 5, born to immigrant parents (Migration Policy Institute 2017) who join the thousands of others born in other countries attending classrooms throughout the country.

How have we met their educational and developmental needs? What are we doing to build our "knowing" about children with immigrant roots? We invite you to reflect on these points and to consider them from the perspective of your role as an educator and early childhood professional.

Seeing the child: Consciously centered practices

For decades immigrant children have been in our classrooms. For many who grew up as immigrant children themselves, the memories are mixed. Many well-intended practices did not meet their needs. Irrespective of these practices, one questions how well their teachers knew them. How much did they know about their experiences and needs, their culture, and their expectations? One wonders about how much empathy and efforts to value their realities and heritage transpired. It causes you to also consider any bias and misconstrued ideas about immigrants that may have influenced decisions and actions. Key to searching and finding answers to these questions, we must insist, is our realization that they are children. Immigrant children share so many things in common with every other child. Yet, they call for thoughtful understanding of who they are. They want us to see them as they are.

"We need to know children," is what has been emphatically stated by many experienced early childhood educators. Firmly supporting their language and heritage, they believe that practices must begin by respecting the children's cultures and own experiences. At the core of their statements is the need for attention to what we are defining as *consciously centered practices* where one can truly see children and their reality. Consciousness about circumstances and realities makes us aware of needs and actions to overcome inequities and ensure equality. This is what Freire ([1974] 2013) postulated as he encouraged reflection and action to fittingly respond to obstacles and realities deemed unequal. Consciously centered practices are intentional and developmentally oriented. They begin by seeing the child as an individual; by knowing their culture; respecting and valuing their knowledge and ways they learn; and supporting and validating the importance of their home language and ways. Practices centered on the immigrant child also happen by recognizing their potential to develop; giving consideration to the social realities and unique circumstances they may have experienced, either personally or together with their family; and equitably safeguarding their rights and opportunities to succeed (Gonzalez, Moll, and Amanti 2005). Consciously centered practices demand consideration for the child beyond ethnocentric views and intentionally centering decisions and practices on what is essential to their well-being. This view is intrinsically anchored in the early childhood profession as a core ethical principle (NAEYC 2011). When children's individual reality and their experiences, circumstances, and needs are consciously viewed as the core of what informs practices, we are centering decisions on what is necessary for their present and future successful development (Figure 4.1).

Coming to live in a culturally different context

Every day is another opportunity for the United States to continue growing as a nation of immigrants. According to the Census Bureau, in 2019, every

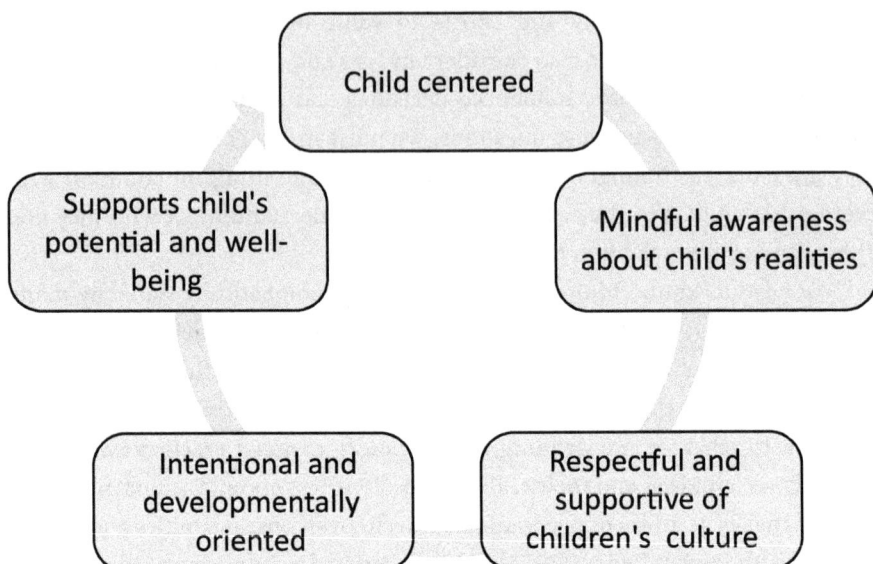

Figure 4.1 Key components of consciously centered practices.

34 seconds, an international migrant was officially entering the country (U.S. Census Bureau 2019). Behind these statistical counts are hundreds of children and their families who continue to enter our country as immigrants just like so many other immigrants already living in our communities. With them, immigrants bring a wealth of ideas, values, and, most importantly, their culture and heritage. Arriving into the country's multicultural society, they encounter a culture, a language, and ways that for many are different from their own. Cultural encounters are among the first experiences for children and their families arriving in the country.

¿Dónde estoy? Where am I? was what an educator born in Cuba said that she kept asking herself during her first experiences at school just after arriving in the United States. She still remembers the feelings she had as a second grader. Besides language, she felt more as a stranger in a classroom so different from the one she previously attended. *¡Sin uniformes!* No uniforms is still one of the experiences she remembers from her first days at school in the United States. Viewing things through the eyes of her cultural lens, what she experienced was seemingly contrary to her previous schooling experiences. No less different are the experiences of so many other children. A young student born in the United States to parents from Jamaica once shared that he remembered how his family instilled in him a sense of formality whenever addressing his teachers

especially in the primary school. He struggled adapting to the more informal interaction with teachers at school and was never able to call them by their first name as some encouraged their students to do. Others remembered standing up whenever called to answer or share a comment in their classroom, something they would learn was not part of the classroom expectations. Even those born in the United States to immigrant families still find some experiences puzzled them as well, especially when families keep following their cultural routines at home. Undoubtedly, culture remains one of the elements central to understanding the behaviors, experiences, and realities of immigrant children and families. It is, also, a factor demanding open-minded and ongoing learning for everyone.

Time to reflect ... *Encountering new cultural ways and routines*

We all acquired ways and respond to routines according to what is learned from one's culture. Take a moment to consider some of the routines or behaviors that may differ from those that children bring to school. What were some of those more commonly encountered? How can we address some of these differences?

Through the lens of culture

As we explore the factors and realities of children with immigrant roots, we take time to ponder the ever-presence of culture. The reality is that "There is no one aspect of life that is not touched and altered by culture" (Hall 1977). A fundamental factor defining individual diversity, understanding, and responding to the needs of immigrant children and their families begins when their cultures are acknowledged and valued (Moll 1992). Using the multidimensional lens of culture, we can appreciate their ideas, practices, and values. This will better enable us to understand the child and families, seeing them through the eyes of what guides their ideas and continues to drive their practices. In every instance, whenever practices and decisions are to be made, culture provides ways to contextualize the needs, expectations, and responses of immigrants in our classrooms and society (Lynch and Hanson 2011; Nieto and Bode 2018). Culture, we must remember, never ceases to influence people.

Efforts to understand and responsively attend to the immigrant child begin when we see them within the context of their culture. The lens of culture guides us as we try to find answers to the experiences faced by children and their families. Children find themselves in a society with expectations and practices, which for many culturally vary from their own. *How much do we know about the role of culture for a child? How does the experience of immigration influence children who come from other cultures? What does it mean to grow up as a child immigrant?* These are some of the questions guiding the discussion in this chapter, trying to gain an understanding about immigrant children in our classrooms and communities. They are also essential to consciously centered practices for children and their families.

The ever-presence of culture

We are because of our culture. (Anonymous)

Culture, broadly considered, provides a sense of belonging and of being to people. A highly complex concept, culture is the shared ways, behaviors, and understandings of a group of people. Culture is what binds people together and gives meaning to their own realities, responses, and behaviors. More importantly, we all belong to a culture from which we derive the sense about ourselves and about our own circumstances. Its overarching influence is present in each aspect of human interaction. People begin to learn about the shared meanings of their culture from birth and continue through experiences and interactions with others—families, relatives, peers, and adults. They carry these meanings and views as part of their cultural repertoire. The multitude of practices, rituals, and routines learned are carried through life, giving meaning to people's lives.

An ongoing and dynamic cultural exchange

The cultural contributions from immigrants, yesterday and today, who call the United States home, enhance and continually transform the culture of the nation. Throughout centuries, immigrants have brought their ways of knowing and doing to the nation they chose to settle and live. Acknowledgment of what people have shared makes us aware of the invaluable ways in which they contribute to build and enrich the nation's character. The blend of ideas, behaviors, and traditions found today across communities is a testimony to the multicultural character of the country's society. This is the ongoing cultural legacy of families and children with immigrant roots. While adapting to the culture of the country, immigrants play a role in the enrichment of the US culture through the contribution of their own culture, experiences, and knowledge. This cultural exchange contributes to keeping the cultural character of the country as a dynamic society.

Two key traits of culture

Cultures are indeed not static, a fact that defies some of the stereotyped views about immigrants and their ways. The fact is that we are continuously learning about the diversity of cultures people bring to our communities. When Clara, a young woman from Guatemala, came to register her 3-year-old child at a center, people found themselves trying to understand what she was saying. Though the young mother spoke some Spanish, her primary language was Quiché, an indigenous language derived from Mayan. It was something new for the staff at the center who soon realized that generalizing what everyone thought was the language common to Latinos did not always apply. Understanding immigrant families and children calls for us to broaden our views about their cultures. Two key traits of culture are the existing diversity within itself as well as its evolving and changing nature (Lynch and Hanson 2006; Robles de Meléndez and Beck 2019). Both are discussed in the section that follows.

Diversity within a culture

Diversity is a main characteristic of a culture. Even though culture implies a commonly shared pattern of understanding, within a cultural group it is not uncommon to find groups of people with diverse ways. While still maintaining some common aspects typical of the culture, a group within a culture may have different parameters defining their shared understandings. Heritage, traditional lifestyles, rituals, life transitions, beliefs, and language are among the diverse traits one may find distinguishing people within the same cultural group. For professionals working with young children with immigrant roots and backgrounds, it is essential to be mindful of existing differences within a group before generalizing their views.

Changing nature of culture

While some key characteristics of culture may remain stable, others evolve as culture adapts to societal changes. Responding to time and its consequent changes, culture actively continues to evolve through generations. Some researchers have pointed out that new communication technologies and ease of transportation have influenced cultural changes, making many more aware about other practices. With easier diffusion of ideas and knowledge, people have encountered other ways that over time influence their outlook on life and behaviors. The dynamic and evolving traits of culture are also what maintain it relevant responding to current realities. Many, even in remote locations, have now become aware of practices in other parts of the world and have adopted their use. This is an aspect that is important for early educators to know, particularly to avoid stereotyped views about a group. Seeing immigrant children and their families with misinformed and biased views hinders appreciation of their cultures and realities (Box 4.1).

Box 4.1 Connecting ideas: *Diversity rules … everywhere!*

Many times, we frequently generalize traits associated with a cultural group. However, one may find that not everyone shares the same views even though they are members of the same culture or ethnic groups. Some aspects of culture are clearly shared among the members of a same group. Others, however, may be specific and differ from what is typically ascribed to a particular culture. Diversity in a cultural or ethnic group is not uncommon, though people frequently seem not to be aware. Some of the more noticeable examples of diversity within a group are seen in our own communities. Indeed, some general traits tend to characterize a culture. It is equally relevant to recognize the existing variety of distinguishing factors. Language and diversity of practices are two among the many inherent factors one may find defining values and ways within a cultural group. For instance, when working with families with Hispanic or Latino roots as well as Asian, acknowledging the cultural and linguistic diversity that defines people within a same group is a first step to ensure appreciation of their individual cultural experience. Both Hispanics as well as Asians are umbrella names designating cultural groups known for their intensively diverse nature, something to always keep in mind.

Seeing the experience of immigration through the eyes of the child

What does it mean to grow up in a different context? This is a question we all need to ponder as we work with children representing a multiplicity of cultures and realities. Much of what has been studied about immigration is typically seen from the viewpoint of adults. However, stories about immigration cannot be fully told without seeing them from the perspective of the youngest immigrants. Only then can we more fully appreciate what it means for everyone.

Think about the feelings we may have when arriving or moving to live in a place unknown or new to us. Consider how it feels when others cannot even recognize or know about your own place of origin. That was the experience of the young student we met, who came at age 9 from a Caribbean island. To his surprise, people could not even recognize his birthplace. In his own words, the experience made him feel like a stranger in the land that his parents had planned for so long to come. Though years have passed, he still remembers that first impression. Another child who came at age 6 from South America still remembers the moment when people tried to say her name. She felt so embarrassed when some of her peers laughed, but would always cherish the way her teacher made an extra effort to pronounce it. Others we heard felt intimidated by comments and expressions they could not understand. Situations similar and many others raise the issue about what negatively influences the immigration experience for the child. Observations; conversations with early childhood professionals, families, and children; and first-hand experiences with immigrant children reveal a multitude of factors influencing their experiences. Culture, issues of language diversity, social status, family immigration status, and, sadly, discrimination are some of the factors playing a role in the child's journey as an immigrant (Adair 2015; Ayón 2015; Robles de Meléndez and Driscoll 2017; Spears Brown 2015; Yoshikawa and Kholoptseva 2013). Some of these factors are discussed in this chapter.

Experiencing immigration

Memories of moving and coming to live in a different place are typically vividly kept in our mind. Even when planning preceded the immigration event, it always leaves its mark on people. Some children that we spoke with shared their memories about their homelands. Some expressed sadness about what they had left behind, especially friends, family members, and even their pets. A young boy from the Caribbean mentioned his surprise when no one seemed to know where he was from: "When I first came here, people didn't know where I was from. Some kept asking me, from where? Where is that?" His disappointment was not uncommon. Like him, others shared similar feelings revealing the emotional intensity of the immigration experience for many children.

In the children's book *The Leaving Morning* (Johnson 2005), the child characters say goodbye to their home with a mix of sadness and enthusiasm for what is to be found in their new home. Some will feel nostalgia for their hometowns, yearning to return, similar to what is expressed by the child character in the story *Angelina's Island* (Winter 2007), when she hopes the airplane would fly her back home again. Similar feelings are evoked by children as they leave their homes and familiar landscapes they have known. Personally, we have heard the same feelings shared many times by children and students alike. A sense of being lost was what we often heard from people who came to the United States during their childhood. One of the authors' former students shared that she still remembered how she felt arriving at age 12 with her family from Asia. In her mind, the gardens and playground of her former school were still cherished memories. She missed not seeing her friends and even some of the familiar plants and flowers she would now try to grow in her own yard.

Time to reflect … *The yearning for our memories*

The yearning for what one left behind is a feeling we may all have experienced. It is a feeling that many foreign-born children and families cherish as they adapt to life in a different context.

Take a moment to reflect on some of your own experiences and think about something that is still so vividly remembered. What emotions and memories does it evoke?

An emotionally charged experience

The experience of immigration is charged with emotions for everyone. Even after years, these feelings still remain and become part of what is shared by generations. Some of the immigrants interviewed who came as children still remembered their first impressions from school and in the neighborhoods where they lived. Among those things remembered by one of them who entered as a refugee was the pets they left behind (personal communication, April 2019). Others mentioned their struggle learning a new language. Educator Cristina Igoa (1995), in her study about immigrant children, postulated that for children, the experience of immigration implies an array of different emotions. Based on

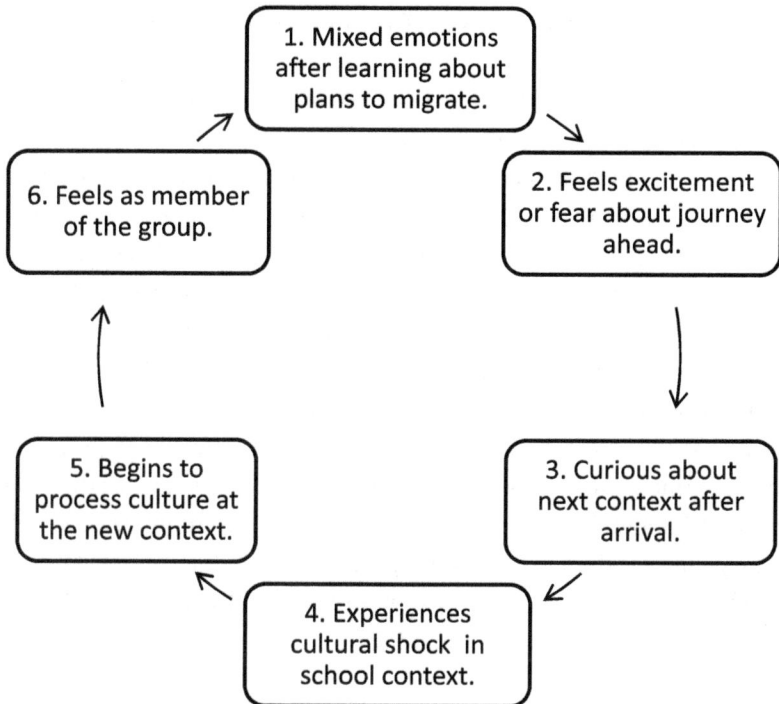

Figure 4.2 Cycle of emotions experienced by immigrant children.
Source: Igoa (1995).

her experiences and observations working with immigrant children, she pointed out that children go through what she described as a cycle of emotions emerging as they experience and process their new circumstance (Figure 4.2).

During the early childhood years, in particular, a sense of stability is one of the elements highly contributing to one's sense of social and emotional wellness (Berger 2018). According to Igoa (1995), the feeling of being uprooted describes the experience of immigration for children as they are transplanted into new contexts. This is an emotion many times shared even by children of immigrants who are born in the country. For them, the reality of immigration transcends, influencing their views as they make sense of life trying to fit in within the larger scope of their neighborhoods and communities. This is especially seen as they struggle with differing cultural patterns and expectations from those learned and followed at home. It is, in many cases, what we have heard people describe as the feeling of trying to define who they are.

Finding self in the context of diverse realities

Imagine the experience of a newly arrived 4-year-old who suddenly finds herself in a community where the language is unfamiliar, the environment different from the one in which she grew up, and where even the food does not resemble the same she is used to eating. Just consider what it means for the child as he or she tries to find self in a diverse context, and you will realize what so many young children experience as they come into our classrooms. This is what Eleana, the child in the vignette in Box 4.2 was experiencing when she was first observed. Seeing her months later revealed how she had managed to adapt to the setting and to its expectations. Navigating oneself in a different culture is a challenge. It begins as one tries to make sense about meanings, routines, and practices in a culture different from your own. This is an experience for many children born in other countries and for the first time entering a US classroom. It is, as well, for so many young children of immigrant parents born in the United States. Many may find themselves encountering a culture different from that at home and sometimes even in their own community.

Box 4.2 Connecting ideas: *Coming to a new setting*

We met 4-year-old Eleana in a preschool classroom. She was busy playing in the block area alongside other children. For the Guatemalan child with expressive brown eyes, being in a classroom environment was still an experience mostly new to her. She had joined the group a month earlier and from what we heard, she used to be at home with her family who lived in a rural community where she spent her time. During those first days at the center, at first, she would stay by herself. In the last few days, we learned, she had started to play with some of her peers, most of which were children of immigrant parents, too. Eleana was rearranging the blocks when her teacher called her. The sound of her name spoken by her teacher was yet somewhat unfamiliar but her soft voice was something she had begun to recognize. One of her peers tapped her and said in Spanish, "Vamos," let's go. She continued playing until her teacher called her, following her, and joining the group outside. It will take her a little bit to learn the routines, her teacher told us. A couple of months later when we visited the classroom again, Eleana greeted us remembering that we had met her before. "Hello" she said as she looked at us and started to talk. We smiled as we heard her words, both in English and Spanish, and saw her more confident attitude. Time, indeed, had made a difference as she adapted to the reality of the classroom.

Making sense of reality

Trying to make sense of expectations and cultural patterns in their classrooms and community is a major task for anyone. Developmentally, experiencing a new environment takes children into uncovering new ways and lifestyles. Using the lens of their own culture, children find ways to make sense and understand realities in the classroom and community contexts. For the 4-year-old in the vignette in Box 4.2, time provided the window into learning and making sense of her new reality in an environment that welcomed her. She also had the guidance and support from an understanding early childhood professional who recognized her need to process and make sense of all the new experiences. Indeed, when children find themselves in contexts that are supportive and where efforts are consciously made to respond to their needs, children's well-being and development are promoted (Copple and Bredekamp 2009; Derman-Sparks and Edwards 2010).

For many immigrant children, facing a culture different from that of their families is one of the first experiences encountered coming to our communities and classrooms—an experience not only for the newly arrived immigrants but also for children born to immigrant families already living in our communities. The dissonance found at times between the culture of the family and that of the environment is a reality they and their families experience. Leila, a young student whose parents came from the Dominican Republic, once shared that she asked herself many times who she was. Born and growing up in a Midwestern state, she felt the struggle between what her peers expected from her and what she had learned from her family. "It's like being in the middle and not knowing what to do," she said during a conversation. Adjusting to new patterns different from those at home is a confusing and many times difficult struggle for children while they try to make sense of themselves in two different environments. Understanding early educators, consciously aware of what the child is experiencing are the key to guide children. They provide continuity and connectedness while children make sense of their own self in their home and classroom contexts (Adair 2011; Wise and da Silva 2007).

Collaborations with families and classrooms intentionally arranged to incorporate elements reflective of the children's home cultures contribute to establishing a sense of continuity as children adjust to the culture of the classroom. Intentionally adding in the classroom resources such as artifacts and realia, representative of what families use at home, provides comfort to children as they find objects familiar to them. They provide a source for validation of their cultures and of what is typical to their lifestyles.

The critical role of culture

Growing up is an active learning experience for every child. During this critical formative period, interactions and encounters with their environments provide the foundational experiences that build a sense about self and their own reality (Berger 2018; Trawick 2018). This is also the time during which children begin to form a sense about culture and about being members of a cultural group. Culture is an influential force on all aspects of development, giving sense to individuals particularly as they develop socially and emotionally. It is also a vital factor in the socialization experience, the process through which the child acquires the social knowledge and conventions deemed valued in one's group (Trawick 2018). Overall, experiences lead children to learn the cultural conventions from home and those of the classroom, which are reflective of the mainstream culture.

Living in a different culture presents both an opportunity and a challenge for immigrant children and their families. It is an opportunity to learn a different way of seeing reality as they adjust to the culture of their environment. But it also poses the challenge of preserving one's culture while the culture of the host environment is acquired. Maintaining the continuity of cultural practices at home is relevant to preserve the family's culture. Interactions at home are powerful learning tools where exposure to their culture introduces children to the tenets of their group. They constitute a dynamic source for understanding the cultural scripts of their settings. Every interaction provides opportunities for learning the cultural conventions, knowledge, and practices followed at home (González, Moll, and Amanti 2005). These ideas or cultural knowledge is what the child uses to make sense of daily happenings in the environment. They are also what makes them part of their culture, giving individuals a sense of stability and certainty knowing the social conventions and expectations within one's context.

Language, too, plays a leading role in building a sense of reality and is instrumental for inquiring and understanding the values and norms of one's culture. The stories, phrases, and unique expressions such as the *refranes* or sayings so common for Latinos as well as in other cultural groups convey the wisdom and values of the culture connecting people with their shared understandings. We learn many of these during childhood and keep us connected to our culture, reaffirming one's heritage. They form part of the funds of knowledge each individual brings into a new cultural environment (González, Moll, and Amanti 2005). When these are recognized and honored, they ease a child's transition into a new environment.

> ## Time to reflect … *Sharing cultural messages*
>
> Every culture has unique ways to convey share understandings through popular phrases, stories, and sayings. Many of these messages are learned during childhood. Reflect on some of those that you still remember and choose one that still speaks to you. What was the cultural message shared?

Facing new cultural scripts

Every immigrant coming to our communities brings a repertoire of ideas and norms learned from their culture. What happens when they find that expectations diverge from those they have known? This is the challenge facing families and children of immigrant backgrounds whose cultural knowledge does not reflect that of their communities or classrooms. To those of us who have experienced immigration, we know how it feels as one tries to make sense of life in a different context. A feeling of uncertainty is not uncommon as children try to accommodate new behaviors with those familiar to them. Coming to live in settings different from those familiar to us presents the challenge of adjusting to new social and cultural codes. This is what is encountered when cultures come in contact (Berry 1980). Reflecting on their childhood as young immigrants, some of the adults we interviewed shared that their first experiences at school were spent trying to figure out every day what to do. Most of them said they kept to themselves and avoided situations while they learned how to navigate the routines and expectations from teachers and peers. Many remembered the warm understanding of their teachers and school staff. Others shared their memories of feeling unwelcomed. Sadly, this is not an uncommon feeling since in many instances people's views are guided by unfounded views about immigrants. The fact is that discrimination and prejudice are part of what immigrant children face and experience (Adair 2015; Ayón 2015; Spears Brown 2015).

Becoming in a new cultural context

Marina was born in the Midwest shortly after her family arrived from an Eastern European country. She remembered her aunt talking with her father in a language she could hardly understand. At home, her parents would always speak to her and a younger brother in English and often reminded them "You are Americans," which she never understood why they repeated. It was years later when Marina learned that they had entered as refugees. All of a sudden, she began to understand them. They wanted their children to feel as part of the community and did what they thought was best to avoid feeling and being seen as outsiders.

The experience of Marina and her parents is not uncommon. When two cultures come in contact, gaining acceptance into a new cultural reality makes one decide whether your cultural scripts remain valid or if these need to be adjusted, that is, balanced out with those of the new culture. During this encounter, cultural change or acculturation occurs. As a process, acculturation takes place when one meets another culture and establishes a continuous contact and interaction (Berry 1988). During this contact, people choose strategies that best suit them in addressing expectations and demands in their new cultural contexts (Berry 1980; Hochhausen, Perry, and Le 2008). Changes in attitudes, responses, and behaviors characteristically occur when individuals encounter more than one culture. For young children, experiences in a new cultural setting are filtered through the family and, indeed, the classroom. Playing a leading role, families interpret and transmit these new cultural tenets to children engaged in what is defined as enculturation. Enculturation occurs unconsciously and takes place through informal and formal experiences and interactions. Here children learn the views and acceptable social and cultural conventions of their settings interpreted by their families (Figure 4.3). Family experiences serve as a bridge into the behaviors deemed appropriate in the contexts where they live. With guidance from families, children gradually acquire the social codes of the context where they now live.

Contextual influences on the process of acculturation

The context plays a significant role in influencing the decisions immigrant families make about their acculturation options (Berry 1980). Berry's research acknowledges that the nature of circumstances surrounding people will weigh into their choices. Whenever there are commonalities among the immigrant culture and that of the receiving community, acculturation is facilitated (Berry 1980; Schwartz et al. 2010). This is the case, for instance, of language where, when this is common to immigrants, it enables their adjustment to the culture of the context. Schwartz et al. (2010) cite the case of Caribbean immigrants and note that those coming from English-speaking countries "may encounter less

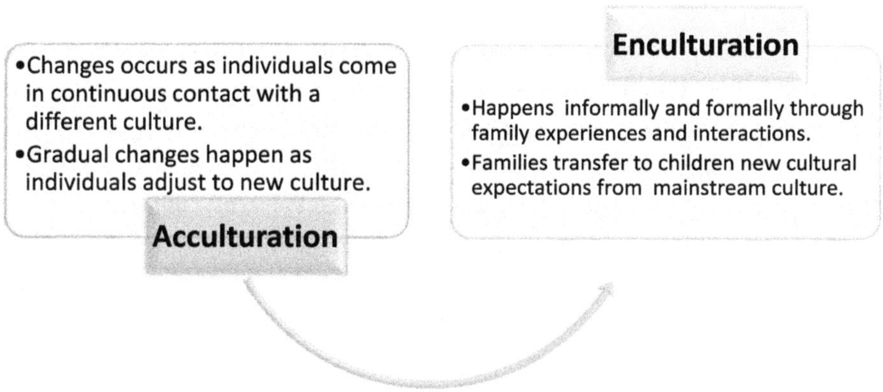

Figure 4.3 Two key processes in adjusting to a new culture.
Source: Berry (1997); Schwartz et al. (2010).

stress and resistance in the United States than migrants who are not familiar with the English language" (3–4). They give the example of Jamaicans whose knowledge of English contributes to an easier entry into the US culture than what Haitians may experience. This may also explain the challenges faced by immigrant children with languages other than English as in the case of Hispanic or Latinos. Barriers surfacing from linguistic differences play a major role in isolating immigrant families in the communities where they live.

Coming to live in ethnic neighborhoods also contributes to easing the stress and challenges of adjusting to a new reality. In these communities, familiarity with language and, to some extent, continuity of cultural expectations provide ways to facilitate the transition. Such communities also facilitate finding and building supports needed by families to help navigate systems and services unfamiliar to them.

Families' role in acculturation

During acculturation, people make decisions about their relationship with the mainstream society. Berry (1997, 2017) postulated that people choose how they will establish relationships in a new cultural context. Choices range from maintenance and integration of their own heritage to assimilation into the mainstream. Decisions made by families about acculturation preferences have implications for what children will experience at home. Individual experiences, contextual situations, and personal beliefs play a role in influencing how immigrants adapt to a new culture.

Living in a culture different from their own place immigrant families in a dilemma, as they are confronted with either adjusting to new cultural scripts or forgoing their ways and acculturate. It brings them to experience daily events and situations that challenge what they have known. This is what was expressed by a Peruvian immigrant in her reflections about her first encounters with a different culture and adapting to life in the United States (see *Voices of immigration*).

Adjusting to life in a different cultural environment implies a series of decisions that are influenced by individual experiences and contextual circumstances. Experiences, both personal and learned from others, and interactions in their social environments play a principal role in choosing decisions. As Berry pointed out, sometimes decisions "are constrained by what a person is able to do in a particular context" (Emamzadeh 2018). For a Peruvian immigrant, it was a process of learning and adjusting to new ideas and ways to conceptualize realities. In her experience, it was a matter of becoming more resilient which, as she stated, "makes you adapt to the circumstances." Options to acculturate for young children, however, are not as obvious as they are for parents and family members who can more knowingly choose the route to take. Children, on the other hand, find themselves facing two cultural parameters, those from home and that of their environment. Influence from adults remains as a leading force for the young child, which gradually is also paired with that of peers. Developmentally, the need to belong is one that drives many decisions while encountering a culture that diverges from our own.

Voices of immigration … Living and getting the best of two worlds

A young professional, who came years ago from her native Peru, in her reflections, shared her experiences about immigration and particularly about her cultural encounters.

Though my circumstances are different from those who had to come over, I still had to endure the differences in culture. In order for me to learn these differences, I had to get involved in a variety of experiences, such as my children's education. I remember how horrified I was when while in one of my volunteer tasks and walking by the classroom, I heard the screams of a teacher trying to quiet her students (quite the opposite from our classrooms in Peru). In this same time when my first born was in Kindergarten, I also learned from our school system of the individuality that is taught since an early age [to children]. Something funny happened in this respect as I was talking to my daughter for something she did wrong: she told me to "not invade her space." You probably know what my reaction was to this exertion of power, lol.

There are of course so many differences that I can't event start to mention, but what I can certainly tell you is that the human being is prone to adapt to any circumstances whether it is language, customs, beliefs, perceptions of others (which are also so different where I come from), habitat, values, and, very important to mention, government. Yes, I feel that at the beginning living in Dallas, I was surprised to find that the so-called "liberty and equity" was not quite the truth. We have so many laws in this country that I find it difficult to catch up. Now I understand it differently .... I feel I can speak freely not only because I am a Hispanic but because I am an American as well. But I know I have changed for the better and mostly it taught me to balance, and, why not say it? To get the best from each world. Resilience is a great word in my vocabulary—it makes you adapt to the circumstances; it allows you to learn and to keep going and it teaches you to be stronger every time.

The need to belong

We all have a need to belong. It is an essential factor for individual well-being. Socially and emotionally, this is one of the developmental challenges faced during the early years. It is as well a challenge for immigrant children as they try to be part of a group. The challenge increases when one's culture is different from that of the group and classroom context. What children experience at home continues as a central force in their social and cultural learning process and, thus, in their development of a sense of self. Family interactions, both formal and informal, play a leading factor in building the sense of belonging and of who we are as members of a cultural group. Language, behaviors, dress styles, and food preferences all gave a sense of identity and creating bonds that tie the child as member of a group. They serve as referents about us as members of a group. Relationships with adults including family members and teachers all provide a source of support for children and contribute to develop a sense of belonging to their settings. Equally relevant are the interactions and relationships children begin to build with peers in the context of classrooms and neighborhoods. Friendships built during this time contribute to establish a sense of belonging. Altogether, they represent the network of social relationships of the child from that which further anchors one's sense of belonging. Table 4.1 highlights some of the factors contributing to support the child's sense of belongingness.

Table 4.1 Some key factors supporting a child's sense of belongingness

Families	Interactions and experiences
	Language
	Routines and practices
Culture	Shared meanings
	Traditions and rituals
	Heritage language
Relationships	Interactions and relationships with parents and family members
	Support and interactions with caring adults
	Interactions with teachers
	Peers, friendships
Environments	Familiar objects
	Language
	Culturally familiar activities

Source: Robles de Meléndez and Driscoll (2017).

Facing different realities

Daily experiences in mainstream contexts bring many children to clash with expectations and social conventions different from those known to them. Trying to find self as part of a new social reality becomes a challenging task when your own referents such as language, customs, or behaviors seem not to fit with those of the environment. One of the students we interviewed shared that her first year at school was an everyday struggle. Coming at age 9 and speaking an Asian language, trying to feel as part of her peer group, was hard. She was trying to keep her family's ways while adapting to those at school. Eventually, as she shared, the friendships she made eased her experience as she also gradually became more linguistically proficient.

In the classroom as well as in their neighborhood, children begin to face the pressure from the mainstream culture. It becomes a constant reality as individuals navigate how to be part of new contexts. For some, it becomes a matter of what to give up, all in an effort to "fit in" society (Ward and Kennedy 1999). Igoa (1995, 131) points out "that feelings of inadequacy can be internalized by the children from exposure to subtle monolingual/monocultural attitudes, implying that one language or one culture is the only way or the best way." Added pressure from peers is often experienced, which increases the challenge of seeing oneself within the context of two cultures. Name calling, rejection, and bullying are among the behaviors targeting immigrants as they make efforts to integrate into the classroom group. These need to be addressed as they emerge not only to counteract their negative impact on the child but also to help children in clarifying views about others. It is relevant to remember that children's views about others are influenced by opinions of adults and what they gather from interactions including the media. Targeted and consciously determined actions are critical to prevent and address unwelcoming attitudes and situations pressing young child immigrants in our classrooms. Because the early years are a time of views and concept formation, adopting an antibias and respectful position for diversity in the classroom is vital to prevent such behaviors and attitudes.

Time to reflect ... *Fitting in*

In the story *The Name Jar* (Choi 2001), the recently arrived young girl from Korea tries to change her name to "fit in" with her new classmates. Coming into a new culture, similar to the character in this story, immigrant children may find themselves trying to fit it. How can we ease the emotional stress of immigrant children as they come into our classroom?

Changing views: Maintaining your heritage culture while adjusting to mainstream culture

In the past, expectations were that immigrants from other cultures would blend and become part of the mainstream culture while leaving behind their culture (McLemore and Romo 2005; Nieto and Bode 2018). Language, an indisputable connector to one's cultural group, was seen as one of the first aspects to be replaced as individuals assimilated. Different from views of the past, this is not the expectation that society has today. We have become more mindfully aware of cultures and about the importance of preserving one's heritage while adapting to the mainstream culture. Undoubtedly, efforts from multicultural education advocates have contributed to recognizing and valuing the heritage and cultures of people in our country. They have advocated for conscious and intentional practices to help children build a sense about themselves as proud members of their heritage while also becoming members of the US society. Becoming a bicultural individual capable of navigating and growing up as members of two cultures is now more readily acknowledged (Birman and Addae 2015). In fact, the language policy recognizing children as dual language learners announced in 2016 by the U.S. Department of Education (2017) implicitly backs the existence of biculturalism.

Unquestionably, while the child makes sense about cultural parameters, efforts from early childhood professionals directed at validating the child's heritage are essential to help them build and affirm their cultural selves. This support from educators remains critical during the early years and throughout the schooling experience. Many times, we have heard from immigrant students and colleagues how they regret losing their heritage language. One student's comment in particular reminded us about the importance of heritage languages and the need to preserve them. She shared her regret for having lost her ability to speak Yiddish, which prevented her to understand so many of the stories her grandmother would share. Reflecting on her teaching experiences, Igoa (1995) recognized the need for concerted efforts to support children's languages and cultures: "If immigrant children are not validated to become bilingual and bicultural, if they do not learn to deal with their bilingual and bicultural selves at an early stage, they come to regret the loss of their language and culture later in life" (131–2).

Language, an anchor of cultural heritage

The critical role of language has long been studied and commonly agreed that it is a significant factor in bonding people to their cultural heritage. Maintaining one's language in an environment where there is another language is also what non-English-speaking immigrants face as one of their challenges. Language emerges as a factor not only relevant to immigrants' adaptation but also essential to maintain themselves connected with their culture. To so many immigrants who grew up in the nation, learning the language is still one of the experiences they remember. Countless stories reveal the embarrassment felt by many as they began to learn English and the many times they simply kept to themselves knowing they would be shunned and frowned upon for using their own language. While today use of one's language is commonly acknowledged as a step in the process of acquiring a second language (Otto 2018; Tabors 2008), practices frowning at the use of heritage languages place many children in a predicament as they begin to familiarize themselves in a setting where they will eventually learn English. In many occasions, we have heard from children how they felt embarrassed and simply remained quiet while they increased their second language skills. "I listened a lot and watched TV programs to get that accent," a colleague from a European country once shared, having come to the country during the 1960s.

Hello, *hola*

Tu lengua eres tú, no lo olvides. [Your language is you, never forget it]
(Anonymous)

Language diversity is one of the elements that sets you apart from the group and also what could bring you together—this is what we heard from some people who opted to change their names, becoming what they thought would be more "American." One of those we spoke with mentioned that she was embarrassed every time they would ask her name because they had a difficult time enunciating it. Some mentioned avoiding using their heritage languages to prevent others from knowing they were immigrants. Knowledge about what others had experienced, feeling like strangers and discriminated by some, has catapulted many to lose some of their own selves and assimilate. "I want my child to be successful" is what we have repeatedly heard from many families when asked why they had stopped using their own heritage language. Awareness about these concerns lead to consciously centering efforts to support and clarify the role of languages in keeping your heritage. Classrooms play a leading role in influencing the child's knowledge of self (Super and Harkness 1986), effectively acknowledging and supporting the children's heritage as they adapt to their communities. Practices such as honoring the child's name and including materials in their heritage languages have been described as some of those helping to encourage children with immigrant roots to feel pride in their own diversity (Copple and Bredekamp 2009; Lynch and Hanson 2011).

Preserving language

This is a country of diversity, of cultures, ideas, and of course, languages.
(Anonymous)

Efforts to safeguard home language, while adjusting to learning the language of the mainstream, is today one of the areas continuously calling for further understanding and culturally conscious support for both the immigrant child and the family. In 2016, almost 10 percent of students in the nation were speakers of languages other than English (National Center for Educational Statistics 2019). Millions of immigrants who are speakers of languages other than English have over the years experienced practices that denied the value of their home languages. Over the years we have heard experiences of many where their language made them the target of prejudice and discrimination. Hundreds of these languages have been lost and with them an invaluable connection to their own heritages (National Center for Educational Statistics 2019). On more than one occasion, we have heard adults regretting the loss of what also connected them to the wisdom of their own cultural roots. The announcement of the dual language policy in June 2016 (U.S. Department of Education 2017) provided a long-waited support to the reality experienced by thousands of children, most of whom are US citizens, who are learning both their home language while also becoming proficient in English. The policy which was announced in Miami, Florida, a city known for its large immigrant population and language diversity, recognized the importance of maintaining one's heritage language as a value-added factor, for the future not only of an individual but also of the nation.

The child character in the story *I love Saturdays y domingos* (Ada 2002) serves as an example of dual language learners and how they successfully connect worlds through language. In the story, the child relishes her relationships with her grandparents, visiting her English-speaking grandpa and grandma and on *domingos*, Sundays, her Spanish-speaking *abuelos*. Although a fictional story, it is reflective of so many children and families who have kept their heritage language while learning English. Supportive and consciously centered practices recognize its use and provide encouragement to preserve home languages as a relevant factor to maintaining one's heritage and cultural knowledge (Gonzalez, Moll and Amanti, 2005; Lessow-Hurley 2013; Moll 1992). Such approach is essential if we are to support immigrant children who are speakers of languages other than English, to grow up as dual language learners. This also takes away the stigma of not knowing or not being proficient speakers of English, a factor which many adults today remembered.

Time to reflect ... *The power of language*

Language has been identified as one of the cultural tools essential for transmitting and sharing the understandings and ideas of a culture. Whether you are or are not a speaker of another language, take a moment to consider what role your language has in communicating ideas. If you were to find yourself in a setting where the language is different from your own, how would you ensure that your ideas are communicated? What would you do to preserve your language?

Growing up as a child immigrant

Living in a culture that is different from that of our families poses multiple challenges. Among those, the challenges of change and adaptation are critical life events children face as they learn to be part of new circumstances in environments many times distant from their own (Schwartz et al. 2010). This is what thousands experience every day. A critical task of the early years, getting a sense about self and beginning to build one's cultural identity is a major developmental childhood event. It is a process of encountering and making sense about cultures, that of their own heritage, and those of the mainstream. Through their interactions, children come across the cultural scripts of the mainstream, where many may find themselves confronting a dissonance with what is learned through their home culture. Awareness for educators about the differing cultural ideas and conceptualizations children may face is critical to understanding and recognizing their social developmental needs.

This is who I am

Unquestionably, as we have seen, culture is a central factor for giving people a sense of identity. Learned and acquired since childhood, experiences with families and others remain as one of the most influential cultural learning forces shaping one's sense about self as members of a culture. All children embark on the task of learning about the cultural ways of their family. Every moment, every experience is central to building a sense about their world as seen through the filter of their own culture. For immigrant children, the task doubles, learning their family's culture and that of the mainstream. This is what we see the author Esperanza Santiago (2006) sharing in her book *When I Was Puerto Rican*, where she tells her own story about coming to live in the mainland from her native Puerto Rico. The cultural shock from what she had learned soon became evident growing up in New York where she was confronted with a different language and the clashing mainstream cultural patterns. Her story is similar to the experiences we heard from families from other countries like Mexico and Haiti who struggled to come to the United States and found themselves with their children trying to make sense of the expectations at home and those in their classroom. Language, we heard from these families, was what they wanted to maintain to keep their family connected. To them, it was also a way to continue sharing their stories and traditions.

Preserving memories, sharing stories, building identity

The experience of growing up as a child with immigrant roots is an individual journey. It can be as varied as people's stories. Perhaps one of the common elements to families is the sharing of stories. Storytelling has long been acknowledged as a tool for keeping alive the events and happenings of the family. To the child, it is also a source for building their own sense about who they are. A meaning-making source, the informal sharing of experiences provides a frame of reference for the child that significantly influences the shaping of one's identity (Huisman 2014). It simultaneously builds a sense of belonging to the family and keeps the family memory alive as stories are passed on to the youngest. Langellier (2002, 57) states that the sharing of family stories contributes to forming a sense of culture while "they imagine and reproduce identity, including their ethnic identity." The informal scenario of the home serves as the stage where the telling of stories maintains the spirit of the family, passing it on to the youngest as incidents, experiences, and ideas that proudly reflect their journeys. The informal sharing of stories in the context of home by parents, family members, and relatives contributes to ascertaining a child's sense of self and identification as member of a group. In many ways, culture becomes palpable as images and examples about moments of pride and sacrifice are shared. The culturally based phrases and sayings of one's language present images and realities that vividly connect and give meaning to who we are. From what is shared at home, one gradually derives a sense about self. For the child, listening to the families' accounts about their struggles, courage, accomplishments, and experiences reaffirms the spirit of their culture's efforts, labor, and successes. Through those special moments when stories are shared, the values and ideals of their culture and life as immigrants are communicated as images children will remember. They remain part of elements cementing a sense of who we are.

The developmental niche of the immigrant child

Developmentally, all elements in the environment play a role in building a sense about self. Experiences whether at home or in the classroom are directly influenced by culture. Socially and emotionally, our culture and our own reality contribute to shaping our sense of individuality. Playing a central role in influencing the formation of a sense of self, culture continues to be a defining factor in the developmental process. Child development principles posit that both culture and what is experienced during the child development process are mutually influencing factors (Copple and Bredekamp 2009; Trawick 2018). Theorizing about the existence of a developmental niche, Super and Harkness (1986) articulated three main forces influencing and contributing to the child's development: physical and social environment, where the child lives, cultural practices, and the views of the child's caregivers where the parents, teachers, and other adults responsible for the care of the child are included. Together, these factors create the cultural context or niche where the child grows and develops. Central to the interaction of these forces are the cultural ideas of the parents who carry these with them as they transplant their lives to other settings.

According to Harkness and Super (1996), one of the challenges facing families is finding ways to maintain what is most relevant to them as they adapt to new realities. Trying to blend both their reality and culture is an everyday experience for countless children and families. Seeing what the child and family's cultural experiences are and valuing what they bring are two essential support elements determining how to provide needed support. In the case of immigrant children, preserving the family's culture is one of the challenges faced while they adjust to the cultural demands of new contexts. Some aspects in the new context may be similar; yet, many others may pose differences from what is known based on the cultural script one may bring. Within the immigrant child's sociocultural environment, language may become another challenging reality, which for speakers of languages other than English emerges as a difficult struggle trying to keep their home language as they adapt to that of the mainstream. Together, both culture and language are two key components inherently present and actively influencing the child's individual development.

Time to reflect … *Preserving one's culture*

Imagine you are living in another cultural setting where you are raising your children. Take a moment and think about the elements from your culture that you would want to preserve and pass on to your children. Which two would be most meaningful to you? Why?

Valuing what each child and family brings

Supporting children and families as they transition into new lifestyles demands an appreciation and understanding about what it means to be transplanted into a culture diverging from that of their heritage. Even today, for thousands of children born to immigrant parents, the urgent need for true and honest valuation of their culture continues as one area demanding our attention. Broadly seen, culture incorporates all the meaning-making elements one learns and carries to understand and interpret reality. Moll (1992) conceptualized the cultural heritage expertise and its components individuals bring with them as *funds of knowledge*. Furthermore, he posited that every child brings an array of ideas and experiences derived from what they have learned as part of their heritage. Based on his research, the funds of knowledge represent the ideas, know-how, ways, and practices one learns and uses to conduct oneself, address daily routine practices, and resolve situations, all the while following the cultural scripts learned at home. Anchored in Vygotskian principles, Moll theorized that cultural practices and knowledge mediated our way of thinking. Implications of his tenets are clear as efforts to support children with immigrant roots are planned and decided. In essence, they call for an appreciation of the culture and life knowledge children and their families bring to our classrooms and communities.

Living in two worlds

Coming to live in an environment where the cultural knowledge differs from those you know challenges immigrant children who find themselves facing expectations unfamiliar to them. When your core set of ideas, that is, your funds of knowledge, are no longer the standard, the result is a feeling of loss and even of rejection to what one has acquired and learned. "It feels like you no longer belong, so isolating," shared a student born to parents from Nicaragua when talking about her classroom experience during her primary years. It took her some time to adapt to the new routines and behaviors people expected from her. "At home, everything continued to be the same. It was like living in two worlds," she added remembering her childhood years. Another person we met from Mexico described her efforts to make sense and fit in, saying that at times it felt as if one was on a swing, always trying to know which way to go. Cisneros, in her book, *The House on Mango Street* (1994), pointedly presents the dichotomy of adjusting to another culture while trying to hold on to what has been learned. Adjusting and making sense of what is expected happens over time. The classroom plays an influential role in the successful adjustment and adaptation to new social expectations. Developmentally, understanding support from early childhood professionals is essential in helping the child to build a sense about behaviors and ways in their new contexts. Intentional planning, both informal and formal, is also needed, aimed at validating children's heritage while facilitating their learning of new social expectations. Maintaining families strongly engaged is also essential as the child adjusts to the ways and routines in the context of their classrooms.

Supporting children's cultures

The role of culture is fundamental in supporting children's needs and positive development. All children are born into a culture, which they come to learn as they interact at home. Families are the main conduit for learning about culture, which explains the role and relevance of interactions at home. This charge continues as families settle in other countries, passing on to their youngest their cultural knowledge and ways. Understanding about the vital relevance of the continuation of home cultural practices is essential to supporting both family and child. The empathetic response from early childhood educators is critical. Continuing practices from one's heritage is one of the ways, we heard, families say help them to preserve their heritage while adapting to the realities of their new home communities. Over the years, this is what we have heard from colleagues and students with roots in other cultures. While adjusting to practices and experiences of the US mainstream culture, keeping themselves practicing some of the traditions and ways carried with them, and learned from family members, is what has kept them tied to their places of origin as they maneuvered life in the nation's communities.

Adjustment to new realities is an experience that immigrants continue to face as they try to make sense of the lifestyle patterns in the mainstream culture. The process is essential as individuals make the efforts to become members of their communities. While retaining their heritage, which reaffirms their individual cultural identity, they struggle to build their sense as members of society. Moll (1992), in his landmark investigation about what he theorized as funds of knowledge, described these as the dynamic ideas, practices, and wisdom that people built and used to make sense in their daily happenings. Shared by family members, the funds of knowledge reflect the practical understandings acquired as individuals address the challenges in their own setting and circumstances.

Time to reflect ... *Culture and you*

"We all belong to a culture" is a statement that describes this shared trait of people. A central part of who we are, culture gives us individual meaning and shared understanding. For immigrants, culture connects them with their heritage as they adapt to the culture of their new environments. We invite you to take a moment and reflect about your own culture. What aspects about your culture would you say characterize you? As an early childhood educator, what could we do to support the child's culture?

Honoring traditions

The role of traditional practices, including those that entail the family's known ways to address needs and find solutions, is undeniable. They provide children with known patterns to resolve and make sense of their encounters with individual realities. Overall, traditional practices offer a sense of stability to the world of the child as families continue to devise ways as they adjust to their environments. For immigrant families and children living in ethnic communities, the transition to new lifestyles is aided as what is known continues to be validated in their environments. Such is the case of families and children living in ethnic communities or in neighborhoods with people with similar cultures. Language, culturally related behaviors, and cultural practices all provide a sense of continuity while children and families adjust to their new life. Others, residing in areas that are predominantly mainstream culture, may not find the same support. The understanding response from agencies and classrooms is essential to recognizing the heritage practices of immigrants. This is vital in supporting children's adaptation to the new norms of the setting, as they may find themselves socially fitting in with the expectations of the classroom context (Brown and Zagefka 2011).

Celebrations and traditions play a leading role in learning and passing on one's cultural knowledge. In the story *Maria Molina and the Days of the Dead* (Krull 1994), the young girl's celebration of her family's longtime tradition to honor their ancestors continues as she settles in her new life in the United States. Even though the child character had transitioned geographically from life in her country of origin, she remained actively honoring her own cultural self. Despite the geographical and lifestyle change, the family of the young girl in the story continued honoring their heritage. The story is similar to that of so many who remain holding practices they grew up with and learned from their families. Like the character in the story, thousands of others have adapted to new ways and yet elected to continue their celebrations, passing them on to their children growing up in the country where they are born citizens. Blending has become a lifestyle of adapting to the mainstream culture while preserving their own cultural identities. This is what we heard from a Peruvian mother who, after more than thirty years, continues to honor her longtime traditions. Navigating and blending her own traditions with those of her adopted country has allowed her to raise her children feeling proud of both their heritage and that of the country where they were born and hold citizenship (Box 4.3).

Box 4.3 Connecting ideas: *Tamaladas*, a celebration of heritage

Traditions play a leading role in keeping people's heritage alive. They are also what ties individuals to their roots, giving meaning to one's ways and values. For immigrants they are a continuous way to reaffirm their culture within the nation's multiculturally diverse society. At a program with over a century of experience serving immigrants in Florida, the celebration of the *Tamaladas*, a gathering to share tamales, has become a way to honor a tradition of children and their families, most of whom are Hispanics, during the December holidays. Tamales are typical to Mexico and Central America where each country and even regions have a special way to prepare the traditional dish served during the holidays. Each year, parents volunteer to prepare tamales representing their regions or countries. Working in teams, each group relives their family recipes long learned and passed on from generations. What started as a simple celebration is now a tradition gathering the community at the school to celebrate their tradition of sharing tamales as they celebrate their culture.

The vital role of the classroom in adapting to new cultural patterns

Classroom experiences play a leading role in facilitating adjustment to new cultural patterns. The nature of interactions and experiences, in turn, becomes instrumental in supporting the child's evolving sense of adaptation and consequent feeling of being part of the group (Schachner et al. 2018). The climate of the classroom sends strong messages to children. Messages can be powerful socioemotional tools either welcoming or isolating children. Some of the immigrant parents we interviewed mentioned having felt at home when they brought their children to a local preschool. One of them indicated still remembering the sign on the door in their heritage language welcoming her 4-year-old child. Another one, who came as a child immigrant herself, talked about the choice of stories read and the songs they taught, which included many familiar ones from her country of origin. Strong support and acknowledgment of the immigrants' culture ease the transition and adaptation process. Feelings of being accepted contribute to facilitating the child's social interactions with his/her peers and teacher in an atmosphere characterized by integration of diversity.

Consciously centered practices with a multicultural orientation, overall, have a positive impact on the social interactions and relationships of both immigrant children as well as their mainstream peers. The role of teachers becomes critical in creating an inclusive environment that invites the immigrant child and encourages relationships as a member of the group. Inclusive environments also provide peers with experiences to build a sense about life in a culturally diverse society, an essential factor in avoiding biases and preventing misleading ideas (Adair 2015).

Families and children: *Todo por ellos*

Todo por ellos, all for them, was perhaps what we more often heard immigrant parents and families shared talking about their children. High hopes were, in fact, the general sentiment expressed by all the families we have met. Similar to the mother in our opening vignette to this chapter, who came wanting to build a future for the children she hoped to have and feels proudly about them now, countless immigrant families continue working and overcoming challenges for their children, all in hopes of a brighter future. For a young woman whom one of the authors met, who recently arrived from South America, her infant daughter was what best justified all the efforts to relocate to Florida. Hopes of a stable and safe place for her baby erased her travails as she thought of what would come for her daughter. This is the same sentiment expressed by a migrant parent from Nigeria who did not hesitate to state that if given the opportunity once again, she would not think twice to come to the United States to work for her children. She later told us that thanks to her remittances, not only her two children—who now lived with her—but also her aging parents were able to live more comfortably. Not uncommon, thousands of transnational families, living in their countries, depend on the support from family members who come as immigrants. They are also participants in the immigration reality through their relatives.

Stories about the efforts made by parents for their children are countless. So many parents continue to dream their best for their children, the children that we work with in our classrooms and communities. Aspirations for a successful future are characteristic of immigrant parents who, according to Fuligni (2012), hold high educational ambitions for their children. In fact, aspiration for their children to receive an education was what led parents to fight for the rights of their children in the *Plyler* v. *Doe* legal case that we further discuss in Chapter 5. Not afraid to claim what they considered their children needed, a group of undocumented parents took to the courts in 1982 to obtain recognition for their children's right to receive an education (Olivas 2012). Their efforts mirror that of thousands of parents who continually work and would give it all for their children. For us, as early childhood educators, they are the families and the parents of the children we meet and work with in our classrooms and communities. They also hold high hopes in us as the educators leading their children to success. Building a sense of trust and respect is what we have repeatedly experienced is vital as we worked together with the children and their families to build a lasting relationship.

Families' immigration status and children's well-being

Feelings of safety are central to the child's emotional development. Many still experience deep and troublesome emotions as they fear the uncertainty of losing their parents. Seeking a future and having high hopes for their children are all common goals guiding parents who have arrived and continue to come into the country. Still, implications surrounding the status of the family's arrival into the country are a reality that must be considered. The path taken, arriving as immigrants, documented or undocumented, plays a major role in the nature of experiences ahead (Suárez-Orozco and Suárez-Orozco 2001). Immigration status has become in recent years a more influential variable and factor in the experiences and life conditions of immigrant parents and children. This has become more evident as greater enforcement of immigration regulations has been observed over the past two decades. During this time, focus on undocumented immigration has become a topic of contentious discussion, which continues to date. As discussed earlier in Chapter 1, since 2014, the increased and continuous arrival of undocumented families elevated the issue to the top of the agenda in the nation. Parallel to the United States, similar arguments are taking place in many countries throughout the world where they are now experiencing a surge of immigrants driven by similar desires for a safer place.

Many scholars (Chavez et al. 2012; Pereira and Ornelas 2013; Punti 2013; Suárez-Orozco et al. 2011; Yoshikawa 2011; Yoshikawa and Kholoptseva, 2013) have raised concerns about the impact of the legality of a family's immigration status on their children. Studies have shown that a family's immigration status significantly influences their own future as a family and the well-being of their children. Families with an undocumented status have been found to more commonly face multiple difficulties and place their families and children at risk (Rojas-Flores 2017; Sidhu and Song 2019). The uncertainty of their undocumented status threatens the overall welfare of the child. Studies have shown that even having one member with an unauthorized status "can generate fear and stress for an entire family, including the children" (Chavez et al. 2012, 3). Fear of detention and deportation and the continuous threat of family disruption are but some of the difficult challenges facing undocumented families (Rivera 2016). Still, the reasons forcing so many to arrive undocumented continue to call for understanding and attention to the needs of their families and children in our communities (Box 4.4).

Box 4.4 Connecting ideas: *Strengths and assets of undocumented families*

Overall, it has become evident that, parents with legal immigration status tend to do better than those with undocumented status (Brabeck, Sibley, and Likes 2016). However, while circumstances of undocumented entry imply risk and difficult experiences, it is relevant to recognize the assets of families arriving under these conditions. Studies have revealed that despite the challenges that they are exposed to experience, they also bring with them several protective factors highly contributing to their children's development. Among the assets, their strong sense of care and obligation stand as key strengths. It has also been found that children tend to live in two-parent families, another asset and protective factor (Sibley and Brabeck 2017). These two factors are particularly evident among Hispanic or Latino parents who comprise a large majority of the undocumented population living in the nation. A strong sense of commitment for their children's education characterizes families. Their resiliency has been identified as one of the main protective factors descriptive of this population (Rivera 2016) whose strength to overcome obstacles is an undeniable factor supporting their families. Their sense of shared purpose contributes to their strong cohesion, which ties family members together as they navigate daily experiences. Even during times of family disruption, families tend to stay together by supporting each other. Cultural continuity is another strength and factor supporting the whole family, particularly through use of their primary language and adherence to their cultural heritage practices.

Facing trauma

Immigration is an experience charged with multiple emotions. Some of its events may be difficult for young children, leaving their emotional mark on them. Though resiliency is a trait that describes immigrants, recognizing the impact of the trauma lived by some children during the immigration experience is central to responding with the support needed. Park and Katsiaficas (2019) posit that young child immigrants "are more likely than their peers to be affected by trauma due to experiences before, during, or after migration" (2). Several different factors can lead children to experience trauma during and after migration. Among the postmigration factors, recent immigration enforcement has resulted in immigration raids in communities and immigrant neighborhoods. Fear of losing a parent, something already experienced by many families, remains as a threatening reality for children of immigrants in numerous communities across the United States. Other factors include the persistent and stressful reality of prejudice and discrimination, sometimes unintendedly, continuing to impact the children's experience (Adair 2015; Park and Katsiaficas 2019). Considerations about the emotionally charged circumstances that some immigrant children have experienced and their implications are crucial.

In her views about emotions experienced during the immigration process, Igoa (1995) pointed out to those emerging during premigration, a phase relevant to consider given the multiple circumstances leading to a family's decision to migrate. For many children, there may be excitement about the upcoming journey, while for others surprise and sadness at the unexpectedness of the event. Still for others, prior experiences may include traumatic circumstances, which demands understanding support and attention. It is important to remember that the process of immigration itself implies many adjustments that may further add additional challenges and stressors to individuals (Perez Foster 2001). Children are as well vulnerable to experience the stress of the changes and of the circumstances surrounding their immigration, both prior to and after migration. Hardships and exposure to violence and threats experienced by many are stressful and difficult circumstances leaving their emotional mark on families and their children. It has also been pointed out that the experience of immigration itself could even lead to posttraumatic stress disorder (PTSD) (Pereira and Ornelas 2013). Among the possible causes, the legal nature of the family entry into the country is one of the stressors to consider placing young children at risk of experiencing traumatic experiences (Chaudry et al. 2010). The fear of losing a family member is itself a difficult situation experienced by thousands of families. With greater enforcement of immigration laws, raids have become more commonly conducted, adding to the stressful situation that many already experience (Park and Katsiaficas 2019). Announcement of immigration raids during July 2019 created fear among immigrants at the possibility of a loved one being detained and deported. Moreover, these have left many children without the presence of a parent or family member. This is what Colato Laínez, an elementary school teacher, shares in the introduction to his book *From North to South*. In his own experience, Colato-Laínez learned how many children, shared the experience of losing a parent, family, member, relative, or even a neighbor to deportation. In each case, family separation became a painful and stressful event (2013).

Recognizing and consciously addressing experiences causing stress and trauma to children is critical (Park and Katsiaficas 2019; Park, Katsiaficas, and McHugh 2018). Actions and understanding efforts are essential to safeguard their development and future while the child and family experience any difficult and traumatic experience.

Time to reflect ... *Traumatic experiences*

Researchers have raised concerns about the difficult events and circumstances that some immigrant children may experience during immigration. Considering the needs of the whole child, reflect on practices and supports available to address the needs of children who may have suffered trauma. How well do they respond to their needs? Are these practices consciously centered on the realities of immigration?

Mixed-status families: A growing trend

Reports show that about four-and-a-half million children born in the United States are living with an undocumented parent (Zayas and Gulbas 2017). For many undocumented immigrant families, whose children were born in the United States, they find themselves as *mixed-status* families. Mixed-status families are those where some members are undocumented—which may include adults and children who came along with their parents—and where some of their children are US citizens (Zayas et al. 2015). An estimated nine million children, most of whom are citizens, live in mixed-status families. This family pattern, according to Chavez et al. (2012), is becoming "very much the norm" (11) for countless families, many of whom are of Hispanic roots. In 2011, 59 percent of undocumented immigrants living in the country were Mexicans (Hoefer, Rytina, and Baker 2012), many of whom were mixed-status families. On average, over 27 percent of undocumented immigrants have been living in the country for more than ten years (Rojas-Flores 2017). More recently, it has been found that many undocumented families with mixed status legally entered the country and ended overstaying their visas. Their status is a factor contributing to their vulnerability. Among the concerns of their status, Vargas (2015) pointed out that many mixed-status families end being marginalized and exposed to stressful circumstances. These, in turn, also make their children vulnerable (Sidhu and Song 2019).

Unauthorized immigrant status and its impact on children

As we discussed in Chapter 2, the impact of the family's legal status on the child has long been a concern for educators and researchers. Given the uncertainty of their parents' status, children are more predisposed to experience various risk factors that threaten their well-being. In their analysis about families with unauthorized status, Capps, Fix, and Zong (2016) identify some of the risk factors they face, which include the following: lower preschool enrollment for children ages 3–4; linguistic isolation, given limited exposure to English at home or in the community; lower English proficiency for children ages 5 and older; higher incidence of families and children living in poverty; and lower socioeconomic progress.

Concerns about the impact of the family's status on children have been the focus of several studies (Suárez-Orozco et al. 2011; Yoshikawa 2011; Zayas and Gulbas 2017). Investigations by immigration scholars revealed that the legality of a parent's entry into the country not only influences the individual adult but also affects the children. In his study of undocumented parents raising their US-born children, Yoshikawa (2011) posited that the stress of knowing about their parents' legal status was a factor hindering children's outcomes. The fear of deportation is a standing threat to the family, affecting all members, particularly children. Studies found that for some children experiencing the threat of their parents' deportation, "school staff, teachers and counselors provided support, guidance, and a trusting community where they felt a sense of belonging" (Gulbas et al., cited by Lovato et al. 2018, 113).

Given the high proportion of children living with unauthorized parents, a policy solution to alleviate their immigration situation was proposed in 2014, Deferred Action for Parents of Americans and Lawful Permanent Residents (DAPA). The policy would have provided opportunities to legalize the immigration status of some immigrant parents living in the country since 2010. Sadly, the proposal that created heated opposition never received approval (Box 4.5).

Box 4.5 Connecting ideas: *For some, their fear has been real*

Conversations with a group of families and early childhood professionals working with immigrant families with mixed status revealed to one of the authors the standing threat of deportation of one of their parents that some young children experience. This fear became a reality for a 10-year-old boy whose father, while driving his son back home after school, was detained by immigration authorities. With his father apprehended by the border patrol, the child found himself alone and feared whether he would ever see him again. An immigrant advocate returned him home to his mother. It was not long before the young boy and his family learned that deportation was going to be initiated. The family soon found themselves struggling to support themselves having lost the income from the father. With the support of advocates and their school, the family was able to overcome some of the ensuing stress and need. Support from understanding teachers and assistance from others in the community provided the needed support for the young boy during the long months while the father remained detained. After months of work from one of the advocacy groups that provided legal assistance, everyone celebrated the good news of the release of the boy's father. Now having an opportunity to legalize his status, it was the new beginning everyone in the family needed.

Further evidence about the adverse impact of the parents' immigration status on children was identified by Suárez-Orozco et al. (2011) in their study, which shows that a parent's undocumented status impacts their children's developmental process. Their findings revealed a range of issues affecting the child that included access to health care, quality of early learning experiences, and impact on the child's cognitive and social development. Of great concern is the fact that the impact of experiences on a child's development is observed not only during the early years but in some cases may become evident later in their life that continues to be impacted.

Situations challenging children living in undocumented families vary but, overall, remain as a factor placing children at risk (Figure 4.4). The current US legal and political climate acts as an inhibiting environment for many immigrant children especially those of Latino descent. Reports show that approximately one-quarter of Latino children living in the United States "have a least one parent who is an unauthorized immigrant" (Clarke, Turner, and Guzman 2017, 1). Moreover, these children live within the context of social exclusion that dominates the lives of their parents (Sibley and Brabeck 2017), further depriving them of resources and experiences essential to their development. This is in light of the US Supreme Court ruling in *Plyler* v. *Doe* stating children of immigrants have the same right to attend public schools as do US citizens and permanent residents. Though

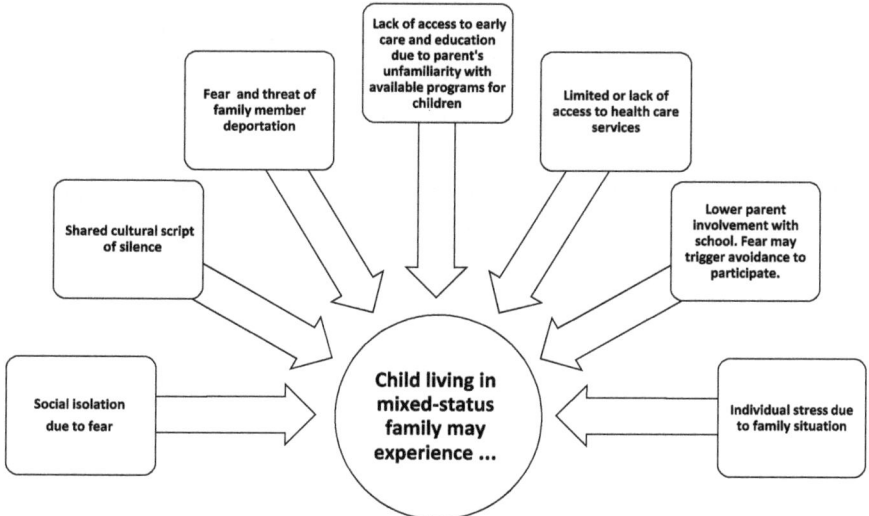

Figure 4.4 Undocumented family status and its impact on the child's well-being. *Source*: Lovato et al. (2018); Suárez-Orozco et al. (2011); Yoshikawa (2011); Zayas and Gulbas (2017).

researchers agree that further investigation is needed to better understand the scope of the impact of immigration status on children, concerns about a child's well-being underline the severity of these implications for the over four million children who find themselves living in undocumented and mixed-status families.

Advocates for immigrants continue to serve as a light of hope for families with undocumented members, assisting and helping adults to navigate their way through immigration regulations and normalize their status. Meanwhile, they represent the support for families, ensuring that they are informed and have access to the programs and services available that their children are legally entitled to receive.

Addressing the needs of immigrant children

Every day is another opportunity to learn more about the hundreds and thousands of immigrant children and families living in our communities. Their realities are multiple and cannot be judged by a singular view. At the heart of responses, the right to experience what every child is entitled to receive must guide decisions. Responding to their situations and continuing to address their needs demands practices centered on what is socially just and directed to responsibly ensuring the child's well-being. This calls for conscious attention to their personal stories, their culture, and for what every child necessitates to develop. Forero (2018) reminds us that "We are all one humanity, and we must start standing up for these children whose voices cannot be heard" (n.p.).

Critical to ensuring equity and responsible attention, it is of utmost need to be mindful about the needs of immigrant children whose voices are clear but many times not heard. But, equally important is to move into action to provide and deliver what children deserve. We need more consciously centered efforts in early childhood to fully address the scope of the needs, whether developmental or cultural, of immigrant children.

Key ideas

- Children are one of the main reasons driving families to immigrate. Safeguarding their opportunities for a better life and future remains at the heart of what families may sacrifice and endure in their journey of immigration.

- Thorough appreciation and knowledge about the needs of the child immigrant is fundamental to providing equitable experiences and to addressing their needs.
- Supporting the needs and safeguarding the well-being of immigrant children are paramount. This is vital to ensure experiences that are socially fair and equal. Addressing their needs calls for consciously centered practices that begin by seeing the child as an individual, respecting and valuing their heritage, recognizing their abilities to unfold their potential, and protecting their rights and opportunities to succeed.
- The lens of culture provides early childhood educators and child immigrant advocates a window to better understand their needs and realities. Through the lens of culture, professionals can better appraise needs and make consciously centered decisions.
- Coming to live in a cultural context different from their own places pressure on immigrant families and their children. Acculturation is the experience of coming in contact with a culture different from our own.
- Legal status of immigrants has been found to impact children. Children of families with unauthorized immigration status may find themselves at risk as compared to peers whose families legally entered the country. Children may have fewer attendance to preschool experiences and tend to be more linguistically isolated.
- The need to belong remains as one of the main developmental needs. Classroom experiences with a diversity orientation can effectively contribute to building a positive sense about self as immigrant children encounter and adapt to a new culture.

To think, do, and reflect …

1. What are some of the main reasons motivating families to migrate? How do they compare to those of families in your community?
2. In your consideration, what is the goal of consciously centered practices?
3. Review the tenets about the developmental niche (Super and Harkness 1986). Considering your own family, identify the factors and individuals playing a role in each of the sections of the developmental niche.
4. Contextual factors influence acculturation. What factors do you consider would influence children's acculturation in your community?

References

Ada, Alma. Flor. 2002. *I Love Saturdays y Domingos*. New York: Atheneum Books for Young Readers.

Adair, Jennifer. 2011. "Confirming chanclas: What early childhood teacher educators can learn from immigrant preschool teachers." *Journal of Early Childhood Teacher Education* 32(1): 55–71.

Adair, Jennifer. 2015. *The Impact of Discrimination on the Early Schooling Experiences of Children from Immigrant Families*. Washington, DC: Migration Policy Institute.

Ayón, Cecilia. 2015. *Economic, Social, and Health Effects of Discrimination on Latino Immigrant Families*. Washington, DC: Migration Policy Institute.

Bateson, Mary. 1995. *Peripheral Vision*. New York: Harper.

Berger, Kathleen. 2018. *The Developing Person through Childhood and Adolescence* (11th ed.). New York: Worth Publishers.

Berry, John. 1980. "Acculturation as varieties of adaptation." In A. Padilla (ed.), *Acculturation: Theory, Models, and Some New Findings*, 9–25. Boulder, CO: Westview.

Berry, John. 1988. *Understanding the Process of Acculturation for Primary Prevention*. ERIC Document. ED 308441.

Berry, John. 1997. "Immigration, acculturation, and adaptation." *Applied Psychology: An International Review* 46: 5–34.

Berry, John. 2017. *Mutual Intercultural Relations*. Cambridge: Cambridge University Press.

Birman, Dina, and Dorothy Addae. 2015. "Acculturation." In Carlos Suárez-Orozco, Mona Abo-Zena, and Amy Marks (eds.), *Transitions: The Development of Children of Immigrants*, chapter 6, 122–41. New York: New York University Press.

Brabeck, Kalina, Erin Sibley, and M. Brinton Lykes. 2016. "Immigrant parent status, parent child relationships, and child socioemotional well-being: A middle childhood perspective." *Journal of Family and Child Studies* 25: 1155–67.

Brown, Rupert, and Hanna Zagefka. 2011. "The dynamics of acculturation: An intergroup perspective." *Advances of Experimental Social Psychology* 44. Accessed June 25, 2019. Retrieved from http://sro.sussex.ac.uk/id/eprint/14150/1/BROWN,_R_Advances_in_Experimental_Social_Psychology.pdf.

Capps, R., M. Fix, and J. Zong. 2016. *A Profile of U.S. Migration with Unauthorized Immigrant Parents*. Fact Sheet. Retrieved from https://www.migrationpolicy.org/research/profile-us-children-unauthorized-immigrant-parents.

Chaudry, Ajay, Randy Capps, Juan Manuel Pedroza, Rosa Maria Castaneda, Robert Santos, and Molly Scott. 2010. *Facing Our Future: Children in the Aftermath of Immigration Enforcement*. Urban Institute. Retrieved from https://www.urban.org/sites/default/files/publication/28331/412020-Facing-Our-Future.PDF.

Chavez, Jorge, Anayeli Lopez, Christine Englebrecht, and Ruben Viramontez. 2012. (2–13). "Sufren los niños. Exploring the impact of unauthorized immigration status on children's wellbeing." *Family Court Review* 50(4): 10.1111/j.1744-1617.2012.01482.x

Choi, Yangsook. 2001. *The Name Jar*. New York: Dell Dragonfly Books.

Cisneros, Sandra. 1994. *The House on Mango Street*. New York: Knopf.

Clarke, Wyatt, Kimberly Turner, and Lina Guzman. 2017. *One Quarter of Hispanic Children in the United States Have an Unauthorized Immigrant Parent*. National Research Center on Hispanic Children & Families. Retrieved from http://www. hispanicresearchcenter.org/wp-content/uploads/2017/10/Hispanic-Center-Undocumented-Brief-FINAL.pdf.

Colato-Laínez, Rene. 2013. *From north to south/Del norte al sur*. San Francisco, CA: Children's Book Press.

Copple, Carol, and Sue Bredekamp. 2009. *Developmentally Appropriate Practice in Early Childhood Programs Serving Children from Birth through Age 8*. Washington, DC: National Association for the Education of Young Children.

Emamzadeh, Aresh. 2018. "Acculturation and migration: Interview with Dr. J.W. Berry." *Psychology Today*. Retrieved from https://www.psychologytoday.com/us/blog/finding-new-home/201803/acculturation-and-migration-interview-dr-j-w-berry.

Forero, Izabella. 2018. "The Cries of Immigrant Children." *The Cavalier Daily*, June 24. Retrieved from https://www.cavalierdaily.com/article/2018/06/forero-the-cries-of-immigrant-children.

Freire, Paulo. [1974] 2013. *Education for Critical Consciousness*. London: Bloomsbury.

Fuligni, Andrew. 2012. "The intersection of aspirations and resources in the development of children from immigrant families." In C. G. Coll and A. K. Marks (eds.), *The Immigrant Paradox in Children and Adolescents: Is Becoming an American a Developmental Risk?*, 211–41. Washington, DC: American Psychological Association.

González, Norma, Luis Moll, and Cathy Amanti. 2005. *Funds of Knowledge: Theorizing Practices in Households, Communities, and Classrooms*. New York: Routledge.

Greenberg, Erica, Victoria Rosenboom, and Gina Adams. 2019. *Preparing the Future Workforce: Early Care and Education Participation among Children of Immigrants*. Washington, DC: Urban Institute.

Hall, E. 1977. *Beyond Culture*. New York: Anchor Books.

Harkness, Sara, and Charles Super (eds.). 1996. *Parents' Cultural Belief Systems: Their Origins, Expressions, and Consequences*. New York: Guilford Press.

Hochhausen, Laila, Deborah Perry, and Huynhnhu Le. 2008. "Neighborhood context and acculturation among Central American immigrants." *Journal of Minority Health* 12: 806–9.

Hoefer, Michael, Nancy Rytina, and Bryan Baker. 2012. *Estimates of the Unauthorized Immigrant Population Residing in the United States: January 2011*. Population Estimates. Office of Immigration Statistics. Washington, DC: U.S. Department of Homeland Security.

Huisman, Dena. 2014. "Telling a family culture: Storytelling, family identity, and cultural membership." *Interpersona* 8(2): 12–19.

Igoa, Cristina. 1995. *The Inner World of the Immigrant Child*. Mahwah, NJ: Lawrence Erlbaum Publishers.

Johnson, Angela. 2005. *The Leaving Morning*. New York: Houghton Mifflin.

Krull, Kathleen. 1994. *Maria Molina and the Days of the Dead*. New York: Simon and Schuster.

Langellier, Kristin. 2002. "Performing family stories, forming cultural identity: Franco American *Mèmëre stories*." *Communication Studies* 53(1): 56–73. doi: 10.1080/10510970209388574.

Lessow-Hurley, Judith. 2013. *The Foundations of Dual Language Instruction* (6th ed.). Boston, MA: Pearson.

Lovato, Kristina, Coruna Lopez, Leyla Karimli, and Laura Abrams. 2018. "The impact of deportation-related family separations on the wellbeing of Latinx children and youth: A review of the literature." *Children and Youth Services Review* 95: 109–16.

Lynch, Eleanor, and Marci Hanson. (eds.). 2011. *Developing Cross-Cultural Competence: A Guide for Working with Young Children and their Families* (4th ed.). Baltimore, MD: Paul Brookes.

McLemore, S. Dale, and Harriet Romo. 2005. *Racial and Ethnic Relations in America* (7th ed.). Boston, MA: Allyn and Bacon.

Migration Policy Institute. 2017. *Children in U.S. Immigrant Families*. Retrieved from https://www.migrationpolicy.org/programs/data-hub/charts/children-immigrant-families.

Moll, Luis. 1992. "Bilingual classroom studies and community analysis: Some recent trends." *Educational Researcher* 21(2): 20–4.

National Association for the Education of Young Children (NAEYC). 2011. *Code of Ethical Conduct and Statement of Commitment*. Reaffirmed and updated. Washington, DC: Author.

National Center for Educational Statistics. 2019. *English Language Learners in Public Schools*. Retrieved from https://nces.ed.gov/programs/coe/indicator_cgf.asp.

Nieto, Sonia, and Patty Bode. 2018. *Affirming Diversity: The Sociopolitical Context of Multicultural Education* (7th ed.). Boston, MA: Pearson.

Olivas, Michael. 2012. *No Undocumented Child Left behind. Plyler v. Doe and the Education of Undocumented Children*. New York: New York University Press.

Otto, Beverly. 2018. *Language Development in Early Childhood* (5th ed.). Boston, MA: Pearson.

Park, Maki, and Caitlin Katsiaficas. 2019. *Mitigating the Effects of Trauma among Young Children of Immigrants and Refugees: The Role of Early Childhood Programs*. Washington, DC: Migration Policy Institute.

Park, Maki, Caitlin Katsiaficas, and Margie McHugh. 2018. *Responding to the ECEC Needs of Children of Refugees and Asylum Seekers in Europe and North America*. Migration Policy Institute.

Retrieved from https://www.migrationpolicy.org/research/
responding-ecec-needs-children-refugees-asylum-seekers-europe-north-america.

Pereira, Krista, and India Ornelas. 2013. "Painful passages: Traumatic experiences
and post-traumatic stress among immigrant Latino adolescents and their primary
caregivers." *The International Migration Review* 47(4). doi: 10.1111/imre.12050.
doi:10.1111/imre.12050.

Perez Foster, Rose Marie. 2001. "When immigration is trauma: Guidelines for the
individual and family clinician." *American Journal of Orthopsychiatry* 7(2): 153–70.

Punti, Gemma. 2013. *Legal Status, Education and Latino Youth's Transition to
Adulthood*. University of Minnesota. ProQuest Dissertations Publishing. 3589144.

Rivera, Claudio. 2016. "Academic risk and protective factors of Latinos of
undocumented status: A narrative approach." Ph.D. dissertation. DePaul University.
Retrieved from https://via.library.depaul.edu/csh_etd/183.

Robles de Meléndez, Wilma, and Vesna Beck. 2019. *Teaching Young Children in
Multicultural Classrooms. Issues, Strategies and Perspectives* (5th ed.). Boston,
MA: Cengage.

Robles de Meléndez, Wilma, and Wayne Driscoll. 2017. *Here I Am! Listening to the
Voices of Immigrant Children and Their Families: An Analysis of Socially just Practices
Supporting Immigrant Children's Sociocultural Development*. Paper presented at
the Annual conference of the European Early Childhood Research Association.
Bologna, Italy. August 29–September 1, 2017.

Rojas-Flores, Lisbeth. 2017. *Latino U.S.-Citizen Children of Immigrants: A Generation at
High Risk. Summary of Selected Young Scholars (YSP) Program Research*. Foundation
for Child Development.

Santiago, Esperanza. 2006. *When I Was Puerto Rican: A Memoir*. New York: Merloyd
Lawrence Book.

Schachner, Maja, Linda Juang, Ursula Moffitt, and Fons van de Vijver. 2018. "Schools
as acculturative and developmental contexts for youth of immigrant and refugee
background." *European Psychologist* 23(1): 44–56.

Schwartz, Seth, Jennifer Unger, Byron Zamboanga, and José Szapocznik. 2010.
"Rethinking the concept of acculturation: Implications for theory and research."
American Psychologist 10(4): 237–51.

Sibley, Erin, and Kalina Brabeck. 2017. "Latino immigrant students' school experiences
in the United States: The importance of family-school-community collaborations."
School Community Journal 27(1). Retrieved from https://files.eric.ed.gov/fulltext/
EJ1146470.pdf.

Sidhu, Shawn, and Susan Song. 2019. "Growing up with an undocumented
parent in America: Psychosocial adversity in domestically residing immigrant
children." *Journal of the American Academy of Child and Adolescent Psychiatry*
58(10): 933–935.

Spears Brown, Christia. 2015. *The Educational, Psychological, and Social Impact of
Discrimination on the Immigrant Child. Reports*. Washington, DC: Migration Policy
Institute.

Suárez-Orozco, Carola, and Marcelo Suárez-Orozco. 2001. *Children of Immigration.* Cambridge, MA: Harvard University Press.

Suárez-Orozco, Carola, Hirokazu Yoshikawa, Robert Teranishi, and Marcelo Suárez-Orozco. 2011. "Growing up in the shadows: The developmental implications of unauthorized status." *Harvard Educational Review* 18(3): 438–72; 619–20.

Super, Charles, and Sarah Harkness. 1986. "The developmental niche: A conceptualization at the interface of child and culture." *International Journal of Behavioral Development* 9: 545–69.

Tabors, Patton. 2008. *One Child, Two Languages: A Guide for Early Childhood Educators of Children Learning English* (2nd ed.). Baltimore, MD: Paul Brookes.

Trawick, Jeffrey. 2018. *Early Childhood Development: A Multicultural Perspective* (7th ed.). Boston, MA: Pearson.

U.S. Census Bureau. 2019. *U.S. and World Population Clock.* Retrieved from https://www.census.gov/popclock/?intcmp=w_200x402.

U.S. Department of Health and Human Services and U.S. Department of Education. 2017. *Policy Statement on Supporting the Development of Children Who Are Dual Language Learners in Early Childhood Programs.* Retrieved from https://www.acf.hhs.gov/sites/default/files/ecd/dll_guidance_document_final.pdf.

Vargas, Edward. 2015. "Immigration enforcement and mixed-status families: The effects of risk of deportation on Medicaid use." *Children and Youth Services Review* 57(October): 83–9. Retrieved from https://www.ncbi.nlm.nih.gov/pmc/articles/PMC4592159/.

Ward, Colleen, and Antony Kennedy. 1999. "The measurement of sociocultural adaptation." *International Journal of Intercultural Relations* 23(4): 659–77.

Winter, Jeannette. 2007. *Angelina's Island.* New York: Farrar, Strauss, and Giroux.

Wise, Sarah, and Lisa da Silva. 2007. *Differential Parenting of Children from Diverse Cultural Backgrounds Attending Child Care* (Research Paper No. 39). Melbourne: Australian Institute of Family Studies.

Yoshikawa, Hirokazu. 2011. *Immigrants Raising Citizens: Undocumented Parents and Their Young Children.* New York: Russell Sage.

Yoshikawa, Hirokazu, and Jenya Kholoptseva. 2013. *Unauthorized Immigrant Parents and Their Children's Development: A Summary of the Evidence.* Washington, DC: Migration Policy Institute.

Zayas, Luis, and Lauren E. Gulbas. 2017. "Processes of belonging for citizen-children of undocumented Mexican immigrants." *Journal of Child and Family Studies* 26(9): 2463–74.

Zayas, Luis, Sergio Aguilar-Gaxiola, Hyunwoo Yoon, and Guillermina Natera Rey. 2015. "The distress of citizen-children with detained and deported parents." *Journal of Child and Family Studies* 24(11): 3213–23.

5

Promising Practices for Immigrant Children

Through this chapter, we will

- Explore practices supporting the needs of immigrant children and families
- Discuss the need for consciously centered practices for children
- Identify selected policies and legislative actions addressing the educational needs of immigrant children
- Discuss some of the factors addressing supportive practices for immigrant children
- Identify some of the elements influencing immigrant parents' involvement in schools

Key terms

- Social justice
- Consciously centered educational practices
- Educational legislative actions
- Well-being of immigrant children

NAEYC standards

- NAEYC #1 Promoting Child Development
- NAEYC #2 Families and Communities
- NAEYC #6 Professionalism

Sharing stories: *A future for my children*

Johan came from an African country together with his two children just like many others seeking a better life. Living in a place where civil unrest was happening almost daily, he made the decision to leave thinking about his children. Violence had already taken too much away from their lives. The morning he received the news about his visa, he went and told his siblings who had been taking care of his children. Leaving, he thought, was never in his plans. It was not an easy decision but was one he needed to make for the sake of his own children. A single father, he soon looked for a place with schools where his children could attend. As he texted his family back home, he started telling them that the school where his children were now enrolled reaffirmed why he had come to America. "It's so different but it is a good school. Children are getting used to being here and that makes me feel happy."

In the best interest of children

In all actions concerning children, whether undertaken by public or private social welfare institutions, courts of law, administrative authorities or legislative bodies, the best interests of the child shall be a primary consideration. (Article 3(1) United Nations Convention on the Rights of the Child [UN 1989])

The story of immigration continues to unfold every day. People wanting to see their aspirations crystalize continue to move across borders with their bags of dreams and experiences. We had mentioned it before and it is similar to what brought the father in the opening scenario: children continue to be one of the main forces leading immigration efforts for many. We have been pondering the life circumstances surrounding the experiences of immigrant children. As we take time in this chapter to examine educational practices and programs for young immigrant children and their families, the premise of ensuring what is best in the interest of the child remains a central principle. Affirmed by the Convention on the Rights of the Child (UN 1989), as the epigraph reads, decisions for children must always adhere to what is best in the interest of the young. The principle, long-standing in our country, has roots in efforts to ensure protection for the child facing challenging situations (Carbone 2014). Today, emerging strongly in recognition of the rights of children, ascertaining what is best for a child reaffirms the integrity of childhood. Consequently, affirming childhood recognizes the human rights ascribed to children by society. Considerations of their rights and needs along the spectrum of their individual experiences and development are the cornerstone of efforts and practices targeted at supporting child immigrants.

An ethical responsibility toward children

Central to actions and practices addressing children's needs is the aspiration to ensure they find the experiences and care essential to reach their successful development. Where do considerations begin? What is the extent of these considerations? They begin with our conscious awareness about the ethical responsibility toward children that guides informed practice in early childhood education. They are anchored in an understanding of what is intended to prevent and protect the child from any harm, a core principle defining and guiding actions for children (NAEYC 2011). Every decision, entailing practice directed at the child, is a reminder of the charge early educators embrace to protect the child. More importantly, their successful development and well-being is of interest to all and "especially important to the nation because they are the fastest-growing segment in the U.S. population" (Tienda and Haskins 2011, 3). Similar assertion is made by Hernández, Denton, and Macartney (2008), who state that immigrant children are a concern to everyone in the country. In their words,

> The sheer number of children in immigrant families, means they will play a major role in sustaining the American economy during the coming decades. This is critical to the well-being of all Americans but especially to the baby boom generation, which will depend for economic support during retirement, on the productivity of all American workers, including those who grew up in immigrant families. (19)

The best interest perspective takes center stage in child protection and in legally bound decisions pertaining to children both internationally and in the United States. As a standard parameter throughout the country, this position gives guidance to practices, services, and programs that safeguard children's needs and future. Beyond custody, as stated by Alston and Gilmour-Walsh (1996), the principle has "far wider applicability than in the custody area alone" (1). It stands at the core of all efforts for the child. From a broader scope, the best interest position brings into perspective any circumstance challenging the rights of children. Such is the case of the guidelines published in 2008 by the United Nations High Commissioner for Refugees (UNHCR) providing direction for a comprehensive determination of best interest in the case of refugee children. The continuing crisis impacting and placing children at risk led to the revision of the guidelines in 2018 (UNHCR 2018). Its premises continue to assert the responsibility that everyone in society must protect children.

In early childhood education, the best interest of the child is a parameter that anchors expectations for practices centered on attaining overall well-being. Vital to delivering quality and equitable services and experiences, embracing the best interest principle places the focus on the child and his/her realities and particular experiences. Rooted firmly in the declaration of the Convention on the Rights of the Child (United Nations 1989), the child rights principle serves as a framework defining the charge for responsible attention to children in need or experiencing individual circumstances that challenge their welfare. Its guidance offers strong focus on practices reflective of ethically based conduct particularly pertinent to the immigration crisis of recent years, which impacted childhood.

The focus in this chapter is on considering practices and experiences for immigrant children and their families. Within the framework of the chapter, the best interest principle is inherent to what we termed earlier as consciously centered practices. Whenever you invoke consciously centered practices your aim is to deter and erase any unfair actions denying children of their rights to equitable experiences. That is what the best interest for children also strives to accomplish. It is what suitably and more appropriately responds to what a child's needs may be accordingly with what respectfully safeguards the integrity of childhood.

As we begin the discussion, we urge you to consider issues and topics through the lens of ethics, that is, what is right to be accomplished for children. We also urge you to reflect on the issues using the lens of what is appropriate educational practice and developmentally appropriate for a child. Both views provide angles that inform expectations for achieving what is best for children.

Time to reflect ... *Following the premise of best interest of the child*

Keeping children safe and facilitating opportunities for their development are goals at the heart of efforts in early childhood. It is also what reflects our commitment to do what is best for children. Consider the implications of the principle *best interest of the child* and think about one or two instances where you have upheld this principle in your work with and for children. Explain what motivated your actions or decisions in the best interest of the child.

Everyday practice: What is best for children

When Mira's family came to visit the preschool center near their home, they wanted a place where their daughter could find "good learning" and understanding teachers. Short of a year earlier, her parents had come from northern Africa after a long journey trying to get to the U.S. They were somewhat hesitant waiting for the director of the center. Just a month before, they had enrolled their daughter at another center where they were explicitly told, "You need to speak to your child only in English" after seeing one of the parents talking to the then three-year old, in their native language. The next day they pulled their daughter out and started searching for another school. The morning they came to a local center they were surprised to find the director of the center who greeted them and interjected words and phrases in their home language. With her was one of the teachers, who seeing the child with long hair, bent down and began speaking to her. "This is the place," the father said watching his daughter, with a shy smile but evidently denoting she felt welcomed. So did her parents, too.

What is best for children must always guide actions and daily activities in early childhood education. Guided by the principle of best interest of the child, efforts and actions addressing the needs of immigrant children and families must be seen through the lens of what is meaningful and essential to their development and overall welfare. This calls for intentionality, focusing attention and consideration on routines, events, and happenings, and their implications, all viewed from the perspective of what is relevant and necessary for the child. The best interest of children implicitly points to providing access and high-quality experiences that equitably respond to needs.

What Mira's parents experienced portrays one of those instances where the best interest of the child needs to be always upheld. Recognizing the value of her heritage language was in her best interest. Language, key to one's culture and identity, in this case, demanded acknowledgment and consideration of the parents' preferences. Keeping the family's perspectives paramount and counting on their participation is also vital to ensuring a focus on what is in the interest of the child's well-being. Another situation experienced by a young child who had recently arrived from Central America portrays emphasis on actions that responsibly meet children's needs and experiences. Traveling with his twin brother and living with relatives while waiting to be reunited with his parents, the 7-year-old child was separated from his twin brother at school. Soon teachers noticed how he was keeping himself away from his classroom peers, searching all the time for his brother at lunch break. On more than one occasion, they found him entering into his brother's classroom. After an interpreter had a conversation with the child and the need to be together with his brother became clear, the decision was made to have both children in the same class.

Through the lens of appropriate educational practices

Looking at services and programs for child immigrants and to what happens in the classroom directs us to use the lens of what are appropriate and essential practices for children's development. Practices supportive of what is best for children take place every day. They arise out of ongoing observations and consciously centered on responding to children's experiences and needs. Responsible practices are also firmly rooted in developmental knowledge and are individually determined to reflect a child's realities (Copple and Bredekamp 2009). Consciously determined, appropriate experiences and practices are intentionally delivered as part of essential efforts directed at securing the well-being of children. More specifically, they are centered on what is critical for their successful development and what is socially just for all children. They are also mindfully determined, considering their families' culture and aspirations. Vandenbroeck (2018) cautions that services and programs must be considered "beyond stereotypical notions," calling attention to ideas held about families that may obscure views about what they want and aspire for their children. Existence of known and unconscious biases remains a challenge, and professionals seeking the well-being of children are all called to set aside those preconceptions. Mindful of culturally appropriate practices for children, discussion in this chapter follows the lens of educational appropriate practices. As a lens, it is centered at viewing experiences that are integral and thoughtfully provided to children with immigrant roots. This is, too, what is ethically appropriate.

Time to reflect ... *Through the lens of appropriate educational practices*

Biases and misleading notions about people may prevent us from seeing what is best and appropriate for child immigrants. As an early childhood professional, consider some of the current misconceptions and views about immigrants that may blur and impact appropriate practices for children. How could this be counteracted?

The rights of children

The United Nations has proclaimed that childhood is entitled to special care and assistance. (Convention on the Rights of the Child, Preamble [United Nations 1990])

The milestone signing of the United Nations *Convention on the Rights of the Child* (CRC) in 1989 officialized recognition of children as individuals with human rights. Ratification of the convention constituted an acknowledgment of the inherent and concomitant responsibility of society to care and protect children. Globally, it represents a victory for childhood. The document provides a thorough description of children as "a subject of law" (Child Rights Hub 2019). Their rightful access to support and conditions conducive to their optimal development stand out clearly in the CRC. Serving as guideposts for the care and responsible attention to the needs of the child, the document details what is ascribed to children to ensure their rights to their well-being. Guidance from the CRC further supports the call for appropriate and socially just actions aimed at providing what is in the best interests of the child, which, as Article 3.1 of the CRC states, "*shall be a primary consideration*" (emphasis added) (United Nations 1989). With this view in mind, we continue examining experiences and legal antecedents leading to practices supporting the rights of immigrant children.

Supporting immigrant children's rights to education

All children in the United States are entitled to equal access to a public elementary and secondary education, regardless of their or their parents' actual or perceived national origin, citizenship, or immigration status. (U.S. Department of Education [2014])

That children have a right to education is a premise at the heart of social justice. It is as well, according to the U.S. Department of Education, what is ambitioned for all children attending schools in the nation. This, however, has not happened so straightforwardly for children of immigrants. Many have experienced the inequities of a system that perpetuated unequal treatment and denied children of what is rightfully owed. It has taken conscious determination and efforts of parents, educators, and advocates to ensure their rights. Their efforts have not been in vain, yielding an array of legal accomplishments on behalf of child immigrants, which today constitute the legal bases ascribing child immigrant rights to education in our communities. One of the most relevant feats happened in 1982 when the US Supreme Court recognized the rights to public education (K-12) for child immigrants irrespective of their immigration status. The ruling came as an outcome of the landmark case *Plyler* v. *Doe*, which is discussed ahead in this section.

As a major social justice achievement of the Plyler case, immigrant children, including those with undocumented entries, are lawfully eligible to an education and supportive services (Salas 2019). The assertion of their right to education constituted a victory for immigrant children and their families as society acknowledged its responsibility toward the youngest ones. This legal milestone is also a reminder about the ongoing struggle for socially just practices for children with diverse backgrounds. Their rights to equal services continue as the focus of countless advocacy efforts. At stake in the nation has always been the education of students who are culturally diverse. Whether subtle or openly, children with diverse characteristics have been exposed to views, opinions, and actions contrary to what is constitutionally underlined as equality for all. The search for fairness in education for all children, for access, opportunities, and quality of experiences, has been a long-standing challenge, continuing today. Throughout decades, the urgent need to ensure, beyond cultural and racial lines, the rightful path to education for everyone has been the very essence supporting diversity and multiculturalism. The same goal remains guiding at present the voice of educators and advocates seeking to ensure access and delivery of experiences equitably preparing young immigrant children.

Legal milestones in the long-standing pursuit for educational rights

The need to address student diversity, particularly given the continuous immigration and increasing diverse demographics, demands fair and equal attention. The current immigration crisis, in our nation and around the world, has elevated the call for clear understanding about the rights of child immigrants for equitable educational practices. Answering the needs and hopes of children is at the core of educational goals in a democratic society. The road, however, to actions and practices supportive of these aspirations has been hindered by many obstacles emerging out of distorted views about the rights of children of immigrants in our nation. Among the challenges, the impact of immigration policies on children's rights and their well-being has also come to the forefront. Yet, the fact is that "Regardless of how one might feel about our nation's immigration policies, there is no turning back the clock on the children of immigrants already living here, most of whom are U.S. citizens" (Shields and Behrman 2004, 4). At stake is how society responds to the needs of young immigrant children to rightfully ensure their well-being. The call is for everyone and weighs heavily on education, especially early childhood education as the nation's children increasingly are of immigrant heritage.

The lawful right of immigrant children to public education is a milestone in the story of immigrants in the United States. This successful accomplishment is rooted in events of the past that served as precedents. Before we look at the Plyler case, it is pertinent to examine some of the legal precedents that illustrate the determined efforts of parents and advocates for their children's equal access to education. Undoubtedly, the key constitutional framework for ensuring equality is found in the 14th Amendment to the US Constitution. Ratified in 1868 after the end of the Civil War, the amendment recognized the right of individuals to due process and their equal protection under the law (McLemore and Romo 2005). Under its umbrella, the road was gradually paved to the Supreme Court ruling of 1982. Among the main cases, the following tells the story and trajectory of the struggle for immigrant children's rights to education:

1. ***Plessy* v. *Ferguson:*** We need to look at the unthinkable decision *separate but equal* that the US Supreme Court ruled in 1886 pertaining to the segregation of African-American students. Though this ruling addressed the existing unfair educational treatment of African-American students, the ruling also impacted the situation of Chinese, Hispanic, and Native American students who at the time were also segregated from mainstream students. The ruling established the principle of equity in educational services for ethnic minorities. However, it still upheld the racial segregationist practice. Debated in the courts for almost six decades, it would be overturned later in 1954 after the momentous *Brown* v. *Board of Education* case.

2. ***Alvarez* v. *Lemon Grove School District:*** In January 1930, Mexican parents in the school district of Lemon Grove in the San Diego area were outraged when their children were denied entrance into the main school building and told to attend a separate two-room building that would serve as classrooms for Mexican children (Alvarez 1986). Refusing to accept the separation of their children from the rest of the school, Mexican parents

obtained legal counsel and fought the order in court. Arguments against the separation clearly based on racial segregation led the parents to a victory. In 1931, the court ruled in favor of the children declaring, on the basis of equality, they were entitled to receive instruction in the regular school building (Alvarez 1986).

3. *Mendez v. Westminster:* Another momentous precedent was the case of the Mendez children in California during the 1940s. Born in Mexico, Gonzalo Mendez became a US citizen in 1943 and lived with his wife, Felicitas, a Puerto Rican immigrant, and their family in Westminster. When his children went to register at the local school, the same one their father had attended, they were sent to a different school, one where all the students were Mexicans. Clearly separating the students based on race, and surprised by the actions of the school, Mendez met with the principal and the Westminster School Board. After conversations failed, Mendez obtained legal advice. Through his legal counsel, he learned that the schools were following the practice of segregation, separating Mexican-American students from their White peers and sending them to different school facilities. Determined to seek fair actions and a stop to this practice, in 1945, Mendez and several other families filed a class action lawsuit against the school board challenging the segregationist practice. The US District Court ruled in 1946 that segregation violated the state laws. In his ruling, Judge McCormick stated that "A paramount requisite in the American system of public education is social equality. It must be open to all children by unified school association regardless of lineage" (Strum 2010). The victory of the Mendez case set the ground for the milestone case of *Brown* v. *Board of Education*.

4. *Brown v. Board of Education:* One of the major legal accomplishments targeted at ensuring fair educational practices dates back to 1954, the *Brown* v. *Board of Education*. This landmark case established the rights of all children to receive equal education, invalidating and prohibiting the racial segregation of African-Americans, until then, existing beyond a century since the ruling of *Plessy* v. *Ferguson*. Its significance for all ethnic minorities including immigrant children continues today.

The quest for equality continues to be vigorously pursued today by educators and advocates who recognize the rights of every child. It was precisely the quest for equal rights that inspired the Civil Rights Movement during the 1960s. Thousands representing ethnic minorities joined African-Americans to pursue the end of unfair practices. Many of the successes achieved in the search for fairness and equality are part of the legacy of the Civil Rights advocates of the 1960s. Their cornerstone efforts are examples continuing to inspire the search for equity for all children.

The Plyler case

No State shall … deny to any person within its jurisdiction the equal protection of the laws. (14th Amendment to the US Constitution)

That every individual has the same rights and protection of the laws is a central constitutional principle in the nation. This extends and includes children of immigrants. The lawful right to education of immigrant children in the country's public schools is the outcome of the efforts and perseverance of parents. Guided by their aspirations for their children and determined to make their dreams happen, they took their fight to the courts. The result led to the current policy, based on the US Supreme Court ruling in the case of *Plyler* v. *Doe*. This decision opened the public schools' classroom doors to all immigrant children. The case emerged after a school district in Texas denied enrollment to undocumented children in an elementary school. They were following the policy approved by the Texas legislature in 1975 denying enrollment to children not legally admitted into the country and allowing school districts to charge tuition if they were to enroll. When the Tyler school district started to charge an annual tuition of $1,000 for each child with unauthorized entry, parents sought legal representation. Working with the Mexican American Legal Defense and Educational Fund (MALDEF), they filed a class action lawsuit against the policy. The district court ruled that the practice was in violation of the Equal Protection Clause of the 14th Amendment (Olivas 2010). Brought to the US Supreme Court, the court ruled in 1982 that the policy violated the rights of students and asserted their rights to free public education (American Immigration Council 2016).

Based on the *Plyler* v. *Doe* ruling, admission into public schools (K-12) is protected. Under state law, immigrant students with unauthorized status are required to attend schools (Intercultural Development Research Association [IDRA] 2014), which in turn is constitutionally recognized as a result of the Plyler case.

Efforts of advocates continue advising families and parents about the rights that their children have to attend and receive an education in the nation's public schools. In times where attitudes and misinformed views about immigrants continue, advocates are actively guiding families about the fact that schools cannot deny their children's right to enrollment. They are also communicating to families about what is not acceptable for public schools to do. Among what is not acceptable, schools cannot:

- Deny enrollment due to immigration status.
- Request the student's social security number.
- Ask students or their parents to disclose or give proof about their immigration status.
- Intimidate parents to prevent their access to educational services.
- Inquire about students or their parents with the intent to expose their undocumented status. (IDRA 2014)

Following the Plyler ruling, the rights of immigrant children to receive a free education were recognized and it stands today as current policy. Furthermore, the privacy of students' information is protected under the Family Educational Rights and Privacy Act of 1974 (FERPA), which establishes that data can only be released with the consent of the parents or guardians (Sugarman 2019). Despite the legally binding rulings, there have been cases where some immigrant families have been asked to document their status, actions that violate the rights of children. Actions and support of immigrant advocates have provided families with needed support to ensure their children's access and enrollment. In 2014, a letter from the U.S. Department of Education to all K-12 educators (U.S. Department of Education 2014) reaffirmed the educational rights of immigrant children and provided clarification about their rights to services and programs. Still, many other actions remain yet to be pursued as advocates for child immigrants remain actively working to ensure their rights and well-being.

The *Lau* v. *Nichols*, the impact of a ruling on language instruction of dual language learners

The milestone ruling in the Plyler case opened doors to child immigrants into the public schools' classrooms. Yet, there were more challenges to overcome. Because many immigrant children had languages other than English, it did not take long for parents to realize that their children needed some additional accommodations. Their concerns emerge mostly due to the focus of instruction and of practices that threatened the loss of children's primary or heritage languages. The fact is that English instruction has always been the focus of school programs early on. However, practices and emphasis have evolved through the years from a focus centered on building English proficiency to today's attention on effective support for dual language learning.

During the 1970s concerns about linguistic practices grew among parents who felt their children were not receiving the needed pedagogical support at school to become English proficient. In 1971, a group of parents of Chinese students in San Francisco, frustrated with the schools' teaching practices, filed a class action suit on behalf of 1,800 students. They claimed that students were not receiving the instructional support needed to overcome their language barrier, leaving them "to sink or swim" in classrooms where all teaching was in English (Wright 2010). In 1974, the *Lau* v. *Nichols* case went to the US Supreme Court where the decision made earlier by a lower court was overthrown, adjudicating the case in favor of the students under the umbrella of Title VI of the Civil Rights Act (Wright 2010). After a thorough review, the court ruled that school districts needed to ensure steps were taken to overcome language barriers faced by non-English-speaking students. The decision, strongly pointed out by Justice William Douglas, stated, "*There is no equality of treatment merely by providing students with the same facilities, textbooks, teachers, and curriculum; for students who do not understand English are effectively foreclosed from any meaningful education... We know that those who do not understand English are certain to find their classroom experiences wholly incomprehensible and in no way meaningful*" (emphasis added) (Lessow-Hurley 2009, 143).

The successful ruling marked another important milestone in the struggle for the rights of immigrants (Figure 5.1) that, taken to the courts, prompted new practices in recognition of the rights of immigrants. The ruling, which asserted the rights of speakers of other languages to receive appropriate

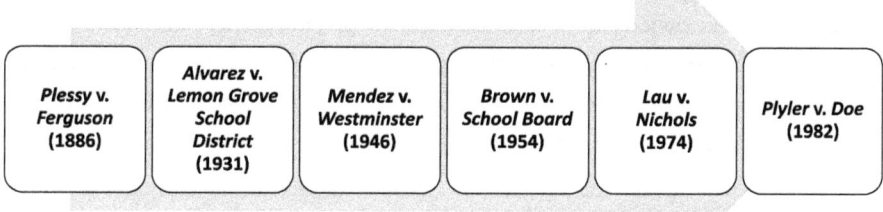

Figure 5.1 Key milestones in the legal struggle for the educational rights of child immigrants.

educational supports, had an important impact on educational policy (Lessow-Hurley 2009; Wright 2010). Following the court ruling, the Office of Civil Rights issued a document with guidance for school districts to implement practices in compliance with the Lau decision. Called the *Lau Remedies*, they defined standards for practices, recommended approaches, and assessments to determine and address the language needs of students (U.S. Department of Education 2018). Under its influence, programs and emphasis on the needs of English language learners gained attention, confirming the rights of students to equal learning opportunities for their educational success.

Equal educational expectations

With the victory obtained in *Lau* v. *Nichols*, other actions followed in support of the language needs of children with diverse linguistic and cultural heritage. The federal education acts of 2001, *No Child Left Behind* and *Every Student Succeeds Act* of 2015 (ESSA), gave further recognition to the rights of all students (K-12) to receive equitable educational experiences, which further supported dual language learners. Both laws established as a goal the need for providing high-quality educational experiences and same academic outcomes for all students, a tenet recognizing equal expectations for speakers of languages other than English as well as students from low-income families. As Sugarman (2019) noted, this requires schools to hold high expectations and provide educational experiences, leading students to successful performance. These expectations have also influenced program quality and expectations for preschoolers.

The announcement in the summer of 2016 from the U.S. Department of Education endorsing practices about dual language learning, which was discussed in Chapter 2, represented another major acknowledgment about students' language diversity and the need for support beginning in early childhood. Acknowledgment about language diversity and need for support represented another milestone in the fight for the rights of immigrant children in the nation. More is yet to come as early childhood professionals and advocates continue to seek equitable and socially just actions for children of immigrants.

Time to reflect ... *Equal expectations*

One of the key goals of the 2015 ESSA education law in the United States is equity for all students (K-12). In particular, it established the need for high-quality practices that equally meet students' needs including those with linguistic differences. Considering its tenets, how do they influence education for young children with immigrant roots?

In our classrooms: Immigrant children and educational experiences

Education is perhaps one of the first reasons people will mention as part of their motives in their immigration journey. Education continues as one of the main ways leading to a future and particularly to make the "American dream" into a reality. This continues to be a shared goal for immigrant parents regardless of their socioeconomic or immigration status. For Hispanic parents, constituting a large majority of immigrants arriving in recent times to the country, education is a major goal as they raise their children, seen as the way for them to become successful. In the views of Hispanic or Latino families, education is perceived as having implications far beyond experiencing education and rather signifying the way to become successful individuals. *Educación*, education for Latino families is seen as an aspiration to better realities and changing lives. Similar ideas and conceptualizations about education have been identified to describe the aspirations and activities of families from other ethnic roots (Barrueco, Smith, and Stephens 2015).

Experiences and interactions at school are an influential component integral to the child's development. They are also part of the powerful forces defining a child's life events. For all parents and families, anticipating the moment when their children will be at school is one characterized with mixed emotions. It is as well for immigrant parents and families. Entry experiences into the school and the education system, usually unfamiliar to many immigrant families, confront immigrants to face a new facet of their life in the country. A young mother from the Caribbean islands once shared that she made sure to dress her 4-year-old boy in his best clothes when she proudly took him to preschool. Similar to what parents everywhere may hope, she also added that she was hopeful to have teachers that would be "as caring as we are at home with him." Bringing their children for the first time to school and entering into a system unfamiliar to them is an emotionally charged experience. In many ways, it is no different than what native-born families feel as their young children come to school.

Immigrant children and families coming to school

Care and love for their children characterize immigrant families. They come to classrooms with high hopes for their young children. At the same time, they arrive eager to obtain the best education for their children, just the same as what US-born parents desire for their children (Gelatt, Adams, and Huerta 2014). Feeling welcome is a first step in establishing relationships with classroom teachers, administrators, and staff. This is what is hoped all children and families will find as they come to schools. Yet, despite legal decisions and policies underscoring the child immigrants' rights to education, how children are received at schools differs across locations, sending confusing messages. Often, one would wonder if they are really being welcomed. According to Adair (2015, 2016), the climate of reception that immigrant families find may range from welcoming support and understanding to one of discrimination and rejection. Undoubtedly, at times, how they are received is reflective of views and attitudes in their local communities. Sometimes unconsciously, behaviors and reactions toward immigrant families and children send unfriendly and hostile signals. Damaging portrayals of immigrants, and little or no knowledge about immigration, have created an unfavorable atmosphere that permeates some places—now and then in subtle ways but still hurtful. Sadly, schools have not been the exception. Microaggressions, a form of subtle discrimination, have been identified as a common incidence in many educational environments. Comments such as "you look different" or "you don't look like one of them" are not uncommon. Many times, unintentional and often not aimed at offending, they are most damaging as they perpetuate biased ideas about others. Discrimination in its many forms continues as one of the experiences common to children with diverse and cultural characteristics.

Time to reflect … *Counteracting biased ideas, mindfully*

Comments about others based on stereotypes and bias remain present in daily interactions. Sometimes we may be unaware about those we are using. Reflect on some of those expressions commonly heard about immigrants. Which ones would you consider that are microaggressions? How would you counteract those?

Facing unfair views and messages

The day she went to the school to enroll her children, Griselda, a young professional from a Latin American country, would always remember the demeaning way in which she was received: "I said, 'Good morning,' and the moment they heard me talk, they didn't see me, they just heard my accent. Gesturing, she pointed me to sit and started to talk louder and very slow. She could not hear that I was talking to her in English. She felt like saying, "Please see me, not my accent!" Though time had passed, her frustration and disappointment remained with her. The reaction to her accent, she said, made her feel so uncomfortable that she still remembers it. Incidents like hers, unfortunately, are not uncommon. Some are unintentional, grown out of little or no experience with diversity. Others are not, reflecting prejudiced understandings guiding actions.

Some parents arrive at school with a sense of apprehension. The experience itself of immigration brings dramatic changes and adjustments to one's life. For immigrant parents, this also includes entering into an educational system unfamiliar to them. Personal impressions from past experiences and knowledge about what others have encountered inevitably build anxiety in many parents. Sadly, many already "know that they are often viewed negatively," which furthers their uneasiness and sense of distrust (Adair 2015, 5). Compounding the challenges, the existence of often damaging views about immigrants further adds to what families and children encounter. Stereotypes about immigrants, particularly due to their ethnic and racial diversity, have also become a source of offensive experiences. Comments and use of derogatory terms are still experienced by many immigrant children. Many times these are used by their young peers, who may not be aware about their hurtful meaning. Interventions in the classroom and at home are necessary to clarify these offensive expressions.

Discourse about immigration in current times, as we have shared before, has inaccurately portrayed the reality of immigrants, projecting messages that diminish the efforts and experiences of families and children. It also continues to feed discriminatory and unfair practices emerging from negative stereotypes. Regrettably, discrimination is present in the life and experiences of many immigrants, something researchers have acknowledged (Carnock 2015; Krogstad and López 2016; Spears Brown 2015). The existence of negative views clouds the efforts of so many educators who consciously center their practices in what is relevant and equitable for the well-being of children and their families (Box 5.1).

Box 5.1 Connecting ideas: *Child immigrants, overcoming challenges and reaching success*

Arriving into a context that, for most, is culturally and linguistically different from their own implies the challenge of adapting to new norms and expectations for both parents and children. Throughout time many have experienced the challenges of having to learn about practices and regulations unfamiliar to them, sometimes without little guidance or support. Overcoming obstacles, parents' efforts continue to be guided by the aspirations they have for their children. Every year, as one sees the smiling faces at graduation, one recognizes the successful stories of thousands of immigrant children. In so many ways, they are successful stories about their families, too. During a meeting at a program supporting immigrants, one of the authors remembers how proudly an immigrant mother came into the room with her son. A former worker in the fields, she was accompanying her now college graduate son. Having attended the program as a child, he came to express his gratitude for the support and encouragement provided. Dressed in his academic gown, he was a palpable example of the promise residing in every child immigrant. Today, his photo is displayed in the program office as a reminder of what everyone could accomplish. Like him, the list of others who continue to overcome and persist is endless.

It is impossible not to mention the existing power differences between school and parents. Unfamiliarity with policies and practices at times places parents in difficult situations. Frequently, this leads to difficult situations due to communication barriers, lack of clarity, confusion about what is expected, and fear brought about by uncooperative attitudes and discriminatory responses from individuals. It is not unusual for many to feel intimidated, particularly for parents and families with language barriers or those with unauthorized immigration status. Fear, lack of trust, and anxiety due to unfamiliarity with system processes are not uncommon feelings for parents and families. Whatever the source of tension, negative impressions remain. As Spears Brown (2015) pointedly stated, the time has come for everyone "to be aware of the negative consequences associated with discrimination" (16).

Where are the children? Participation in early childhood programs

In the United States, "providing all children with a quality education is the foundation of the American dream" (Schneiderman 2016). This has directed efforts through the years and continues at present with attention to the role early childhood education plays for a child's future. Studies have confirmed that early childhood programs are a foundational experience for later success in life. This is a well-known fact today and a reason underlining the programs and services available for child immigrants (Karoly 2016; Karoly and Gonzalez 2011). Moreover, early childhood learning constitutes a critical social justice experience, leading to successful schooling, and driving elimination of social inequalities (Ansari and Crosnoe 2011). Yet, levels of participation of immigrant children in early education programs remain as a concern. Reports from states and local communities show that enrollment of immigrant children in early childhood programs continues to be low in comparison to that of their peers (Greenberg, Michie, and Adams 2018). The continuing underenrollment of immigrant preschoolers has been marked as a serious issue. Lower levels of participation are especially evident during the preschool years, creating concern about the educational success of the youngest immigrants. Representing the future workforce generation in a society, demographical projections show immigrants will be key to the nation's population growth (Crosnoe 2007).

Participation of child immigrants in early childhood programs continues to show gaps, even though, irrespective of their immigration status, they are eligible to receive educational programs and services. Overall, immigrant children ages 3–4 continue to have lower enrollment in preschool classrooms than their native-born counterparts (Fortuny, Hernandez, and Chaudry 2010). Even in recent years, with the increased number of prekindergarten programs, participation continues to be lower than for native-born children. Ironically, although almost 90 percent of immigrant children are US citizens, reasons behind their lower enrollment continue to puzzle educators. This is an aspect still calling for further research to determine the issues and factors impacting decisions (Miller, Votruba-Drzal, and Coley 2013).

Lower participation of immigrant children in early childhood

Despite efforts to provide access to programs, participation of immigrant children continues to be at a lower level. What accounts for the lower participation in early childhood programs? Reasons explaining lower participation of immigrant children vary. Some reasons responsible for the lower enrollment include the fact that many families seem to be unaware of what their children are entitled to receive, including local programs and services. Despite efforts made to reach families, some of the barriers continue to be the same. Language barriers remain as one of the factors inhibiting the spread of information for many families who only speak their heritage languages. Reports show that 60 percent of children have at least one parent who speaks languages other than English, while over a third of children live with linguistically isolated families where no one was proficient in English (Fortuny, Hernandez, and Chaudry 2010). This further accentuates language as a challenge added to the fact that many local programs continue to lack staff that can speak the languages of families in their communities (Andrew and Jang 2007). Approaches used for dissemination of information about programs and enrollment have been identified as another reason for lower enrollments (Adair 2015). Strategies, in some cases, have proven ineffective in reaching parents when they fail to send the message in ways consonant with the cultural practices of those in the community. In one case, one of the authors spoke with a group of Hispanic parents participating in a literacy program and inquired how they have learned about services for their children. The majority mentioned that it was through their neighbors, and word of mouth, that they had found out about the programs for their young children. Radio broadcasts, still a practice in many ethnic communities, was also found to be an effective dissemination method when trying to reach Hispanic families, as well as families from other cultures. Using what is familiar and common practice to the ethnic group to spread information is relevant to ensure parents and families are informed.

Time to reflect ... *Welcoming programs*

In their report about immigrant children's participation in prekindergarten programs, Gelatt, Adams, and Huerta (2014) call for creating immigrant-friendly programs to increase participation. Reflecting on the programs in your community for preschoolers, what would you suggest for making your programs more inviting to immigrant families? What changes or change would you consider to be most relevant?

Cultural practices have been listed as one of the other reasons keeping young immigrant children at home rather than in preschool. Though participation is increasing, some families, as in the case of Hispanics, consider caring for their young children at home as one of their cultural parenting expectations (Takanishi 2004; Zuniga 2011). Although parents are becoming more conscious about the importance of preschool experiences, many immigrant children remain at home, receiving care from parents or are being cared for by trusted relatives or trusted neighborhood individuals (Crosnoe 2007). Trust is another issue challenging participation in early care and education programs. The meaning of *confianza*, trust, particularly for Hispanic or Latino families, implies a profound feeling and sincere conviction that their children will be well cared for. This would help explain parents' preference for having children in more informal types of care where there are higher levels of trust and already established relationships.

For those with undocumented status, fear emerging from their immigration situation results in isolating their children. In a large number of cases, anxiety about what schools may do elicits distrust, fearing the threat of deportation. Others face the challenge of obtaining the necessary documentation to prove their children's eligibility (Gelatt, Adams, and Huerta 2014). Still others, as gleaned from conversations with parents, continue to encounter insensitive remarks and unfair treatment from some individuals that discourage families from using their services. Awareness about the uncertainty and unfairness some families experience is essential. Understanding responses are necessary to end the disparity of preschool participation of immigrant children. This would also make certain that children gain access to programs and receive the services that they are rightfully entitled to enjoy (Box 5.2).

Box 5.2 Connecting ideas: *A bigger issue, distressing feelings of fear*

Throughout our discussion we have underlined the fact that immigration status of children and families in recent years has gained greater interest. This has also elevated its attention across the nation's schools, thus elevating it as a concern for schools. In particular, it has become an evident concern for educators who recognize the existing stressful circumstances surrounding the lives of so many immigrants. Increased enforcement of immigration has brought a sense of fear among immigrant children and families with unauthorized status. Early childhood teachers have reported their concerns as they notice children becoming distracted and disengaged (Kugler 2017). Fear of deportation has become common among those whose parents or family members' entry into the country was unauthorized. Impact of immigration status places children at risk as they experience the tension and anxiety that permeates "all aspects" (Sibley and Brabeck 2017, 144) of family life. Many parents have limited or avoided their involvement and participation at school, which further affects children's experiences at school. In some cases, adults' fear of detention and self-imposed seclusion isolates children and denies many from receiving services that parents are fearful to request. The result is that efforts promoting equitable experiences and opportunities for immigrant children are at risk. Living in contexts where they are not welcome works against their well-being. Actions are needed to eliminate practices that continue to exist to the detriment of young immigrant children.

Supporting school readiness of the youngest immigrants

Programs serving child immigrants are found throughout the country. Attending school remains as an aspiration of immigrant parents just like all parents want for their children (Gelatt, Adams, and Huerta 2014). This is something we have learned from parents we met at meetings and during visits to centers. Participation, however, remains lower than from their US-born peers during a period critical to their successful schooling experience.

School readiness, preparation for successful kindergarten experiences, continues today as one of the priorities guiding programs. Policies and curricular directions in preschool programs such as Head Start and Early Head Start and state-funded prekindergarten programs as well as center-based child care programs today are aimed at providing children the foundational experiences that serve as a predictor for schooling achievement. Irrefutably, preschool experiences potentially contribute to preparing child immigrants for later schooling and it is especially relevant for those from low-income families (Crosnoe 2007). Findings from de Feyter and Winsler (2009) in their study about school readiness of immigrant children revealed that participation in child care and prekindergarten programs effectively contributed to their progress in various domains of school readiness.

The need for responsive practices that appropriately meet children's cultural learning needs emerges as another challenging area impacting teaching and learning experiences. With a large participation of child immigrants in early childhood, defining approaches or emphases to follow continues as part of the debate on how to best teach children whose cultures and languages are other than English (Tienda and Haskins 2011). At the core of the continuing priorities in the education of young immigrants is the support needed to ensure their effective attainment of learning outcomes. Emphasis on appropriate practices shows that key to their success is the high-quality nature of instruction experienced by children (Copple and Bredekamp 2009; Takanishi 2004). While the child immigrant population is very diverse, a large number live in low-income families. With limited resources, the need for access to higher quality programs is heightened as an investment in the well-being of immigrant children and their peers (Crosnoe 2007).

Welcoming practices and actions in support of the child immigrant

When Therese, a young Haitian parent, came to the local preschool, she was hesitant to enter. Born in Haiti, she had come as a child to live in the United States. Memories of her years at school were not always the most pleasant ones and she had not forgotten. Now as a parent herself, she wanted her child to have the best experience. Though she had moved over a month earlier to the community, she was still unsure as to what programs she would find for her 3-year-old child. That morning, she went to a local center she heard about from some neighbors. The moment she entered, she was greeted by the sounds of the children playing outdoor. She could distinctively hear the echo of the children's voices in familiar languages and others unknown to her. That drew a smile on her face as she walked to the director's office. Years later, she shared that seeing especially the sign that read in various languages, "Welcome children, welcome families," made her feel it was the place for her child and that indeed it was.

Impressions are always long-lasting experiences. Fortunately, for Therese, finding a center for her young daughter proved to be a successful experience. This helped erase what she had experienced during her childhood. Many times, we may not be aware of the importance of those impressions emanating from the multiple messages in a classroom, center, or even in community environments. Yet, they are very powerful. They are especially powerful for families and children coming from other places and cultures, where for many, they are their entry experience into mainstream society. They are, too, for immigrant families and children already living in our communities. Environments inviting children to learn and families to feel welcome are precisely the settings envisioned in early childhood education. They are also where diversity is celebrated as attention is on the development, care, and well-being of the child. Such settings are also the ones that welcome immigrant children.

The multiple facets of early childhood classroom environments

Coming into a classroom is an experience and an important transition in the life of a child. This transition is even more important when the child comes from experiences and cultural contexts different from those of the school. Such is the case of immigrant children, entering a new social and cultural situation where their development will continue to unfold. A sixth-grade immigrant student shared comments about her experiences, saying, almost melancholically, that "At home it was so different. They always knew my name and had friends. Here they changed my name and sometimes I don't' even know if it is me anymore."

Vygotsky (1978) considered environments as social and cultural contexts that promote children's learning and where they develop a sense about self (Michell 2016). In her study of child immigrants, Guo (2018) highlighted the importance of a sociocultural view on the role of environments as an influential element. She further posited that the children's relation to the environment or social situation is an influential element in their development, calling for its consideration in the teaching process. Moll (1992) also recognized the role of environments as a leading element on children's adaptation to the classroom. The use of funds of knowledge is in itself a way to insert familiar elements into an environment new to the child. How children see themselves in an environment goes beyond just the physical space or materials. It rather calls for a broad angle perspective at those factors that influence one's sense of belonging and relationship in the social environment of the classroom.

Multidimensional character of classroom environments

The classroom is more than just a physical space. It is rather multidimensional. Classroom environments can be seen as having five dimensions: emotional, cognitive, physical, cultural, and what happens at home (Figure 5.2). Dimensions are interrelated across experiences, calling for intentional consideration and purposeful planning. The first four dimensions must respond to what is developmentally appropriate and consciously centered on children, as experiences are built to meet their needs and individual realities. Together, they form the ecology of the child's day-to-day experiences and emphasize goals supporting development that foster their success.

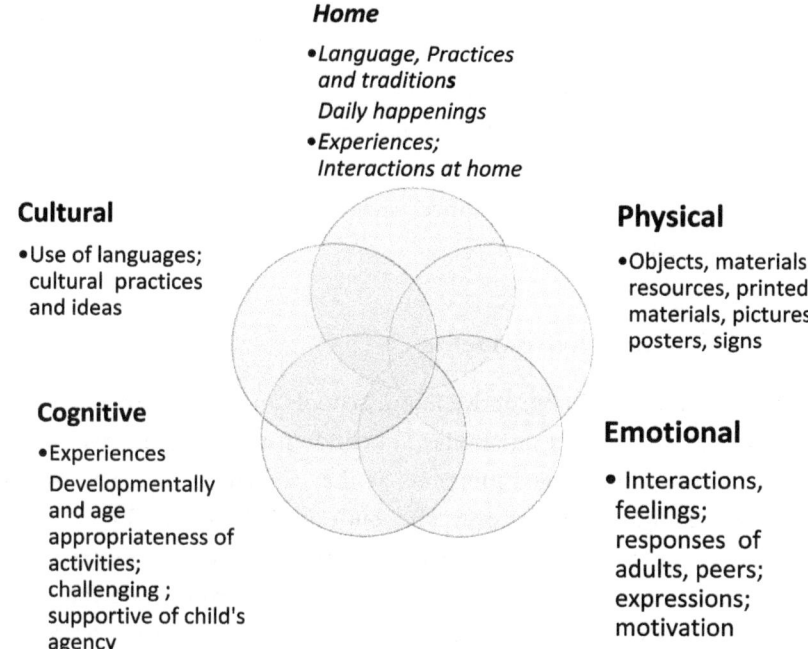

Home

•*Language, Practices and traditions*
Daily happenings
•*Experiences;*
Interactions at home

Cultural

•Use of languages; cultural practices and ideas

Cognitive

•Experiences Developmentally and age appropriateness of activities; challenging ; supportive of child's agency

Physical

•Objects, materials , resources, printed materials, pictures, posters, signs

Emotional

• Interactions, feelings; responses of adults, peers; expressions; motivation

Figure 5.2 Five dimensions of classroom environments.
Source: Guo 2018; Robles de Melendez and Beck (2019).

Including home as another key environment

A note about including home as an environment is pertinent. Guo (2018) considered the home culture environment as another setting central to consider given its influence on children's learning experiences and outcomes. Everyday events taking place at home are undeniably influential in a child's life. For that reason, home is also added as another environment integral to the spectrum of experiences influencing the child. What happens at home is of relevance to early educators to better inform decisions and practices. It is particularly relevant, too, when working with immigrant children. Awareness of the challenges encountered as families navigate their realities and make sense about daily experiences helps us in understanding children and their needs as these arise. It also helps us in considering the many assets coming from home that children bring to the classroom.

Knowledge about what happens at home and the child's culture is what informs us about the multiple funds of knowledge children bring to the classroom, which Moll (1992) pointed out as a critical element in addressing children's cultural heritage. Home interactions and the network of happenings and events reveal the abilities and special ways families have to address and adjust to life (Abo-Zena 2018). They also allow us to learn about their sense of care and commitment to children that defines interactions and responses to their young. So is as well their high regard for education conveyed in their support for their children. Collaborative work with children's home is integral to early childhood education, a practice that is underlined when working to address the needs of young immigrants.

Finding self in new environments

Every day immigrant children arrive in our schools and begin new experiences in contexts that for many are unfamiliar. For children and certainly their parents, these are emotionally charged moments as they transition into new settings. Transitions are always hard for everyone, but especially for children. They are even harder when children are coming into environments where culture, setting, arrangements, people, and language may be different from those familiar to them. In their analysis of migrant children's classroom experiences, Picchio and Mayer (2019) indicated that coming into our classrooms is where many child immigrants encounter the spectrum of diversity for the first time. This fact is another challenge children face as they begin to process new experiences and new cultural frameworks. It further challenges how they see and find themselves in the setting.

New experiences always bring new challenges. As children begin to make sense of new realities and contexts, fostering opportunities for children to feel emotionally connected is critical. Responsive attention and understanding are vital to ease their adjustment to new realities. Social and cultural principles posit that impressions, the feeling of belonging, and the overall cues and climate of the environment can directly influence the behavior, performance, and socioemotional state of the child (Berk 2015; Trawick 2018). The nature and quality of interactions and social relationships that child immigrants establish with peers and teachers has been seen to be a contributing factor in their adaptation to new routines and patterns (Adelman and Taylor 2015; Picchio and Mayer 2019).

Intrinsic to the child's success in a new setting is the nature of relationships they build, which gradually becomes their emerging social network. Friendships contribute to supporting their sense of belonging for children in a new setting. This is a relevant factor pointed out by researchers (Katz 2014; Sime and Fox 2015) as central to the success of child immigrants. The child's own agency and motivation is instrumental in establishing relationships and connections with peers. Buddy system, a strategy long used in classrooms, is an effective way to support interactions with peers. As children begin to feel they belong, their own feelings contribute to building and establishing relationships with peers. These, in turn, support their interest and motivate their participation. Undoubtedly, and as Guo (2018) contends, consideration to the child's ability to build relationships is relevant given its implications on their learning and progress. With the classroom forming part of the ecology of the child growing up, the character of relationships with peers and teachers is a leading influence on the child's sense of belonging. Following what is best for children, deliberate efforts to make immigrant children feel as part of the group are vital to supporting children's social and emotional needs in an environment where they feel welcome with caring and trusting early childhood educators (Figure 5.3).

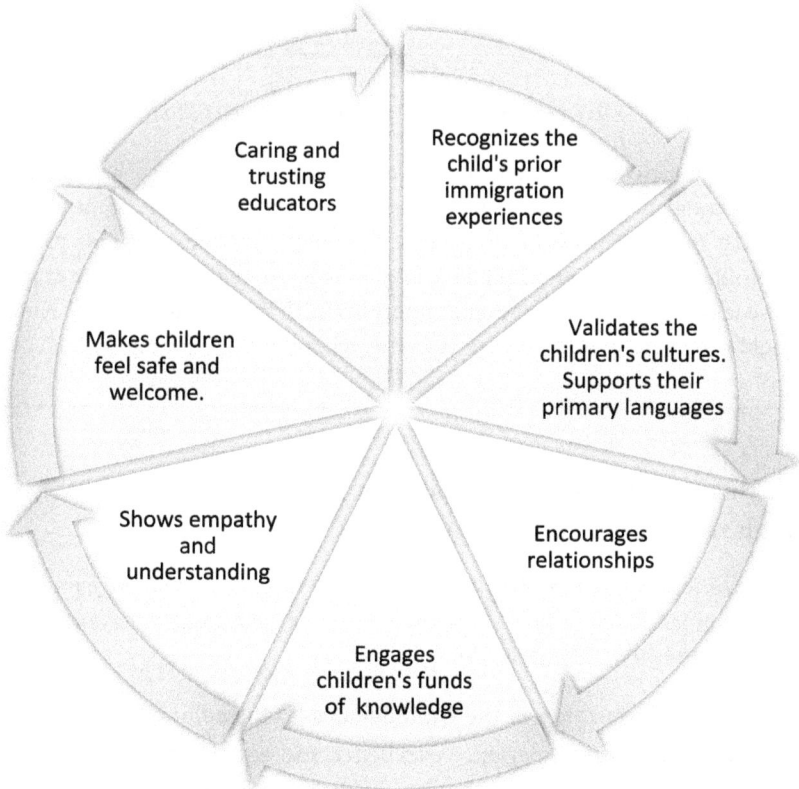

Figure 5.3 Child immigrants need emotionally supportive environments.
Source: Guo (2018); Moll (1992); Robles de Melendez and Beck (2019).

All children need emotionally supportive environments

Emotionally supportive environments welcome children and lead them to see themselves as part of the group. For child immigrants, an emotionally supportive setting begins with consideration of the diverse immigration experiences and to how they weigh on children. In some cases, distressful experiences may have marked the period prior to or after their entry into the country for the child and the family. It may as well include difficult events for children of immigrants born in the United States due to their own family experiences. Transitioning into a new school or starting school for the first time adds another experience to the overall stressful nature of what children may have already endured. This reality demands conscious consideration and attention to the child's needs during a vulnerable time. Keeping in mind that their experiences vary across the range of possible life events, whether they are foreign born or born to immigrant parents in the United States, attention to the emotional needs and sense of belonging is fundamental to their success.

Time to reflect ... *Encountering diversity*

Coming to new places is an exciting experience. It could also become an intimidating one as we encounter diversity. From the perspective of the child, consider for a moment the things in a classroom or center that may prove unfamiliar to an immigrant child recently arriving from another culture or for those familiar with different home cultures. Which ones would they be? How would you lessen or address their impressions and possible feelings?

In the classroom: Promoting learning through responsive experiences

[The] mission is to promote student achievement and preparation for global competitiveness by fostering educational excellence and ensuring equal access. (U.S. Department of Education [2011])

The aspiration of education in the United States, as the epigraph to this section reads, is for students to experience excellence and equal opportunities. As the aspiration of the nation, this implicitly establishes inclusivity, that is, for every child to find responsive and high-quality experiences fostering their potential.

This is, too, what is hoped will guide the experience of immigrant children in our classrooms.

Socially just efforts call for responsive practices that value and respect the learning potential of the child. This is a central tenet in early childhood education. It also addresses what is in the best interest for children. That every child brings assets and a capacity to learn is a premise guiding our teaching and learning efforts. At the same time, every child has individual experiences we must recognize and consider as classroom activities are planned to support their learning. Effective practices for child immigrants call for experiences that build and support their cognitive capacities. Because learning is empowering and a right for all children, learning experiences for all children must be guided by what is meaningful and challenging to the child. This is the same premise defining learning activities and expectations for young immigrant students. Moreover, this is what must permeate the classroom learning environment. High expectations are inclusive of all children and demonstrate respect for their capacities (Lundy-Ponce 2010). Views about curricular modifications due to language and cultural differences are many times misinterpreted. Often these end in diluted activities that deny the child's potential and capacity to learn.

Teaching for children's success

Building a positive, challenging, and meaningful cognitive environment begins with knowledge about the child. Robles de Meléndez and Beck (2019, 175) point out that early childhood educators "need to incorporate both the perspectives of diversity and developmentally based practices into their instruction in an effort to respond to the whole child." Consciously centering practices on what every child immigrant needs demands thorough knowledge about the social and cultural realities experienced by the child and family. They also call for presenting activities that are relevant and that challenge the child, fostering growth accordingly to the children's capacities. Awareness about the child's culture and own funds of knowledge provides a source for anchoring experiences in what is familiar to children while making experiences appropriate and inviting. Emphasis on learning outcomes and preparation for future schooling success should be paramount as experiences are planned. The success principle that guides efforts in classrooms must be what leads teaching and learning practices for young immigrant children. Such orientation regards and asserts what is fair and equitable for children.

Supportive and responsive practices

The environment remains an influential force in what individuals experience. It is as well for young children coming to experience schools in the nation's communities. Every year, thousands of immigrant children begin attending schools for the first time. Encounters in environments where the culture of practices and expectations differs from that of their neighborhoods and home are an impactful experience for the young child. Beginning school in a new place and new culture continues as challenging transitions for children. Elenna, an experienced primary teacher born to immigrant parents, shared that over the years working with child immigrants, she learned and understood how emotionally challenging those first days were for children. She began a practice of having in the classroom an object, a picture, or simply something familiar to children, she pointed out, that would "ease their fear." Remembering her own schooling days as a child, her practice was a way to address the emotions evoked by new experiences. Familiar objects, materials in their home language, and music related to their cultural knowledge (Moll 1992) help children to feel connected to what is known to them while they begin to build experiences. Developmentally, they are important elements helping individuals to feeling emotionally safe. They also provide experiences with lasting memories. This is what we heard from an educator, born in Nicaragua, who came as a child with his family. Now a professional health educator, he shared that he still remembers how his primary teachers made him feel welcome. His third-grade teacher would always include something about his country. He cannot forget the day he came to school. The flag from his country of birth was in the classroom. Perhaps just a detail, but one that he still cherishes. Teacher's knowledge about the impact of changes on the child drives many actions. Just like what José experienced as a child, which eased the emotional transition into a new culture and reality. These are times when children are more vulnerable, which warrants our understanding and support (Box 5.3).

Box 5.3 Connecting ideas: *Easing transitions into the classroom*

Arriving into a classroom in a culture different from that of your own or from that of your family is always a challenging experience. Transitioning into a context where expectations may differ from those familiar to the child can be frustrating for children. In the children's book *Cleversticks* (Ashley 1995), the main character is a young Chinese child experiencing some frustration adjusting to his classroom just as what many immigrant children may experience. While it was challenging for him to master some of the same activities as those of his peers, the observant eye of the teacher noticed his ability to use chopsticks, something characteristic of his family funds of cultural knowledge. Tapping on these as a strength made the child feel proud about his own abilities. Though a fictional story, the message clearly highlights the importance of recognizing the special abilities and strengths each child brings from their cultures. In turn, a child's special abilities and strengths can become vital in supporting the children's social and emotional needs in the context of their classrooms.

Considering the needs of immigrant children and of their peers

At all times, consideration of the developmental needs of both immigrant children and their peers is paramount. Early childhood is a period where their social and emotional skills are emerging and developing. The feelings perceived in a classroom may send strong social and emotional messages. Those feelings children perceive as they enter and participate every day in the classroom are powerful moments influencing one's sense about who we are. One may perceive "a sense of welcome and acceptance or of something quite the opposite, such as fear and rejection" (Robles de Meléndez and Beck 2019, 229). The implications are clear. Concerns about the child's social and emotional development heighten the need for intentional attention to the climate of classrooms and settings, where both child immigrants and their peers must feel safe and emotionally comfortable. It is essential to remember that often it is not only the child immigrant who faces diversity but also their peers who may be experiencing it. Such cases continue to occur and are not uncommon, particularly as immigrants settle in communities in new destination states throughout the nation (Terrazas 2011). In some of these communities still adapting to work with immigrants, individual experiences may send confusing messages to children and families. Many times these are unintentional as people learn more about cultures of immigrants. Consciously adopting practices anchored on antibias and multicultural tenets contextualizes the children's experiences and interactions in environments that promote inclusiveness and diversity. Such environments serve as places where child immigrants together with their peers experience the diversity present in their new communities and where they learn about their own diverse ways and that of others (Guo 2018).

Proactive contexts: Counteracting prejudice and discrimination

Given the influential role of the media on society, including children, we cannot dismiss exposure to the many mixed messages presented about immigrants. Similarly, it is relevant to consider what adults may share about immigrants. Sadly, children are exposed at times to comments with misleading views and opinions. This makes it imperative to take deliberate steps to prevent any misguided impressions to which children may have been exposed and which may be shared in the classroom. Social justice efforts remind everyone that "It is important to move away from conceptualizations of immigrant students as taking up resources, and toward a view that they are deserving of an investment of resources" (Perez 2011, 150). Valuing the contributions of immigrants is central in a society solidly rooted in the efforts of immigration. Making that happen begins with efforts consistently aimed at stopping offensive actions and behaviors.

The classroom: Where we can counteract bias and discrimination

As contexts of reception, classrooms and school grounds play a role in the types of discrimination children and their families may encounter (Adair 2015). Discrimination in its many manifestations is a rejection to the reality of diversity that defines us as individuals. While every immigrant could become the target of discriminatory practices, it has been found that threat of discrimination increases, in particular, for families that feel rejected and for those with lower resources (Adair 2015; Tobin, Arzubiaga, and Adair 2014). Many times, discrimination happens in subtle ways, many times disguised as simple comments. Whatever their form they all hurt and offend the same way. Becoming aware of comments, expressions, signs of rejection or isolation helps to address discriminatory behaviors. More importantly, it will prevent these from happening. Presence of unfair discourse about immigration and immigrants calls for our attention to how they may influence experiences when children are encountering diversity and how we take steps to address incidents as they arise. Though difficult, consciously centering practices on addressing these incidents as they happen is essential to prevent prejudice formation. Responses to incidents as these occur will set the tone for fair interactions in the community environment of the classroom. Classrooms and schools are a significant influential factor in the experiences of young immigrants and their families. This makes practices directed at preventing formation of misleading concepts to be of utmost relevance.

At the heart of early childhood practices is the child's well-being. Peers play a major influential role in what children experience and how that contributes to feeling as part of the group. Preparing children to receive and welcome peers from immigrant backgrounds is essential. Just as we mentioned earlier, attending school may be a first encounter with cultural diversity for child immigrants. It may be as well for peers (Guo 2018). For classroom peers, it may also be an initial experience facing diversity or where they find themselves confronted with new diverse traits. In other words, it becomes an experience for both. How they respond varies. It depends on how steps are taken to support and address the needs of both child immigrants and their peers.

Time to reflect ... *Misguided views and blind spots*

Everyone needs to reflect on actions, comments, and expressions that may send confusing signals about diversity and, indeed, about immigration. Recognizing that blind spots may exist in people is a step to becoming consciously aware about the implications of our very own misunderstandings about diversity. Take a moment to reflect on your own views about immigration and honestly identify any *blind spots* in your thinking or in your expressions.

Classrooms where a multicultural and an antibias orientation permeates experiences promote a sense of commonalities, shared needs, and celebrate individual diversity. This climate, in turn, frames interactions among peers where immigrant children and peers meet and learn about each other. More importantly, it prevents discrimination, a negative and damaging behavior that, unfortunately, is present in the repertoire of experiences of immigrant children (Adair 2015; Carnock 2015; Waters and Eschbach 1995). Studies showed that often immigrant children experience rejection from peers and are considered as having a lower social position (Neitzel, Drennan, and Fouts 2019). Linguistic differences including gestural language, ridiculing because of accent, food choices, dress codes, and appearance describe some of the aspects becoming targets for discriminatory behaviors experienced in classrooms (Adair 2015; Carnock 2015) and in neighborhoods. Intervention and consideration to the ill-effects of discrimination are essential. Memories about discriminatory experiences remain forever and are one of the adverse childhood situations children may encounter. They are preventable and demand from everyone intentional interventions as they occur.

Time has come to eliminate misguided ideas about immigrants, and the early childhood classroom is an environment where prosocial actions find its starting place. With consciously centered practices guiding efforts of educators, they can positively contribute to eliminating prejudiced and devaluing views.

Time to reflect ... *Multicultural and antibias practices*

Today's community and classroom contexts are characterized by what has been called *superdiversity*. This heightens the need for an approach promoting understanding and respect for differences across the spectrum of multiculturalism and diversity. Consider the current teaching practices in your setting and find out if these reflect an antibias perspective. If they do not, what would you propose to amend them?

Resiliency and the immigrant child

Resiliency, a trait depictive of individuals who overcome challenges, is a factor characterizing many immigrant stories. It is, in fact, a basic human capacity, nascent in all children (Grotberg 1995, 3). Despite the challenges and difficult experiences faced during the immigration experience, the achievements and success of some individuals and families continue to highlight their resiliency (Adelman and Taylor 2015). Deemed as a protective factor, resiliency guards and counteracts some individuals during stressful situations fostering skills "that augment an individual's potential to rebound after trauma" (Arnetz et al. 2013, 7).

The resilient capacity exhibited by immigrant children to deal with and overcome obstacles in the face of adverse circumstances has been evident over time. Studies show that children who are resilient shared as a common factor having at least one constant and a dedicated relationship with a supportive adult, whether a parent, caregiver, or any other important adult (Center on the Developing Child 2017; Masten 2018). In schools and centers, teachers play a pivotal role in providing supportive relationships with children that encourages their capacity to cope with challenges. To many, relationships with teachers during their schooling experience remain the factor that provides opportunities to build their own sense of efficacy as they adapt to new realities (Box 5.4).

> ## Box 5.4 Connecting ideas: *Resiliency as a strength of immigrant children*
>
> Resilience loosely defined is the ability to overcome trauma or challenging experiences positively while exposed to social and emotional challenges. It has been pointed out that resiliency is a factor explaining the ability of immigrants to overcome some of their difficult circumstances. Most young children are emotionally buoyant, bounce back quickly, and live resilient lives as they mature (Masten 2011; Petty 2009). Difficult situations, unfortunately, are not excluded from happening to a child. Whenever these happen, the circle of support that a child has is instrumental in fostering their emotional strength to overcome difficult circumstances. Through family support, extended family support, caregivers, and quality early childhood programs responsive to their feelings and strengths, resilience will flourish. Most importantly, young children need at least one caring adult with whom they can attach to offset the challenges they face each day (Petty 2014). Understanding educators play a role in becoming that person who cares for the child's well-being and can offer the support needed for them to become resilient.

Self-efficacy is the belief that one is capable of managing situations and persevering even if faced with stressful and anxiety-producing situations (Santrock 2005). Self-efficacy is an internally developed factor used to overcome challenging situations. It significantly influences a child's success or failure in the future (Masten 2018). Stories in communities everywhere in the country continue to evidence the successful outcomes of immigrants whose sense about self has led them to overcome realities and obstacles.

See me as I am!

All children have special gifts—this is a statement heard many times. At its core, it reflects the need for valuing who and what children are, what they bring, and the promise they embody. This is the thought that should emerge every time we see and talk about child immigrants. It is also the aspiration and hope of immigrants in classrooms and communities across the country. But, important to remember is that child immigrants are simply children. Seeing them as they are is what many have expressed, reflected in what the authors once heard from a 9-year-old. He firmly said, "Que me vean como soy y lo que puedo, that they see me as I am and what I can do."

Indisputably, we must remember the challenges they face before their migration and afterward. The varying levels of vulnerability to which so many are exposed, sometimes only because they are immigrants, cannot be ignored. In fact, stereotyped views about immigrants continue to send distorted messages to society. Sadly, these messages extend themselves to children, compounding or adding to their vulnerable circumstances. Because of the promise that each child embodies, it is time to begin seeing child immigrants not from the point of what they lack but rather from a strengths-based perspective. The stories and experiences of child immigrants are as diverse as life could possibly be. Conscious about their multiple realities, we need to refocus our views and consider the capacities and potential they have brought and continue to bring into our communities and classrooms. Rather than seeing weaknesses and deficits, the call is to see potential and strengths (Doucet and Adair 2018). This position underlines views not only about their resiliency, as discussed earlier, but also of agency, determination, and, most importantly, equality. They all describe some of the many strengths they bring. Takanishi (2004) called for leveling the playing field with respect to child immigrants. She firmly advocated for socially just efforts that provide balanced and fair access and services to immigrant children. If we are to level it, education and society must begin by ascertaining the numerous strengths and inherent qualities of children and families of immigrant roots. It also needs to take a focus on empathy and understanding to value and appreciate their efforts and what children represent for the future of the nation.

Seeing strengths: Agency, determination, and aspirations

Perhaps one of the strengths characterizing immigrants is precisely their aspirations, which also power and drive their own sense of agency. Esmeralda Santiago's account of her experiences as a Puerto Rican immigrant (1993) illustrate the will to overcome the challenges she faced. Coming during her early adolescence to New York City, she faced multiple challenges and negative experiences. Yet, these did not deter but rather fueled her own will to overcome her reality. She writes in her book, *When I Was Puerto Rican*, "And now here you are, about to graduate from Harvard" (Santiago 1993, 270), graduating from college and becoming a known author. Like her, many others have also shown their strong sense of agency, their determined will to act and to effect changes.

Similar stories continue today to be written in classrooms of young and older children throughout the nation.

Voices of immigration: *My story*

The quest for safety and stability continues motivating families to immigrate. The experience of living and growing up in a country different from that of your birth takes you into a journey of hard work and encounters with new realities in a different cultural context. This is what we hear in the reflections shared by an educator who came to the United States as a toddler.

My parents decided to leave Cuba and immigrated to West New York, New Jersey before Castro took power. They left my older brother and sister with my grandparents in Cuba. At the time, I was 17 months old. My siblings would come two years later once we were established. My parents and I went to live with my aunt, uncle, and cousins, already set in West New York, New Jersey. My father worked factory jobs, and then he was able to find work in embroidery. They also worked long shifts; my mother worked days, and my father worked the graveyard shift. My brother and sister were both placed in first grade even though my brother was older than my sister by almost two years. The result was that my older brother would graduate high school later than most students.

My mother had a 5 or 6th-grade education and my father a third-grade education; both worked fulltime at an early age. Due to their limited education and English language skills, they rarely went into the public schools their children attended. We knew, though, that if the school called, we would be in big trouble. My mother watched Italian movies and worked predominantly with Italian immigrants. She understood Italian, and they understood Spanish; therefore, my mother learned very little English but understood Italian.

New Jersey was fascinating, populated almost exclusively by immigrants. The population was composed predominantly of Italian immigrants, but I remember friends that spoke Greek, Polish, German, and Spanish at home. Their parents answered the phone in a myriad of languages. West New York, New Jersey, was a beautiful place to grow.

After winter snow storms and spring rains, the long summer days were welcome to all. In the summer, I was allowed to play outside from morning until night. We played bottle caps, marbles, hopscotch, raced, manhunt, and many other fun active games as we ran up and down our block. My father soon informed me that girls should not be playing outside at my age. I was restricted to playing on my porch. I couldn't understand why my older brother, only a year and a half older than my sister, could leave whenever he wanted to. My sister and I could not; this was part of our Hispanic culture.

My grandparents moved to Hialeah, and my parents decided to follow. I decided to come along first. Hialeah was when I experienced discrimination first hand. There were few Hispanics attending school at the local high school in 1972, but the Hispanic migration was beginning. The following school year there were many more Hispanics. My mother was a factory worker doing finish work for clothing all her life both in West New York and now, in Hialeah, Florida. When I graduated from high school, I worked one summer with her in the factory. I do not know how my poor mother worked so many years in such poor conditions. Finish workers stood at a table all day trimming string off of garments as quickly as possible. No talking was the rule unless as some did, you talked to yourself.

My older brother studied art and then received a full scholarship to the University of Miami and graduated as an art major. Later he would enter the fire department, ride rescue for many years and became a Captain. I became a teacher and later a university professor that strongly values diversity.

Many immigration scholars have brought attention to the child immigrants' own sense of agency. Undeniably, the ability demonstrated by child immigrants to successfully address circumstances in their communities and classrooms proves their sense of agency. Daily experiences reveal how child immigrants navigate and find ways to socially construct their understanding of new experiences and expectations. Their actions also reveal their determination in exerting actions. This is what is observed in the actions of children who become their parents' translators and whose determination helps their families navigate life in their communities. Coming as a young child and today a teacher educator, she shared her experiences as her parents' translator. She says,

At first, my older brother or sister were my parents' translators. Then as my brother became more involved in cross-country track and my sister began working at 13 for a local dry cleaner, I was usually the one to accompany my parents as the translator for jobs, social security, banks, etc. (Personal communication, March 12, 2019)

We see children's agentic behavior in so many facets of their experiences in the classroom. We see it as well in young immigrant children coming with no knowledge of English and, yet, find ways to communicate with peers and adults and make themselves understood as their linguistic proficiency develops. Some of us marveled during a visit to a kindergarten classroom where we met a young 5-year-old talking with his teacher in English. Just a few months earlier, as we learned from his teacher, he had arrived from a non-English-speaking country and was now eagerly talking to everyone in English. No less impressive is the ability displayed by countless children who become the language connector with their families and the school and community. Knowledge of languages is, in fact, another right of the immigrant child, positioning them to be able to understand cultural nuances of both their culture and that of their classrooms and communities.

That children have the ability to initiate efforts and changes is a fact recognized by those endorsing the child's own sense of agency, that is, of action (Duggin 2011). We see the children's agency and determination and who, despite the experiences, although sometimes dramatic, continue to reach their goals. A commitment to their aspirations both personal and for the family is a strength noticeably observed among immigrants. For Mariana, whose family came from the Philippines, the day she entered her primary school classroom was the beginning of her road to making her parents' dreams come true. This is what she still remembers years later as she shared while waiting to graduate from university. Unquestionably, she persevered through her school years, both to meet her own goals and to honor her parents' aspirations for her, too. There were difficult moments, as she shared, but though shaken up at times, she never doubted she would make things happen. We also heard a student from a rural community in Mexico who struggled with the attitudes she encountered but whose determined attitude guided her to "demostrarle a todos que llegaría a tener éxito, show everyone that it was possible for me to succeed."

Building bridges and engaging families

During a parent meeting with migrant parents mostly from Central America, the comments shared by many echoed what one of the mothers said: "*Me hacen sentir que puedo y que me necesitan*, they made me feel that I can and that am needed." Her comments were a statement of what is expected when families and schools are engaged. "*No sabía que tenía tanto poder*," I did not know that I had so much power, was the comment heard from a father during a meeting at a rural center. Wanting to know if more could be done to support children at the center his children attended, he was encouraged to share his concern at the board meeting. His comment is an example of respectful and participatory parent engagement, where parents' needs and ideas are welcomed and considered. This is the vision of programs pursuing what is best for young immigrant children, building bridges of understanding with families. This is, as well, what was envisioned by Ira Gordon (1979), a pioneer educator whose visionary efforts laid down the tenets of family engagement. His thoughtful work underlined the shared and equally respected role of parents and teachers working together for children. Gordon's ideas influenced the parent partnerships views of the budding Head Start program at the time, continuing today to set the course for true partnerships.

Efforts in early childhood education have always recognized the role and need for parent and family participation in schools. Intrinsic to children's successful experiences, collaborations of parents and teachers have been marked as instrumental in yielding positive learning outcomes (Berger and Riojas-Cortez 2019; Jung and Zhang 2016). Studies have shown a definite link between students' achievement and parent and family involvement. This has also been identified as an influential factor in the educational success of immigrant children (Jung and Zhang 2016; Poza, Brooks, and Valdes 2014; Turney and Kao 2009). Interest and concerns about the developmental and educational success of immigrant children remain as one of the goals emphasizing collaborations with parents and families. Together, they can better meet and address their holistic needs.

Interest in school involvement of immigrant families has yielded valuable findings, though more remains to be researched with specific attention to this population, especially as it grows more ethnically diverse. Some studies have indicated that the dedication and commitment of immigrant families to their children's success is one of the reasons responsible for their resilient character amid challenges (Suárez-Orozco and Suárez-Orozco 2001). However, when it comes to school involvement, the image that continues to arise is one of lesser participation (Berger and Riojas-Cortez 2019; Poza, Brooks, and Valdes 2014). Many staff and teachers often consider their "lack of active involvement" (Thao 2009, 4) as signaling disinterest in their children's education. Others, however, see the level of their involvement as an indication of their concern and care for their children's success (Turney and Kao 2009). Contrary to these opinions, parents and families hold the education of their children in high regard (Jung and Zhang 2016; Li et al. 2016; Poza, Brooks, and Valdes 2014). The ongoing sacrifices made by parents are the best testimony about their decided aspiration for children to receive a good education and to have a better future. Still, we cannot discount the fact that parents and families continue to face barriers that obstruct their fuller engagement. Existing and prevalent deficit views about immigrant families continue to negate appreciation of their rich experiences and diverse cultures (da Silva Iddings and Reyes 2017; González, Moll, and Amanti 2005).

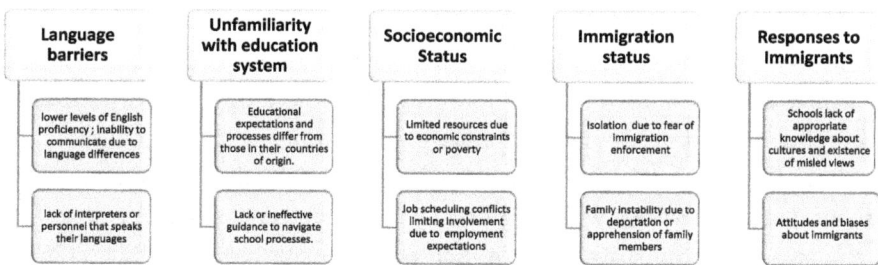

Figure 5.4 Barriers impacting immigrant parents' school involvement.

Barriers to parent and family engagement

While research confirms the commitment of immigrant parents for their children, in the view of many, their participation remains as a challenge. Undoubtedly, the experience and conditions of their immigration journey weight into how families integrate into the realities of their new communities and schools (Beauregard, Petrakos, and Dupont 2014). Circumstances surrounding their arrival, ability to speak English, location and knowledge about the system influence their level of engagement with their children's schools. Along with this, a series of factors have been identified as responsible for the apparent lower involvement. Ranging from language issues to immigration, these are obstacles continuing to impact immigrant parent and family participation in schools. Some of these are listed in Figure 5.4. Some of the main barriers gathered from the literature are discussed in the section that follows (Abo-Zena, 2018; Jung and Zhang 2016; Nyemba and Chitiyo 2018; Poza et al. 2014; Takanishi 2004; Turney and Kao 2009).

Language barriers emerging from linguistic diversity has been shown as one of the main obstacles impacting communication with schools and teachers. It has been identified as well as one of the factors influencing lower levels of involvement in schools. On the other hand, studies have revealed that immigrant parents with English proficiency tend to have higher involvement in schools, thus impacting their children's opportunities for success (Jung and Zhang 2016). In some cases, parents with lower levels of English proficiency abstained from participating in school meetings, adducing frustration since meetings were held only in English (Turney and Kao 2009). Some have cited feeling less confident and embarrassed to talk due to their lower proficiency levels.

Unfamiliarity with the educational system, which in many cases largely differs from those of their home countries, also becomes another obstacle for many parents. Difficulty understanding schools' expectations and processes adds to the lack of support networks that some families experience. This aspect, in fact, has been identified as an obstacle for immigrant parents in other countries. In Spain, a study of immigrant families revealed that lack of familiarity with the education system was found to hamper parents from participating in the local settings (Hernández-Prado et al. 2017). In many cases, the lack of knowledge about practices paired with linguistic barriers deters them from accessing services and programs available for their children. Nyemba and Chitiyo (2018) in their study about Zimbabwean mothers found that parents might experience a cultural shock as they encounter practices that differ from those known to them. However, as they noted, adapting to these varies across groups. Still, this makes efforts difficult for many parents who, even wanting to participate, find themselves hitting some grave obstacles. In addition, cultural views held about education also influence how families see and consider their role, position, and relationship with schools (Lynch and Hanson 2011). In some cases, experiencing bias and sometimes facing discriminatory responses, many times stemming from misconceptions about immigrants, was pointed out as another factor for lower involvement (Adair 2016).

Box 5.5 Connecting ideas: *Promising engagement practices*

Over the years, a number of programs have successfully responded to the needs of child immigrants and their families. Centered on the goal of engagement of families with diverse roots, numerous school programs already target practices that welcome families. One of these is the Head Start program that true to one of its building principles follows an engagement framework to anchor practices. The Head Start Parent, Family, and Community Engagement Framework (2018) provides a holistic view of contributing elements to ensure the well-being of the child and the family. Guiding practices and collaborations with families, the framework anchors activities on what is equitable and respectful to the child and family's heritage. Many schools and agencies offering services and programs directed at assisting immigrant families also emulate their principles. Efforts are needed to build the supportive niche for immigrant children in the country.

The social and economic status of immigrants has been highlighted as another factor affecting their involvement and participation (Jung and Zhang 2016; Karoly and González 2011; Takanishi 2004). While the social and economic spectrum of immigrants in the United States is very diverse, along that continuum, many immigrants continue to face challenging socioeconomic realities including living in poverty. According to McHugh (2016), immigrant families living in poverty are more predominant in some states, with the southern states having the highest number. In many of the communities where they live, resources available to families are limited, which further adds to their challenges. This limitation, in some cases, also reflects what is available at the schools where their children attend. Work schedules, which sometimes may include more than one job, many times limit their participation due to the timing of school activities. Still others face inadequate transportation or services to care for younger children that further impedes efforts to attend and getting involved in their children's schools. Despite the challenges, experiences of the authors have revealed to them the resilient character of parents and families who, despite difficult situations, go the extra mile to support their children.

The parents' immigration status continues as one of the obstacles affecting their engagement in schools' events and activities. As mentioned earlier, many families with undocumented immigration status and their children end up isolating themselves from community and school activities. In the majority of cases, their children were born in the United States and may not enjoy all the educational benefits they are rightfully entitled to receive (Yoshikawa and Kholoptseva 2013). Declining enrollment in schools and day care centers has been on the rise with the increase in deportations (Lovato et al. 2018), further impacting the educational opportunities of children.

The reality of their immigration status remains as a barrier and as a challenge to the integrity of the family. Recent emphasis on immigration enforcement, as pointed out before, drives many to stay away because of fear of deportation or prosecution (Zayas and Cook Heffron 2016).

Bias and discrimination: A persistent issue

Though there are countless stories and exemplary practices of school engagement and collaboration with immigrant families (see Box 5.5), the existence of continuing biases and prejudiced behaviors cannot be discounted. This is yet a continuing barrier deterring the best intentions of immigrant parents from participating and supporting their children's schools. These manifest themselves in a myriad of ways, with all being equally damaging and hurtful. Open and subtle disregard of parents' efforts and collaborations by school staff ends up sending unwelcoming messages. In some cases, responses to parents' accents and lower English proficiency discouraged many immigrants from attending activities and failing to build relationships with their children's schools. Biased responses, anchored in misleading views and lack of knowledge about the cultural experiences of parents and their children, absence of understanding, and inability to prioritize the needs of children all remain as detractors from engagement and involvement.

Hopeful and equitable outlook

In their study about inequality, Lee and Burkham (2002), referred to the need for "equality at the starting gate" as the way to end disparities and promote advanced opportunities for young children. Indeed, their words resonate with the idea of fairness, the guiding principle in practices consciously centered on meeting the needs of immigrants. Achieving success for children begins with determined efforts aimed at balancing opportunities and services where access is equitably provided. In today's US society, young child immigrants are a growing population not only in numbers but also in their diversity. While their realities are as diverse as their ethnicities, they represent one-quarter of the children in the country (Child Trends 2018). They are the seed for a hopeful future. Continuing efforts of advocates for the rights of immigrants remain as a hopeful promise. But, for this to happen, the call is for concerted actions that will make equity the feature descriptor of every immigrant child's experiences and opportunities.

Still needed …

Though there are many promising practices that continue to set the path for equity for young immigrant children, more remains to be done in the agenda for socially just actions. Among those actions, continuing efforts aimed at erasing bias and discrimination are central if we are to aspire to equitable experiences and opportunities for all children.

Key ideas

- Practices and decisions for immigrant children should be guided by the best interest principle. This principle entails the ethical responsibility that individuals and early childhood professionals must ensure that children's well-being is at the center of any action proposed or taken.

- Internationally, the rights of children are recognized by the United Nations' Convention on the Rights of the Child, which are extensive to immigrant children. They acknowledge the inalienable rights ascribed to childhood.
- Parents and advocates fought and won the rights to education in the United States for immigrant children through various landmark rulings. These legal victories recognized the value and the educational rights (K-12) of all children regardless of their immigration status.
- Many programs continue to serve and address the developmental and educational needs of the growing child immigrant population. Programs and services for immigrant children call for responsive attention and consideration to the experiences and needs of children.
- Despite the role of immigration in the historical trajectory of the country, discriminatory practices and prejudiced behaviors continue to be part of the realities of immigrants.
- Emphasis on collaborations with parents and families continues as one of the goals guiding programs and services. There are still many barriers to be overcome to fully ensure engagement of immigrant parents.

To think, do, and reflect ...

1. Using the framework of the *child's best interest*, identify some of the practices in your community that fit under this premise. Explain your reasoning on how that practice depicts the framework.
2. Many legal battles continue to assert the rights of immigrant children. Consider the implications of those victories discussed in this chapter and choose the one that in your view has been most relevant. Discuss the reasons for your selection.
3. In what ways would you make your school or community a welcoming place for immigrant children?
4. Review the barriers to immigrant parents and family involvement and identify the one that you consider to be most challenging in your community or school. What steps would you propose to erase that barrier?
5. What efforts would you suggest are needed to ensure successful and equitable experiences for immigrant children?

References

Abo-Zena, Mona. 2018. "Supporting immigrant-origin children: Grounding teacher education in critical developmental perspectives and practices." *Teacher Educator* 53(3): 263–76.

Adair, Jennifer. 2015. *The Impact of Discrimination on the Early Schooling Experiences of Children from Immigrant Families*. Washington, DC: Migration Policy Institute.

Adair, Jennifer. 2016. "Creating positive context of reception: The value of immigrant teachers in U.S. early childhood education programs." *Education Policy Analysis Archives* 24(1). Retrieved from http://dx.doi.org/10.14507/epaa.v24.2110.

Adelman, Howard, and Linda Taylor. 2015. "Immigrant children and youth in USA: Facilitating equity of opportunity at school." *Education Sciences* 5: 323–44.

Alston, Philip, and Bridget Gilmour-Walsh. 1996. *The Best Interest of the Child: Towards a Synthesis of Children's Rights and Cultural Values*. UNICEF. Retrieved from https://www.unicef-irc.org/publications/108-the-best-interests-of-the-child-towards-a-synthesis-of-childrens-rights-and-cultural.html.

Alvarez, Robert. 1986. "The Lemon Grove incident." In T. Scharf (ed.). The Journal of San Diego History. *San Diego Historical Society Quarterly* 32(2). Retrieved from https://sandiegohistory.org/journal/1986/april/lemongrove/.

American Immigration Council. 2016. *Public Education for Immigrant Students: Understanding Plyler v. Doe*. Retrieved from http://americanimmigrationcouncil.org/research/plyler-v-doe-public-education-immigrant-students.

Andrew, Hannah, and Deeana Jang. 2007. *The Challenge of Change: Learning from the Child Care and Early Education Experiences of Immigrant Families*. Foundation for Child Development. Center for Law and Social Policy.

Ansari, Arya, and Robert Crosnoe. 2011. "Immigration and the interplay of parenting, preschool enrollment, and young children's academic skills." *Journal of Family Psychology* 29(3): 382–93.

Arnetz, Judith, Yoasif Rofa, Bengt Arnetz, Matthew Ventimiglia, and Hikment Jamil. 2013. "Resilience as a protective factor against the development of psychopathology among refugees." *Journal of Nervous and Mental Disease* 201(3): 167–72.

Ashley, Bernard. 1995. *Cleversticks*. New York: Crown Publishers.

Barrueco, Sandra, Sheila Smith, and Samuel Stephens. 2015. *Supporting Parent Engagement in Linguistically Diverse Families to Promote Young Children's Learning. Implications for Early Care and Education Policy*. New York: Child Care & Early Education Research Connections.

Beauregard, France, Harriet Petrakos, and Audrey Dupont. 2014. "Family–school partnership: Practices of immigrant parents in Quebec, Canada." *School Community Journal* 24(1): 177–210. Retrieved from http://www.adi.org/journal/2014ss/BeauregardPetrakosDupontSpring2014.pdf.

Berger, Eugenia, and Mari Riojas-Cortez. 2019. *Parents as Partners in Education* (9th ed.). Boston, MA: Pearson.

Berk, Laura. 2015. *Infants and Children: Prenatal through Middle Childhood* (8th ed.). Boston, MA: Pearson.

Carbone, June. 2014. "Legal applications of the 'best interest of the child' standard: Judicial rationalization or a measure of institutional competence." *Pediatrics*, *134*, Supplement 2, S111–20. Retrieved from https://pediatrics. aappublications.org/content/pediatrics/134/Supplement_2/S111.full.pdf.

Carnock, Janie. 2015. "How young children of immigrants face discrimination at school" (blog post), September 18, 2015. Retrieved from https://www.newamerica. org/education-policy/edcentral/early-discrimination/.

Center on the Developing Child. 2017. "Resilience." Retrieved from https:// developingchild.harvard.edu/science/key-concepts/resilience/.

Child Rights Hub. 2019. *The Convention*. Retrieved from http://childrightshub.org/en/ the-convention/.

Child Trends. 2018. *Immigrant Children*. Retrieved from https://www.childtrends.org/ indicators/immigrant-children.

Copple, Carol, and Sue Bredekamp. 2009. *Developmentally Appropriate Practice in Early Childhood Programs Serving Children from Birth through Age 8* (3rd ed.). Washington, DC: NAEYC.

Crosnoe, Robert. 2007. "Early child care and the school readiness of children from Mexican immigrant families." *International Migration Review* 41(1): 152–81.

da Silva, Ana Christina, and Ileana Reyes. 2017. "Learning with immigrant children, families and communities: The imperative of early childhood teacher education." *Early Years* 37(1): 34–46.

de Feyter, Jessica, and Adam Winsler. 2009. "The early developmental competencies and school readiness of low-income, immigrant children: Influences of generation, race/ethnicity, and national origins." *Early Childhood Research Quarterly* 24(4): 411–31.

Derman-Sparks, Louise, and Julie Olsen Edwards. 2010. *Anti-Bias Education for Young Children and Ourselves*. Washington, DC: NAEYC.

Doucet, Fabienne, and Janet Adair. 2018. "Introduction: A vision for transforming early childhood research and practice for young children of immigrants and their families." In *Supporting Young Children of Immigrants Prek-3*. Bank Street Occasional Papers Series 39. New York.

Duggin, Shaun. 2011. *The Development of Sense of Agency*. Master's thesis. Georgia State University.

Fortuny, Karina, Donald Hernández, and Alan Chaudry. 2010. *Young Children of Immigrants: The Leading Edge of America's Future*. Washington, DC: Urban Institute.

Gelatt, Julia, Gina Adams, and Sandra Huerta. 2014. *Supporting Immigrant Families' Access to Prekindergarten*. Washington, DC: Urban Institute.

Gordon, Ira. 1979. "The effects of parent involvement on schooling." In I. Gordon (ed.), *Partners: Parents and Schools*, 4–25. Washington, DC: Association for Supervision and Curriculum Development.

Greenberg, Erica, Molly Michie, and Gina Adams. 2018. *Expanding Preschool Access for Children of Immigrants*. Washington, DC: Urban Institute.

Grotberg, Edith. 1995. *A Guide to Promoting Resilience in Children: Strengthening the Human Spirit. Early Childhood Development: Practice and Reflections. Number 8.* Hague, Netherlands: Bernard Van Leer Foundation.

Guo, Karen. 2018. "A comparative study of immigrant children starting childcare." *Exceptionality Education International* 27(2): 72–93.

Hernández, Donald, Nancy Denton, and Suzanne Macartney. 2008. "Children in immigrant families: Looking to America's future." *Social Policy Report* 22(3). Retrieved from https://files.eric.ed.gov/fulltext/ED521704.pdf.

Hernández-Prados, María Ángeles, María Paz García-Sanz, Joaquín Parra, and María Angeles Gomariz. 2016. "Involvement of immigrant families in the school life." *Procedia-Social and Behavioral Sciences* 237(21): 157–63.

Intercultural Development Research Association [IDRA]. 2014. *Immigrant Students' Rights to Attend Public Schools-School Opening Alert*. Retrieved from https://www.idra.org/resource-center/school-opening-alert-2/.

Jung, Eujoo, and Yue Zhang. 2016. "Parental involvement, children's aspirations, and achievement in immigrant families." *Journal of Educational Research* 109(4): 333–50.

Karoly, Lynn. 2016. "The economic returns to early childhood education." *The Future of Children* 26(2): 37–55.

Karoly, Lynn, and Gabriella Gonzalez. 2011. "Early care and education for children in immigrant families." *Future of Children* 21(1): 71–101.

Katz, Janice. 2014. *Guiding Children's Social and Emotional Development: A Reflective Approach*. Boston, MA: Pearson.

Krogstad, Jens, and Gustavo López. 2016. "Roughly half of Hispanics have experienced discrimination." *FactTank*. Pew Research Center. Retrieved from https://www.pewresearch.org/fact-tank/2016/06/29/roughly-half-of-hispanics-have-experienced-discrimination/.

Kugler, Eileen. 2017. "Supporting families in a time of fear." *Educational Leadership*. September: 26–32.

Lee, V., and D. Burkham. 2002. *Inequality at the Starting Gate: Social Background Differences in Achievement as Children Begin School*. Washington, DC: Economic Policy Institute.

Lessow-Hurley, Judith. 2009. *The Foundations of Dual Language Instruction* (5th ed.). Boston, MA: Pearson.

Li, Xuemei, Antoinette Doyle, Maureen Lymburner, and Needal Ghadi. 2016. "Parental support for newcomer children's education in a smaller centre." *Comparative and International Education/Education Comparee et Internationale* 45(3). Retrieved from http://ir.lib.uwo.ca/cie-eci/vol45/iss3/6.

Lovato, Kristina, Corina Lopez, Leyla Karimli, and Laura Abrams. 2018. "The impact of deportation-related family separations on the wellbeing of Latinx children and youth: A review of the literature." *Children and Youth Services Review* 95: 110–16.

Lundy-Ponce, Giselle. 2010. Migrant students: What we need to know to help them succed. ¡*Colorín colorado!* Retrieved from http://www.colorincolorado.org/article/migrant-students-what-we-need-know-help-them-succeed#h-strategies-for-success.

Lynch, Eleanor, and Marci Hanson (eds.). 2011. *Developing Cross-cultural Competence. A Guide for Working with Children and Their Families* (3rd ed.). Baltimore, MD: Paul Brookes.

Masten, Ann S. 2011. "Resilience in children threatened by extreme adversity: Frameworks for research, practice, and transitional synergy." *Development and Psychopathology* 23(2): 493–506.

Masten, Ann. S. 2018. "Resiliency theory and research on children and families: Past, present, and promise." *Journal of Family Theory and Review* 10: 12–31. Retrieved from https://onlinelibrary.wiley.com/doi/epdf/10.1111/jftr.12255.

McHugh, Margie. 2016. "New data resources can help improve targeting of state early childhood and parent-focused programs." *Commentary.* Accessed November 2018. Retrieved from https://www.migrationpolicy.org/news/new-data-resources-can-help-improve-targeting-state-early-childhood-and-parent-focused-programs#.

McLemore, S. Dale, and Harriet Romo. 2005. *Racial and Ethnic Relations in America* (7th ed.). Boston, MA: Pearson.

Michell, Michael. 2016. "Finding the 'prism': Understanding Vygotsky's *perezhivanie* as an ontogenetic unit of child consciousness." *International Research in Early Childhood Education* 7(1): 5–33.

Miller, Portia, Elizabeth Votruba-Drzal, and Rebekah Coley. 2013. "Predictors of early care and education type among preschool-aged children in immigrant families: The role of region of origin and characteristics of the immigrant experience." *Children and Youth Services Review* 35: 1342–55.

Misra, Tanvi. 2015. "The immigrant kids are not all right." *City Lab*, September 1. Accessed May 4, 2019. Retrieved from https://www.citylab.com/life/2015/09/the-immigrant-kids-are-not-all-right/403258/.

Moll, Luis. 1992. "Bilingual classroom studies and community analysis: Some recent trends." *Educational Researcher* 21(2): 20–4.

National Association for the Education of Young Children. 1995. *Responding to Linguistic and Cultural Diversity: A Position Statement of the National Association for the Education of Young Children*. Washington, DC: Author.

National Association for the Education of Young Children. 2011. *Code of Ethical Conduct and Statement of Commitment. A Position Statement of the National Association for the Education of Young Children* (2011). Reaffirmed. Washington, DC: Author.

Neitzel, Carin, Kelley Drennan, and Hilary Fouts. 2019. "Immigrant and nonimmigrant children's social interactions and peer responses in mainstream preschool classrooms." *Journal of Educational Research* 112(1): 46–60. doi: 10.1080/00220671.2018.1437529.

Nyemba, Florence, and Rufaro Chitiyo. 2018. "An examination of parental involvement practices in their children's schooling by Zimbabwean immigrant mothers in Cincinnati, Ohio." *Diaspora, Indigenous and Minority Education* 12(3): 124–38.

Olivas, Michael. 2010. *Plyler v. Doe: Still Guaranteeing Unauthorized Children's Rights to Attend U.S. Public Schools*. Retrieved from https://www.migrationpolicy.org.

Perez, William. 2011. *Americans by Heart: Undocumented Latino Students and the Promise of Higher Education*. New York: Teacher College Press.

Petty, Karen. 2009. "Using guided participation to support young children's social development." *YC: Young Children* 64(4): 80–5.

Petty, Karen. 2014. "Ten ways to foster, resilience in young children-teaching kids to bounce back." "Discover how caregivers can use activities to assist young children in building resilience." *Dimensions of Early Childhood* 42(3): 35–9.

Picchio, Mariacristina, and Sussana Mayer. 2019. "Transitions in ECEC services: The experience from migrant families." *European Early Childhood Education Research Journal* 27(2): 285–96.

Poza, Luis, Maneka Brooks, and Guadalupe Valdés. 2014. "'Entre Familia': Immigrant parents' strategies for involvement in children's schooling." *School Community Journal* 24(1): 119–48.

Robles de Meléndez, Wilma, and Vesna Beck. 2019. *Teaching Young Children in Multicultural Classrooms. Issues, Concepts and Strategies* (5th ed.). Boston, MA: Cengage.

Salas, Rachel. 2019. "What all teachers should know: The laws that provide undocumented, unaccompanied minors the right to an education in the United States." *Teachers College Record*. Retrieved from http://www.tcrecord.org ID number:22709.

Santiago, Esmeralda. 1993. *When I Was Puerto Rican: A Memoir*. Cambridge, MA: Da Capo Press.

Santrock, John. 2005. *Children* (8th ed.). New York: McGraw-Hill.

Schneiderman, Eric. 2016. "Immigrant children have a right to a good education." Commentary. *Education Week* 35(24): 18. Accessed May 3, 2019. Retrieved from https://www.edweek.org/ew/articles/2016/03/16/immigrant-children-have-a-right-to-a.html.

Shields, Margie, and Richard Berhman. 2004. "Children of immigrant families: Analysis and recommendations." *The Future of Children* 14(2): 4–15.

Sibley, Erin, and Brabeck Kalina. 2017. "Latino immigrant students; school experiences in the United States: The importance of family-school collaborations." *School Community Journal* 27(1): 137–57. Retrieved from http://www.schoolcommunitynetwork.org/SCJ.aspx.

Sime, Daniela, and Rachael Fox. 2015. "Migrant children, social capital and access to services post migration: Transitions, negotiations and complex agencies." *Children and Society* 29: 524–34. doi:10.1111/chso.12092.

Spears Brown, Christia. 2015. *The Educational, Psychological, and Social Impact of Discrimination on the Immigrant Child*. Washington, DC: Migration Policy Institute.

Strum, Philippa. 2010. *Mendez v. Westminster. School Desegregation and Mexican American Rights*. Kansas: University Press of Kansas.

Suárez-Orozco, Carola, and Marcelo Suárez-Orozco. 2001. *Children of Immigration*. Cambridge, MA: Harvard University Press.

Sugarman, Julie. 2019. *Legal Protections for K-12 English Learner and Immigrant-Background Students*. Issue Brief. Migration Policy Institute. Retrieved from https://www.migrationpolicy.org/research/legal-protections-k-12-english-learner-immigrant-students.

Takanishi, Ruby. 2004. "Leveling the playing field. Supporting immigrant children from birth to eight." *The Future of Children* 14(2): 60–79.

Terrazas, Aaron. 2011. *Immigrants in New-Destinations States*. Migration Policy Institute. Retrieved from https://www.migrationpolicy.org/article/immigrants-new-destination-states/.

Thao, Mao. 2009. "Parent involvement in schools. Engaging immigrant parents." *Snapshot*. Accessed May 9, 2019. Retrieved from https://files.eric.ed.gov/fulltext/ED511597.pdf.

Tienda, Marta, and Ron Haskins. 2011. "Immigrant children: Introducing the issue." *The Future of Children* 21(1): 3–18.

Tobin, Joseph, Angela Arzubiaga, and Jennifer Adair. 2014. *Children Crossing Borders*. New York: Russell Sage Foundation.

Trawick, Jeffrey. 2018. *Early Childhood Development: A Multicultural Perspective* (7th ed.). Boston, MA: Pearson.

Turney, Kristin, and Grace Kao. 2009. "Barriers to school involvement: Are immigrant parents disadvantaged?" *Journal of Educational Research* 10(4): 257–71.

UNHCR. 2018. *UNCHR BIP Guidelines. A Quick Guide to the New 2018 Guidelines on Assessing and Determining the Best Interest of the Child*. Retrieved from https://resourcecentre.savethechildren.net/node/11569/pdf/bip_guidelines_quick_guide_-_external.pdf.

United Nations. 1989. *Convention on the Rights of the Child*. Retrieved from https://www.ohchr.org/Documents/ProfessionalInterest/crc.pdf.

U.S. Department of Education. 2014. *Educational Services for Immigrant Children and Those Recently Arrived to the United States*. Fact Sheet. Retrieved from https://www2.ed.gov/policy/rights/guid/unaccompanied-children.html.

U.S. Department of Education. 2018. *Developing Programs for English Language Learners: OCR Memorandum*. Retrieved from https://www2.ed.gov/about/offices/list/ocr/ell/september27.html.

U.S. Department of Health and Human Services, Administration for Children and Families, Office of Head Start, National Center on Parent, Family, and Community Engagement. 2018. *Head Start Parent, Family, and Community Engagement Framework*.

Vandenbroeck. Michel. 2018. "Diversity in early childhood services." Revised edition. In *Encyclopedia of Early Childhood Development*. Retrieved from http://www. child-encyclopedia.com/sites/default/files/textes-experts/en/857/diversity-in-early-childhood-services.pdf.

Vygotsky, Lev. 1978. *Mind in Society: The Development of Higher Psychological Processes*. Cambridge, MA: Harvard University Press.

Waters, Mary and Karl Eschbach. 1995. "Immigration and ethnic and racial inequality in the United States." *Annual Review of Sociology* 21: 419–46.

Wright, Wayne. 2010. *Landmark Court Rulings Regarding English Language Learners*. Retrieved from http://www.colorincolorado.org/article/ landmark-court-rulings-regarding-english-language-learners.

Yoshikawa, Hirokazu, and Jenya Kholoptseva. 2013. *Unauthorized Immigrant Parents and Their Children's Development. A Summary of the Evidence*. Washington, DC: Migration Policy Institute.

Zayas, Luis, and Lauren Cook Heffron. 2016. *Disrupting Young Lives: How Detention and Deportation Affects Young lives Affect US-born Children of Immigrants*. CYF News. November. American Psychological Association. Retrieved from https://www. apa.org/pi/families/resources/newsletter/2016/11/detention-deportation.

Zuniga, Maria. 2011. "Families with Latino roots." In Eleanor Lynch and Marci Hanson (eds.), *Developing Cross-cultural Competence. A Guide for Working with Children and Their Families* (3rd ed.), 179–217. Baltimore, MD: Paul Brookes.

6

Advocacy Efforts for Immigrant Children: A Framework for Action

Tell me, what can we do for children? We owe our own future to them. (Anonymous)

Through this chapter, we will

- Examine the concept of advocacy from the perspective of social justice
- Identify the ethical parameters of advocacy efforts
- Explore the reasons supporting advocacy efforts for immigrant children and families
- Describe the traits of advocates for child immigrants
- Identify actions needed to address supportive practices for immigrants.

Key terms

- Advocacy
- Child well-being
- Social justice
- Equity
- Ethical conduct

NAEYC standard

- NAEYC #6 Becoming a Professional

Sharing stories: *Language challenges*

The young girl in the back of the classroom was only five when she started attending the local school. Native born and living in the same community as her school, she was more comfortable speaking her mother's Mayan language.

For about a semester, she was waiting for an evaluation to identify some suspected "behavioral and communication disabilities." Her teacher shared with her colleagues that she would hardly talk and would exhibit some anger. While waiting for the evaluation, an observer her teacher had invited, visited the classroom. The observer soon noticed a blank expression on the face of the child with long braided hair. After a quick conversation with the child's teacher, the observer set aside her notes. She sat next to the child and looking at her greeted her in Mayan. The girl's eyes opened wide in surprise. An immigrant herself, it did not take long for the observer to realize what the issue was. She needed someone to communicate in her primary language! Later that day, the observer wrote to the teacher dismissing any apparent disabilities and suggesting dual language services for the young child.

Calling for action

Every day is a time to continue the quest for what is socially just for children. For early childhood educators, our determination grows stronger every moment we see the faces of young children. We hear their families speak with great hope about their future. We learn about the dreams that children have for their future—they tell us with excitement! However, we cannot forget that many are still faced with challenges to overcome if their own dreams and their parents' hopes are to come to fruition. One rejoices whenever we hear about the successful achievements of children. So many immigrants we met as children are now grown up and on the road to success. They are the promise-turned-reality that continues to sustain the future of a nation built from the labor of immigrants.

Despite efforts of professionals and advocates that over the years have obtained rightful services and attention to the needs of child immigrants, there are countless others who are still experiencing the bitter reality of indifferent attitudes and inequitable practices. Whether overtly or guided by misinformed views, what they experience is obscuring the journey of children of immigrants in our communities, the majority of whom are US citizens (Zong, Batalova, and Burrows 2019). Issues of immigration in our times continue to underline serious concerns about fairness and equitable responses for immigrant children and their families. While legalities of entry into the country continue to be discussed, the focus of attention needs to be reshifted and placed on the thousands of immigrant children who remain waiting for actions. We echo the words of Nobel poet laureate Gabriela Mistral once again when she said that children cannot wait. Now, the urgent need is to recognize the rights that every child has to mindfully receive services and programs that meet their individual needs (Toczydlowska and D'Acosta 2017). Moving into action begins with recognition of their rights to a future of bright success.

Children of immigration continue as an important reality of our century (International Organization for Migration 2020) and an integral component of our nation. So is the need for more clarity and targeted attention to their circumstances and future. Fair practices and equal attention to all children are particularly critical in light of the distorted discourse that has vilified immigration. Far from an understanding of the important role of immigration in society, which is central to the US societal soul, arguments remain divisive, blurring the immigrants' work and contributions, their hopes, and even their critical role for their future. In the midst of this divisiveness, the realities of child immigrants, both recently arriving and those of generations already in our schools and communities, continue to demand immediate action. Meanwhile, 26 percent of the nation's children who are children of immigrants (Zong, Batalova, and Burrows 2019) remain waiting for firm and determined actions to safeguard their development and future.

Similar to the young child in the opening scenario, hundreds of children linger in the classroom, left without the attention, experiences, and services they are entitled to receive. Their situations are among the many examples where actions are needed to ensure fair attention and consciously centered responses that will support their development and overall well-being. We have repeatedly stated it before. The issue at stake is the responsible and equitable attention owed to every child. Undeniably, many times some are unintentionally victimized by people's lack of knowledge or unawareness about their needs and ways to assist. Others experience prejudice and discrimination because of their language diversity, origin, and cultures (Adair 2015), leaving them to confront multiple challenges at school and in their neighborhoods. These and many other difficult situations continue to echo the call for action to support children and their families. As others had shared, they are waiting for Superman to come to save the day (Driscoll 2017).

Immigration: A continuing topic demanding attention

In the atmosphere of recent years, as pointed out throughout the preceding chapters, immigration has become a highly controversial and contentious topic. At present, it continues to be heatedly argued in our nation and globally. Opinions and positions have made the discussions complicated. Discussions about caravans of immigrants coming from Central America, news about vessels overflowing with people fleeing dangerous and hopeless situations crossing the Mediterranean, arrivals of immigrants in fragile boats from Caribbean countries, and desperate families crossing the US borders have not stopped. It is a continuous flow of humanity asking for recognition and empathy. Among the faces of weary travelers are hundreds of children together with parents and others alone, asking for strong consideration and attention to the circumstances they each experience. Meanwhile, the tone of arguments continues to impact the contributions and opportunities of long-time immigrant families and of their children, many of whom for generations living in our communities continue to contribute to our nation's future. At the moment of completing this work, arguments and issues facing children of immigrants and their families have not stopped. Rather, these have taken new directions while policies remain unclear about what is best for children.

Time to reflect ... *Journeys*

In the story *The Journey* (Sanna 2016), the characters evoke the stories of thousands of people leaving their homelands in search of a safe place. Reflect on the images of immigrants and their children arriving in the country. As an early childhood educator, what actions should be considered for children and their families?

Today, children of immigrants are a growing part of the nation's demographic landscape. They bring to our communities and classrooms invaluable wealth of their diversity, culture, and heritage. As diverse as their cultural profile, so is the immigrant socioeconomic character, including many children continuing to live in poverty, a fact that increases their vulnerability (Robles-Meléndez and Driscoll 2017). Past and present accounts of immigrants continue to raise awareness of the tribulations experienced by families and children coming to the nation. They tell about the harrowing efforts of many as they begin or continue their life in our communities and forge their future.

Even with the many challenges faced by immigrant children and their families, society continues to express surprise at the multiple immigrant success stories. Crosnoe (2013, 13) points out that "Overall, the children of immigrants in the United States are doing better than expected in the educational system, given the many disadvantages they face." Indeed, the point that Crosnoe makes about their success despite the challenging circumstances many encountered simply continues to demonstrate their tenacity and determination to excel. How they are able to overcome challenges is a perplexing reality for many who, given the multitude of issues that are experienced, are able to overcome and succeed (Feliciano and Lanuza 2017). Their resilience and energy to move ahead is what for many remains as a question difficult to answer. We can see the spirit of their commitment and purpose that views challenges as an opportunity to move ahead.

Paradox of immigrant success

The smiling faces of students receiving their degrees during graduation ceremonies whose roots are from all parts of the world continue to be a testimonial to the resilient character of many. The humble beginnings and difficult experiences are all but a reminder of what many immigrant children endured to achieve success in the nation they now call home. During a recent visit to a rural center we were once again reminded about the successful experiences of the executive program director, an immigrant herself, who grew up as a child following the harvests alongside her Mexican parents, migrant workers themselves. Now, she leads an education program giving hope to many who like her aspire to the dreams that brought them and their families to the United States. Similar to her, hundreds of immigrant stories continue to reveal the energy and determination to overcome challenges and become successful examples of what immigration represents to a country. Any time we look at the future of the nation, the accounts of immigrants emerge telling about their contributions that remain shaping our times and what is yet to come tomorrow.

We are continuously reminded about the success of countless immigrants who today have leading roles in our society and whose stories started humbly as children of immigrants. In education, we are witnesses to the multiple accounts representing the accomplishment of children despite the challenges many times present. How can this happen? This is what many have termed as the immigrant paradox (Suárez Orozco and Suárez-Orozco 2001; Vaughn et al. 2014). Success, despite the multitude of challenges, remains an intriguing fact about immigrants. How they are able to adapt to a new culture and successfully meet its subsequent expectations continues to baffle those unable to understand the strength and determination guiding immigrants. Simply guided by their will to overcome challenges, continue to make their dreams a reality.

Time to reflect ... *Successful immigrants*

Take a moment to consider some of the accomplishments of immigrant students or of immigrant adults you may know. If you are an immigrant yourself, what do you consider that may explain their success as well as your own?

Advocacy for all children

Many reasons and factors explain the countless accomplishments of immigrants. Undoubtedly, the work of advocates, people dedicated to the cause of immigrant children, is one of the contributing factors. Committed to support children and to defend their rights, advocates continue to make the difference for so many of our youngest immigrants. Guiding the efforts of advocates is the search for justice. They intentionally place their efforts in what is rightfully relevant to address the needs of children (Royea and Appl 2009). They have learned about their needs and mindfully approach actions to answer their challenges.

Defining advocacy

Advocacy is not a term easy to define. Overall, it entails the thoughtful and selfless work of dedicated individuals, who seeing the needs of others come to their assistance and support. Their response entails empathy and the ability to act in resolute ways to help and bring about changes for what is right and fair (Figure 6.1). This is precisely what individuals and groups pursue as they engage in advocacy for immigrant children and families. To them, engaging in advocacy work is a call for doing what is essential to halt unfairness. Its outcomes bring attention to situations in need of change or lead to concrete changes (Mevawalla and Hadley 2012). Furthermore, advocacy responds to a mindful and conscious awareness about one's responsibilities to ensure fairness.

Advocacy occurs in many ways. Sometimes in quiet ways, which many times no one realizes the efforts made (Kieff 2008; Royea and Appl 2009). The classroom is one of those places where endless advocacy efforts continue to take place through the unwavering efforts of educators responding to the needs of the children they teach. Both authors have witnessed countless examples of the dedicated work of early childhood teachers responding to their students'

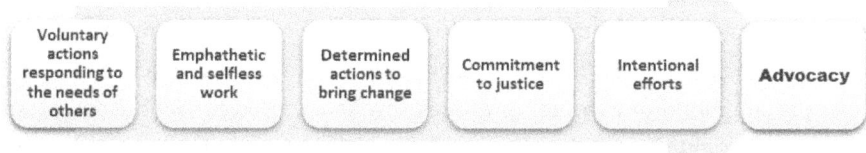

Figure 6.1 Key descriptors of advocacy.
Source: Kieff 2008; Royea and Apl 2009; Mevawalla and Hadvey 2012.

needs. Their leadership and selfless dedication to children guided their actions, which made a difference for their students. There are other times when advocacy happens through the resolute work of educators, groups, agencies, and organizations including the government. The lawful recognition of the rights of immigrant children to receive an education is a milestone accomplished by the perseverant actions of advocates. One of those recently celebrated was the recognition of the role of primary languages while acquiring a second language. The document on *Dual Language Learners in Early Childhood Programs*, released in June 2016 by the U.S. Department of Education, was indeed an outcome of the advocacy efforts of many who together led the government to make such a significant policy statement. Irrespective of the approach, these are examples of action-oriented responses to what is socially just.

Time to reflect … *About advocacy*

To advocate, according to the literature, is to defend and plead for a cause. Reflect on your own role in early childhood education. Think about what would be worthy for you to defend. What would make you take a stance and argue for children?

Stories of advocates confirm the determined attitude that guides their efforts sometimes taking years, yet unrelenting. Simply stated, it is not an easy road to travel. Nonetheless, outcomes of their efforts continue to demonstrate the what and why of their energies and for whom they sought fairness. The road of advocacy efforts to ensure equity is long and continues everyday as efforts are needed to ensure the rights of children with culturally diverse roots. Socially just advocacy is anchored in the multicultural educational efforts of those promoting consciously centered equitable practices. Advocacy actions begin whenever individuals perceive barriers that threaten what is due to others. It is also driven by actions denying equitable opportunities and experiences for others. Threatening and unfair circumstances, whether these emerge out of the actions of others or because of legally supported or common practices, invoke the need for actions to ensure what is justly right (Kieff 2008; Royea and Appl 2009). Cases of outright violation, lack of protection, or denial of rights are at the core of advocacy actions addressing child immigrants and their families. Support, protection, and promotion of a child's well-being have guided actions of individuals and organizations in our country and globally. Today, the calling is for these to continue in earnest.

Accounts about advocacy efforts abound, demonstrating the thoughtful and noble actions of numerous individuals and agencies. These actions have been translated into classroom practices, responses to the unique needs of children and their families, or legislative victories such as what led to the landmark *Plyler v. Doe* decision, which was discussed earlier in Chapter 5. They have also laid the foundation for early childhood policies and program models for immigrants. One of these policies is the early intervention programs and services for children with exceptionalities, irrespective of their immigration status.

Determined advocacy actions to address inequities

The flow of immigrants continues in the United States as a marker of what the nation represents for individuals and families from all parts of the world. "*Busco lo que todos merecen, una oportunidad* [I'm seeking what everyone deserves, an opportunity]," voiced a parent echoing what, perhaps, almost all immigrant families would say whenever asked about their journey into immigration. At the heart of their motivations is the search for equity. Equity is still a precious reality yet absent from the lives of so many people. Stories about unfair situations are constantly being broadcasted by media and discussed publicly. Despite the awareness society has on existing inequities, many circumstances and actions continue to defiantly deny the rights of individuals to receive equal treatment and opportunities. Sadly, this is what has also been experienced by many immigrants in our classrooms and programs. The recent NAEYC position statement *Advancing equity in early childhood education* (2019) has strongly identified the need for educators of young children to ensure equitable opportunities for all. Furthermore, it stated the need for establishing and pursuing equity as an obligation of professionals in early childhood education. The call to advocate for equity was firmly laid out in the document as part of its recommendations for action to the profession. Specifically, it asked for early childhood professionals to denounce unfairness and to collaborate with others seeking just and equitable practices for children and their families. These actions are at the heart of what guides advocacy for children.

Time to reflect ... *Are you an advocate for children?*

Advocacy is action for what is right. It takes efforts from everyone calling for what is just for children. Reflect on what you do to ensure fairness for children. What actions would describe you as an advocate for children?

This is for children

Safeguarding children is everyone's responsibility. Society owes children protection to ensure their development across the span of childhood. It is, after all, an investment in the future of humanity itself and of the nation. This time, the urgent call responds to the need for attention to what is rightful for children with diverse experiences and backgrounds. In fact, demand for their attention has been long denounced by advocates and educators conscious of the uneven opportunities and exclusion from equitable conditions experienced by many children (Abo-Zena 2018; Banks 2015; Nieto and Bode 2018). Their realities "implore educators to consider issues of diversity and equity" (Swindler Boutte 2008, 165).

Concerted efforts for children's well-being are what guide and define advocacy in early childhood education. By itself, advocacy is the actions taken on behalf of others where the cause pursued is socially just and clearly anchored on fairness (Kieff 2008; Wright and Wright 2016). Equal rights is a basic tenet guiding efforts in our nation. Equality is inclusive of everyone, beyond individual diversity or origins. The law already recognizes the rights of young immigrant children, including those who may have arrived unauthorized. It is the conscientious awareness about the inequities that children experience that drives advocates into action. Expected as an individual response to address the needs of children, advocacy is central to professional conduct in early childhood education practice (NAEYC 2011).

Why we need advocates

Even though recognition exists to equality of opportunities, many unfair and unethical situations are still occurring in our communities. In so many occasions, the voices of children and of their families remain silent or their needs fail to be conveyed to others, preventing people from realizing the impact of the lack of actions or of decisions on the child. Efforts to ensure the needs and actions for children accentuate the role and need for advocates. Becoming the voice for children (Wright and Jaffe 2014), advocates direct their efforts to what is right and fair. This is what also describes what advocates for child immigrants do. Advocates are in search of what is right and considered critical for the youngest immigrants and for their families to ensure their support and welfare. More importantly, it is to be remembered that "All children of immigrants are part of our society, regardless of our personal stance on immigration" (Takanishi in Hernández, Denton, and Macartney 2008, 12).

Who is an advocate for child immigrants?

The work of those who advocate for immigrant children and their families is constant, every day and everywhere. The need and outcome of their efforts is evident any time we consider that immigrants are part of the fabric of the nation. Advocacy efforts for immigrants emerge through people who believe in fairness and equity. They are determined to focus their energies and will toward assisting others in obtaining what is rightfully owed to them. Their work has made it possible for countless immigrant children and their families to receive widespread recognition as contributing members in our society.

Perhaps what best defines who is an advocate for child immigrants is the fact that they care. Advocates, beyond the cause they defend, sincerely care about children of immigrants and recognize the need to stand for what is justifiable and fair. They also defend the entitled rights of children within the framework of the law. This is what has guided people to lend their voices to defend what is rightfully owed and essential for a child's successful development. Advocates are also people who care about the well-being of the youngest immigrants. They recognize the potential and promise for society's future in every child and dedicate efforts to make these come true.

Early childhood educators: Advocates for young children

Among those who advocate for children are early childhood educators. It is integral to their profession. Aware of what is ethically responsible, they dedicate their voice and efforts to children. Their sense of caring has long described efforts in our classrooms and beyond. Reasons for caring and advocating for young children of immigrants are intrinsic to the profession and practice in early childhood. Early childhood education embraces and recognizes the diversity of experiences defining children and the need to ensure what is in their best interest (NAEYC 2011). Current times, with the continuously increasing change in the nation's demographics and diversity, have demarcated a greater need for making sure equity defines every child's experiences. Professionally, early childhood educators remain a source of continuous support for immigrant children and their families. Their efforts made the difference for children in their classroom just like what the preschool teacher did for her 4-year-olds in Box 6.1. Others may engage in far-reaching endeavors benefiting their communities and beyond. All efforts are equally relevant and welcome for the child. They simply say that someone cares.

Box 6.1 Connecting ideas: *Reflections from a preschool teacher*

Advocacy efforts for children happen every day. They can take the shape of many distinct activities. What distinguishes advocacy efforts is the nature of the children's needs that are addressed. As you read the reflections below that a preschool teacher made, think about the efforts you make in your classroom in response to the needs of children.

The school year was coming to an end and, as every year, the preschool center in the rural part of town was holding a special ceremony. This celebration of children's achievements was a moment of joy for all. It was for me, too. After a year, it was so special to see now the group of children coming to the center with their families. Dressed in their best outfits, the line of smiling and excited PreK students began to march across the room. Their parents, mostly farmers and field workers, stood up, cameras in hand to grasp the special moment. One by one, the children were called. With each child, memories of what we had experienced throughout the year came to mind. There they were, singing as my heart pounded remembering the stories of some of the children. I looked at the child that used to be very shy and who now was there standing so proud. Next to her was the short-haired girl who blossomed after we found out she needed glasses. Singing out loud was the youngest child who came to the center not saying a word in English. She was now leading everyone to sing. Seeing all of them made me realize all that we had accomplished for them and with them. This was the best reward. Yes, I will surely do it again and again.

Regardless of the magnitude of the advocacy efforts, early childhood educators are true to the professional commitment to respond and stand for children. This is what the NAEYC postulates in its *Code of Ethical Behavior and Statement of Commitment* (2011), asserting the obligation of early childhood educators to attend and become advocates to secure what is best for children. They further call for professionals working with young children to become the voice for children.

Time to reflect … *Advocating for children*

Advocacy is one of the ethical commitments of early childhood professionals. Reflect on the needs of children in your community and in our nation. Consider ways in which you have advocated for their rights. What advocacy efforts are still needed to meet the needs of immigrant children?

All efforts count for children's ongoing needs

Nobel peace laureate Malala Yousafzai pointedly said that "when the whole world is silent, even one voice becomes powerful." At her young age, she had already proven to be that voice, calling and advocating for what is fair and right. Again, we must reiterate, no advocacy effort is ever too small. They all remain pertinent to the children and families they intended to assist. Efforts come from individuals or collectively in response to needs or actions that threaten the quality of life for children (Larocco and Burns 2005; Royea and Appl 2009). We call for your efforts to address and bring equity to the experiences of children.

Unfairness: A reason for advocacy

Consciously determined practices and efforts are essential as continuing challenges are faced by our youngest immigrants. This work advocates this calling for every child immigrant. Recent and continuing circumstances experienced by immigrants emphasize the need for advocacy efforts. One-sided, slanted comments about immigrants and discriminatory practices and actions have reemerged in many communities demanding greater attention to circumstances that may threaten the rights of children and families. In some cases, child immigrants encounter discriminatory behaviors right at school, sometimes from peers and staff (Adair 2015; Spears Brown and Chu 2012). How and when this is manifested varies. The outcome is the same, hurtful and denying children and their families of what is fair. Sadly, there is a multitude of accounts and incidents of unfairness marked by intimidation and indifference to their needs and experiences. Families separated due to deportation or because of their entry into the nation remain, leaving many children without their parents or frightened at the possibility of what may happen. Other times, families are asked about their status or for documentation, adding to their intimidation and distressing experiences. In many instances, immigrant parents, fearful and aware of attitudes and views, may even interpret requests from schools and agencies with fear, abstaining from using services (Sugarman 2019). Linguistic differences have long been the focus of numerous unfair actions shifting language into barriers, preventing children from receiving entitled services. These and many other situations are actively compelling advocates into action.

Addressing children's diversity: Moving beyond awareness

Immigration has been an open door driving diversity in our communities. At present, it continues even more strongly to increase the myriad of diversities in society. Now, more than ever, early childhood education needs to respond to the realities of diversity as mandates to effectively support the child's learning and integral development (NAEYC 2019). Diversity is as well what characterizes child immigrants. Cultures, languages, origins, experiences, and traditions are all traits of the distinctive diversity that describes young children and their families with immigrant backgrounds. Though much has been accomplished in building an awareness about diversity, much more is mindfully needed to be done to move beyond the point of awareness. The reasons for moving beyond awareness are obvious. Day to day experiences in communities, classrooms, and the national arena confirm the views still present denying and rejecting behaviors and ways that differ from those in the mainstream (Banks 2015; Lynch and Hanson 2011; Nieto and Bode 2018; Spears Brown and Chu 2012). Such has been the experience of people with diverse characteristics and immigrant backgrounds yesterday and today. They insult the dignity of individuals that constitutionally is owed to them.

Time has shown us that we must move beyond just having an awareness about the existence of biased and discriminatory attitudes and behaviors. Addressing respect and attention to the diversity of children and families is essential and a responsibility inclusive of everyone. Within the scope of a democratic society, long-standing practices denying equal experiences emphasize a call to action These practices need to be eradicated if we are to affirm educational equity in our early childhood programs. This is what Delpit ([1995] 2006) boldly denounced when she stated, "If we are to successfully educate **all** [emphasis added] of our children, we must remove the blinders built of stereotypes, monocultural instructional methodologies, ignorance, social distance, biased research, and racism" (182). These actions are particularly relevant when demographically the nation's population growth is largely predicted by the growing number of children of immigrants (Pew Research Center 2015). The time calls for conscientious response leading to establish actions supportive of children's right to equitable experiences. Actions aimed at ending inequities because of individual differences are essential and demand everyone to respond. Discrimination never has room or justification (UNESCO 2007).

Responding to the needs of child immigrants

Many continue today answering to the need for erasing discriminatory and unfair actions. Awareness about inequities and unfairness has moved them to take action to end practices against the rights of families and children and their diversity of experiences and ethnicities. The trail of efforts on behalf of immigrants is long and robust. It continues to be strong as people learn more about the experiences of families and children. At the same time, the need and role of advocacy remains crucial for immigrant children and their families. Today, in a society deemed global, the call for supporting immigrants touches everyone in what the UNICEF indicates is "a shared responsibility—shared because no one is untouched by the impacts of the multiple crises in the world" (2016, 2). The challenge is on each one to respond to the collective realities and experiences to better support children. At the same time, we are urged to consider the implications of inaction on the overall society.

Protecting children

Protection of children remains as a common duty for a society projecting itself to the future. It is also what drives early childhood education in its unending call for action. At stake is the well-being of the child. The United Nations' *Convention of the Rights of the Child* itself is a standing call for the inherent responsibility everyone has to protect children. Integral to it is the recognition that children, beyond labels or categories, require and demand protection. Protection begins recognizing their rights to equal attention and experiences. Legal mandates in our nation stemming from milestone court case decisions (such as *Mendez* v. *Westminster*, *Plyler* v. *Doe*, *Lau* v. *Nichols*, among others) establish the overarching rights and responsibilities toward children of immigrants including those with unauthorized arrivals. The agenda to safeguard children begins with mindful understanding about the actions needed to provide equitable care and attention. Equity recognizes the dignity of childhood. This has been a driving force in the work of countless educators, individuals, groups, and agencies supporting child immigrants. Same aspirations continue guiding and motivating work in early childhood, which, today, with more emphasis, pursues what is best and developmentally appropriate for children.

Continuity of educational experiences, high-quality experiences accessible to all, and attention to health and safety are all elements critical to support children during a time when they are most vulnerable—their childhood. These are pertinent to all child immigrants, foreign born and born to immigrant parents in our nation. In fact, the need has emerged vigorously since the 2014 humanitarian crisis at the southern borders of the country (American Academy of Pediatricians 2013; Linton, Griffin, and Shapiro 2017). The call remains today for efforts directed at guaranteeing their integral well-being with conditions that promote children's successful development.

Time to reflect … *The dignity of childhood*

Children are the reason for advocacy efforts in early childhood education. Consider some of the current challenges that threaten the dignity of childhood. What efforts are needed to ensure respect for the dignity of children?

Ongoing efforts of national organizations

Current immigration issues demand everyone's attention and efforts to ensure fair and equitable responses to the needs of immigrant children and their families. Whether recent arrivals or long established in our communities, the call for efforts on their behalf is continuous. The work of individuals and of civic and professional organizations has made possible countless achievements in the recognition of the rights of immigrants and of people with diverse cultures and languages. For instance, active support from Unidos US, a national organization advocating for Latinos, NAEYC, and the Division of Early Childhood of the Council for Exceptional Children, has brought to light immigration issues of children. Nonetheless, issues of fairness and just responses to children remain, despite legal victories and policies that have asserted their rights.

Immigration issues have shed light on the ongoing work of organizations across the country. Since the earliest time, government agencies and organizations born out of the initiative of socially conscious individuals have been responding to immigrants' needs. Their work continues today and remains vital for the well-being of children and their families. It would be hard to list all the organizations that have currently taken a stand for immigrant children and their families. Their work continues in support of families and children throughout the country's communities.

Time to reflect ... *Advocates for children of immigrants*

Take a moment to consider the groups and organizations, whether government led or private initiatives, that advocate for children in your community. Which ones do you know? In what ways does their effort support children of immigrants?

A multitude of goals targeting immigrants' needs guide the missions and efforts of advocacy groups and organizations. Some focus attention on early childhood development and education, while others address a myriad of related immigration issues including assistance with immigration status. Box 6.2 highlights the work of The League of United Latin American Citizens (LULAC), one of many whose efforts have supported the educational rights of immigrants, benefiting students across all ethnic groups. The work of each group and organization remains vital for children and families. Leadership of various organization has brought to the forefront the experiences and circumstances surrounding arriving and already established immigrant families. Their efforts continue to also highlight the presence of immigrants as a contributing and constituent element of US society.

Box 6.2 Connecting ideas: *The League of United Latin American Citizens*

Historically, one of the first organizations formed in response to the needs of immigrants and the oldest serving Hispanics was The League of United Latin American Citizens (LULAC). A national organization established in 1929, the group was founded with the goal of addressing the civil rights of Mexicans from a wave of prejudice and discrimination. Having received US citizenship in response to the annexation of Mexican territory after the Mexican War, Mexicans became victims of a series of discriminatory and segregationist practices. Among the many concerns of the newly formed organization was educational equity, which became one of its main targets. Many of their efforts to ensure equal educational treatment led them to take legal action. In the 1940s, LULAC went to court to end the practice of segregation of Mexican children. At the time, Mexican children were not allowed to sit in the same schools as their peers, forcing them to attend what came to be called as "Mexican schools" (LULAC n.d.). Legal action was taken in 1946 in the landmark *Mendez* v. *Westminster* case, previously discussed in Chapter 5. The US Supreme Court voted in favor of LULAC, which set a precedent for the historic victory of the *Brown* v. *Board of Education*. In 1990, LULAC went to court to defend the civil rights of English language learners (ELL) in Florida, to receive equal educational opportunities and "the delivery of the comprehensible instruction to which ELL students are entitled" (Florida Department of Education 2019). The court settlement provided the grounds for the Consent Decree that guides services for students with culturally and linguistically diverse backgrounds in the State of Florida.

Source: LULAC (n.d.)

Responsive actions

The voices of organizations advocating for young children's well-being have become louder. Advocate efforts have been crucial in the pursuit of the rights and well-being of incoming and already established immigrant children and families. Calls to eliminate existing disparities hindering equitable experiences have brought forward the need for addressing what every child needs to reach their optimal development. This is what lies at the core of socially just efforts urging everyone to responsibly consider what is still needed to be done for children. Critically conscious now about the existence of disparities denounces the need for action that can bring forward equality of opportunities and experiences for children.

The well-being of a child depends on a variety of factors, where efforts from families are joined with those of society. Education, health, family, social and economic realities are among the components determining children's optimal development (Child Stats 2019). Safeguarding the right of children with diverse backgrounds to find equally supportive conditions remains driving efforts for responsive programs, resources, and practices. Many voices have responded and continue to contribute to defend the rights of the child with immigrant backgrounds. Early childhood national organizations have joined the voices calling for fairness and parity in educational experiences, programs, and services. They remain vigilant today about the welfare of immigrant children.

Incidents of recent years have not been ignored by professional organizations. In October 2018, the NAEYC and its affiliates released their statement expressing their concern and opposition to immigrant family separations and calling everyone to continue advocating for the protection of immigrant children and families. This was followed by their statement in June 2019, where NAEYC (2019) firmly reiterated that based on research-based knowledge about what is best for children and following what is ethically responsible, they denounced the humiliating and detrimental effects of policies and practices on immigrant families and children arriving through the country's borders. Support and action from over a hundred other organizations throughout the country continue advocating for the rights of immigrant children and their families. The clamor for safer and humanitarian ways to respond to children remains driving advocates mindfully aware of the serious consequences of what is experienced.

Supporting efforts for young immigrants

Though more support is always needed, countless programs currently support the needs of young children. It would be impossible to name them all here. Many emerged out of the efforts of citizens and agencies including the government. Their work continues to be a response to actions and inequities based on children's diverse experiences and backgrounds. Common to their work is supporting and assisting child immigrants and their families to receive and find equitable experiences. They are also strong supporters of the cultural heritage of the thousands of immigrant families and children. The diversity of individuals who are advocates is as diverse as the children they defend. In common, they all share their determination for fair and just treatment. They zealously fight to stop unfairness, prejudice, and discriminatory behaviors.

One of the multiple examples of advocates is the actions taken to provide quality child care to the children of migrants working in the fields. It was this goal that led to the development of The Redlands Migrant Christian Association (RCMA). Established over fifty years ago, the program serves over six thousand children in Florida, mostly immigrants in its sixty-six centers and two charter schools. Central to their successful efforts was empowering families to share in their common goal for children. Recruiting teachers from among the immigrant families firmed up a trusting relationship with the program. Additional details about its services are discussed in Box 6.3.

Box 6.3 Connecting ideas: *Responding to the needs of migrant children*

Over fifty years ago the sight of migrant worker parents bringing their infant and toddler children to the fields in Florida inspired a group of local citizens to take action. With the passing of the 1965 immigration reform that emphasized family reunification, an influx of immigrants, particularly Hispanics mostly from Mexico, arrived and settled in the farmlands of South Florida. Working in the farmlands and with no resources to cover care for their children, parents were forced to bring them to the fields. Conditions were severe for the children due to exposure to inclement weather, pesticides, and the possibility of even suffering life-threatening accidents. It did not take long for a local group of Mennonite volunteers to respond after a series of serious accidents. Opening a child care center for the workers' young children in the Redlands farming area, soon it became clear that parents were refraining from leaving their children at the newly established center. Calling for assistance, the Mennonites contacted Wendell Rollason, a known immigrant advocate. He realized that a cultural disconnect was hampering their efforts. Noticing the need to address issues of trust and culture, the center was urged to begin the practice of hiring immigrant mothers as caregivers at the center. The response to the new practice did not take long to create successful stories. With parents enrolling their children in the center, the program became a trusting place for migrant workers to bring their children while at work. Through Rollason's insights, the actions of volunteers, and the support of local farm owners in the area, the RCMA model blossomed into a reality. Central to the success of the program was the empowerment of immigrant parents to serve as caregivers and support their professional development as early childhood educators. Today, a large percent of the teaching staff caring for children are of immigrant origin. Many of them were working in the fields at one time or were children of migrant workers. Critical to the model was also the trust placed in the migrant parents who were welcomed to collaborate as partners in the centers.

Barbara Mainster, the program's first education director, continued the tradition of Rollason, honoring immigrants' culture and leading the program to expand its services throughout the state of Florida. In 2018, a migrant early childhood educator assumed the leadership of the program. Currently, the program continues to promote its core ideals, serving children and families and honoring their culture. These core values have garnered the respect and trust of immigrant families and of low-income families for over fifty years. It offers programs to over six thousand children of immigrants and low-income families throughout rural communities in Florida. Expanding their services to offer continuity of attention to children beyond early education, RCMA operates two charter schools in rural Florida communities. The program has been nationally recognized for its exemplary efforts and responses to the needs of immigrant families and their children. It continues today its work for children and families honoring its motto, "*opening doors to opportunities.*"

Source: Brammertz et al. (2012)

Federal programs for young immigrant children

Head Start, the longest-running and successful early intervention program for children, has also been responding to the needs of young immigrants since its inception. Developed to provide experiences for low-income children during the War on Poverty of the 1960s, Head Start has been serving countless immigrant children living in poverty and with limited resources. Speaking with one of the teachers who taught during the summer of 1965 in a rural community in Puerto Rico when the project started, she remembers the program as a beacon of hope for the children in rural communities (personal communication, May 2019). Similar comments were made by one of the assistants that volunteered during that summer in Chicago. Aimed at closing gaps in services and opportunities for children, historical records from Head Start show that in 1966, the first Head Start child of the year was a 6-year-old immigrant child of Mexican heritage (Office of Head Start 2019b). Today, thousands of immigrant families continue to find support and high-quality services for their children, opinions gathered from several families who shared their observations with the authors show. The comprehensiveness of program services has been vital to the thousands of low-income and immigrant children served since its inception.

Head Start program enrollment reflects the growing ethnic diversity of the country's demographics. Serving more than a million children from birth to age 5 in 2018, 37 percent of children in their programs were Hispanic (Office of Head Start 2019b). Linguistically, Head Start's children and families revealed its compelling diversity, attesting to the changing US demographical pattern. Linguistically, in addition to Spanish, spoken by 22 percent of participants, children's home languages exhibited a marked diversity. Table 6.1 details the diversity of home

Table 6.1 Home languages of children in Head Start programs (2017–18)

Home Primary Language	Percentage
English	72.1
Spanish	22.1
Central American, South American, or Mexican indigenous languages	0.3
Caribbean languages	0.4
Middle Eastern or South Asian	1.3
East Asian	1.1
Native North American or Alaska Native Languages	0.7
Pacific Island	0.3
Slavic	0.7
African	0.9

Source: Office of Head Start (2019a).

languages spoken by Head Start children during 2018 (Office of Head Start 2019a). The increasing cultural and linguistic character of the children attending their programs reflects the growing presence of children with immigrant backgrounds.

Emphasizing on children's diversities and culture, in 1991 Head Start adopted *The Multicultural Principles*, which has since continued to guide educational experiences, centered around the principle of culture and its influence on the developing child. The concept furthers acknowledgment of the diversity of children and families receiving services as well as that of their staff. The principles provide guidance for meeting Head Start program goals and for multicultural programming (Office of Head Start 2018). Each principle is relevant to delivering culturally responsive practice and address consciously centered practices directed at supporting children's developmental and holistic needs (Table 6.2). In particular, the principles recognize three fundamental and integral components of diversity: culture, identity, and heritage language. These are essential for the responsive attention to the child and family and especially relevant for immigrant children and their families.

The Migrant Seasonal Head Start Program

The needs of the thousands of children of migrants and seasonal farmworkers led in 1969 to the creation of the Migrant Seasonal Head Start Program. An immigrant-specific program, it is anchored on the principles of Head Start, providing comprehensive services to children of migrants in thirty-eight states (Office of

Table 6.2 Head Start multicultural principles

Principle 1: Every individual is rooted in culture.

Principle 2: Cultural groups in the communities and families of each Head Start program are the primary sources for culturally relevant programming.

Principle 3: Culturally relevant and diverse programming requires learning accurate information about the cultures of different groups and discarding stereotypes.

Principle 4: Addressing cultural relevance in making curriculum choices is a necessary developmentally appropriate practice.

Principle 5: Every individual has the right to maintain his or her own identity while acquiring the skills required to function in our diverse society.

Principle 6: Effective programs for children who speak languages other than English require continued development of the first language while the acquisition of English is facilitated.

Principle 7: Culturally relevant programming requires staff who both reflect and are responsive to the communities and families served.

Principle 8: Multicultural programming for children enables children to develop an awareness of, respect for, and appreciation of individual cultural differences.

Principle 9: Culturally relevant and diverse programming examines and challenges institutional and personal biases.

Principle 10: Culturally relevant and diverse programming and practices are incorporated in all systems and services and are beneficial to all adults and children.

Source: Office of Head Start (2010).

Head Start 2019a). Program services are provided to children 6 weeks old through 5 years old at centers located throughout the country. Parents' voice is encouraged and valued as evidenced by their participation as members of the center's policy councils at each location. During one of the meetings of a migrant parent policy council, one of the authors recollects a parent who, after discussing a need at the center where her child was enrolled, was invited to present her request during the program regional meeting. Surprised by the invitation, the parent remarked that she never thought she was so important, "no sabía que era tan importante." This example is precisely what has distinguished the migrant program's main goals, family empowerment, and engagement in the center's activities and decisions.

Time to reflect … *Empowering programs for child immigrants*

Early childhood programs for young immigrants place emphasis on children's well-being during the critical early years of a child's development. Consider the early childhood programs in your community or state. Identify those programs currently conducting culturally responsive practices directed at addressing the needs of immigrants. What principles do they address? Taking into consideration the Head Start multicultural principles, what aspects remain as action items for programs in your area or state?

Early childhood educators: Responding to the needs of children

Organizations and agencies continue to take action for the rights of children of immigrants. However, undeniably, it is the day-to-day response from educators that remain as the strongest force contributing to defend children with their work and caring response to their diverse realities. They are in the front as first responders in classrooms, schools, neighborhoods, at home, and communities. They have first-hand knowledge about the multiple circumstances, both positive and challenging, facing the child and family. Their work brings justice into the experiences of children. In fact, what teachers do in the classroom—their support, respectful response, interest in their learning growth, and caring understanding—influences how children cope with experiences as immigrants. Today, with the prospects of an increasing diversity drawing from immigration, the role of early childhood educators is integral to achieving equity in the education of immigrant children.

Beyond awareness about children's diversity

Someone once asked one of the authors, "How can I help children who are immigrants?" To that we answer, you have already taken the first step, the next step is moving into action. Truly, the first step is our own internalization of a reality experienced by children whose backgrounds are rooted in immigration and defined by their own diversity. But we cannot stop there. What comes next is to become their voice stepping into actions to responsively defend their right to education and provide equitable experiences. What happens in the classroom, the interactions and supports provided, continues to be a major denominator in enriching the experience and potentializing the immigrant child's opportunities for successful development (Delpit [1995] 2006; Ladson-Billings 1995; Votruba-Drzal et al. 2017). This is, after all, what defines child-centered education, mindful of individual realities, circumstances, and, most importantly, intentionally acting with those in mind.

The voice of educators remains one of the strongest supporters and advocates for children. Their understanding and support for children are a reflection of the ethical and empathetic practices defining their commitment and responsibilities. Their response to the crises experienced by many in the past and now during deportation and immigration raids reaffirms the belief and dedication of early childhood educators to protect and uphold the integrity of childhood. Their voices resonate in defense of children and their families who are suffering the consequences of immigration policies still in need of change both in the United States and in other parts of the world. Effective, culturally conscious teaching practices, bridging children's needs with supportive experiences, and identifying ways to reach each child are testimonials to the efforts transpiring every day across many classrooms. Still, much remains to be done to eliminate unequal practices and disparities children find in some classrooms. Needed also to responsively address practices supportive of children are intentional efforts and practices, empathy and caring attitudes, strong advocacy skills, and deep-rooted knowledge about children's realities and rights (Figure 6.2). Each one is integral to efforts promoting a child's well-being.

Calling for intentional and responsive practices

While we still hear some in education say, "but I do that for all of them," it is recognized that for some children what is done for all will not help, and the calling for responsive practices will remain a priority. One size does not fit all. Every child brings unique experiences that may not fit into one mold. Generalized practices that ignore individual needs simply place immigrant children at risk of not reaching their full developmental potential (Copple and Bredekamp 2009; da Silva Iddings and Reyes 2017; Takanishi 2010). It is not helpful either to maintain practices anchored on a deficit orientation and that disregard children's heritage and experiences (Moll 1992; Sims 2015). At the heart of practices anchored on equity is ongoing consideration to the inherent responsibility of educators to do what is best and right for each child (NAEYC 2011; NAEYC 2019). The charge is on us to make a difference and justly ensure contexts where fairness and equality surround children. Teachers continue to constitute an influential and integral role in the journey of a child's development (Super and Harkness 1986). They are vital to making children feel safe with someone they can trust and share experiences about their immigration journeys (González et al. 2017).

Both of us as authors and as teacher educators have witnessed for years the important role of teachers and how their work continues to impact children.

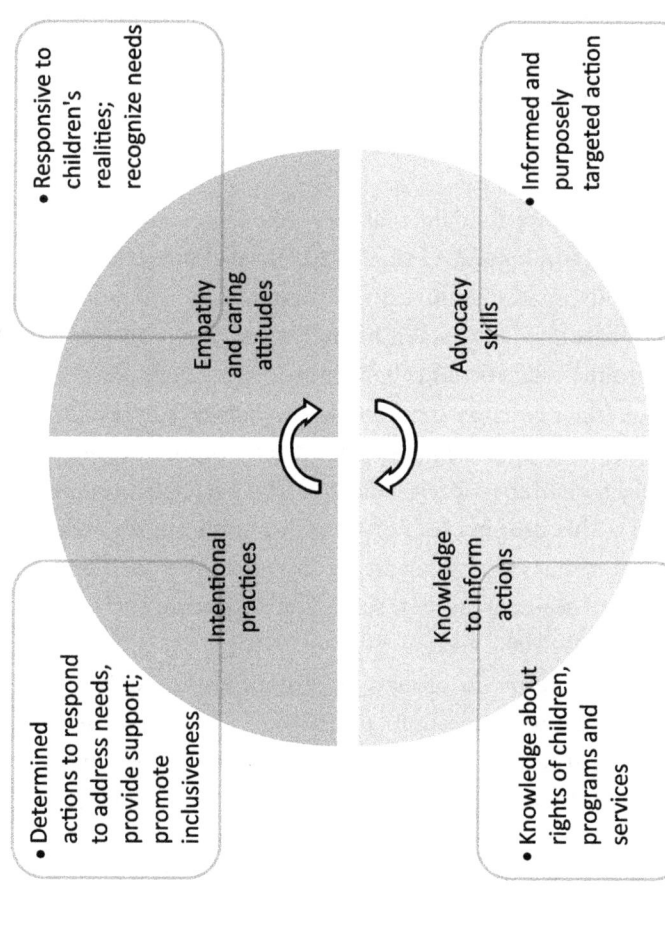

Figure 6.2 Elements influencing responsive practices for immigrant children and their families.
Source: Abo-Zena (2018); Chezare (2017); González et al. (2017); Kieff (2008).

We learned from our conversations with early childhood educators teaching young immigrant children what they have uncovered concerning the multitude of situations and adversity that some children are experiencing. We have seen how the knowledge teachers gained about each child made their decisions more intentional and consciously directed toward what the child may need (Freire [1974] 2013). Knowledge learned from and with the child and families is what informs and changes the direction of practices adding intentionality to what is planned for their success. As educators of young children, making our efforts intentional begins with clear determination to provide excellence for the child. Excellence is anchored on quality and counteracts inequities.

Empathy and caring dedication

Empathy and a sense of care are fundamental to working in early childhood education (Chezare 2017; Cummins and Asempapa 2013). Working with children of immigrant backgrounds continues to call for determined and mindfully oriented efforts. Mindfulness implicitly establishes reflective caring consideration about their individual realities. Efforts also call for empathy, gaining a perspective and understanding about their circumstances and lived realities (Chezare 2017). In every instance, it is essential for teachers to impart their sense of caring and responsibility toward each child they teach, reflective of a principled stance for children (NAEYC 2011). This defining trait of their caring insight for children is vital in a profession aimed at responsibly answering to children and seeking simply what is just, fair, and essential for their successful development (Derman-Sparks and Edwards 2010; Gay 2000; Ladson-Billings 1995).

The caring attention and response of early educators well describes what represents the early childhood education profession. These qualities are especially relevant given that teachers are so many times the first ongoing and enduring contact child immigrants and their families have in our communities. Memories of their interactions remain vividly in a child's mind, serving as hopeful inspiration as they embark on their life journey in a new context. So many times observed, one of the authors had an opportunity to once again confirm the dedication and unmistakable empathy of early childhood teachers. During an informal conversation, when asked what kept motivating them to work in a program serving mostly immigrant preschoolers, some teachers stated they do this "because they [children] need me," while others stated, "how can we say no when we know we can help." Their statement resounded with their care and love for children. Irrefutably, their words revealed a sense of obligation, so clearly representative of what is embedded in the early childhood profession. Their words also showed their feeling of justice and a desire to promote change for children. These traits are intrinsic to advocacy, which Fenech and Lotz (2018) found to be characteristic of what drives the efforts of early childhood educators. Indeed, it is as well what the early childhood field underscores for professionals working with children and their families (Kieff 2008; NAEYC 2011). Early childhood teachers are a powerful force in advocating for what is fair and socially just for children's well-being. Their position and direct interaction with children and families give them a crucial position (Taylor 2006) to engage in advocacy efforts for the young.

Teachers as advocates: Building capacity for advocacy

Guided by their caring dedication and commitment to children, teachers are one of their best advocates. New challenges and difficult circumstances for immigrants have sparked early childhood educators to more strongly stand for children. Personal experiences, inspired by their professional commitment to children, motivate their advocacy efforts.

One of the authors vividly remembers how years before one of her graduate students called after an immigration raid in the community where she worked. The shock and panic in the voice of the student was evident after witnessing migrant parents desperately seeking protection for their children in the center where she worked. She observed that she never thought it would ever happen in their community. Sadly, this experience has continued to be an occurrence in the life of many immigrants who entering unofficially find themselves to be the target of unexpected deportation and separation from their children. With these practices and many others, including discriminatory practices, continuing to occur, the need is heightened for educators to learn about persisting circumstances challenging the lives of immigrants. Policies, regulations, and societal attitudes toward immigrants during recent years pose difficult challenges to immigrant children and their families (Lovato et al. 2018; Yoshikawa 2011).

The need for sustained and determined advocacy efforts in early childhood education is clearly underlined today. More efforts are constantly needed to make the voice of early childhood stronger. Correspondingly, the need exists for early childhood educators to enhance their knowledge about emerging life realities confronting immigrant students. Conscious awareness and knowledge about inequities still present experiences for many children with diverse and immigrant roots, accentuating the need for action. This is what is voiced by NAEYC in their statement on equity (NAEYC 2019) that reaffirms why advocacy efforts must be directed at eliminating existing disparities and inequalities.

Informed advocacy efforts call for enhancing professional knowledge

Key to support the caring and advocacy efforts of early childhood educators is the need for building and expanding knowledge. Learning about changes in policies and practices and taking time for reflection on the significance of issues all contribute to increasing knowledge on issues of immigration. Knowledge deepens the reasons for efforts and sustains their need for children. They simply make your efforts more effective. Informing advocacy efforts with knowledge is critical as children and their families navigate and process experiences and events in their communities. Increasing knowledge is guided by our personal commitment to bring our efforts to address issues facing children and their families. It also depends and calls for opportunities from educational agencies to facilitate ongoing inservice opportunities that support teachers to gain perspectives on the diverse implications of immigration on children.

An agenda for child immigrants: Issues still calling for action

There is much that remains to be done to bring equity into the experiences of children and families with immigration backgrounds. Equity in the experiences and opportunities of young child immigrants is the aspiration guiding efforts for children. We are cognizant of many issues that challenge the rightful delivery of practices addressing children's diverse needs. Unfair and discriminatory practices, unrealistic expectations that disregard individual diversity, uncertainty about the future of families and children due to deportation, and fear about family separation all continue to call for concrete actions in support of young children of immigrants in our communities. They continue as obstacles in erasing inequities and discriminatory practices. The nature of many of these issues is complex and depends on multiple factors. They each call for an agenda of support focused on what is relevant to address and provide child immigrants what is equitable and socially just for everyone.

In the preceding chapters together we had explored, pondered, and reflected upon the nature and implications of immigration. Actions to ensure fair treatment and equitable opportunities are still needed if we are to erase inequities and bring about what is socially just for every child. Where to begin is a question that educators and many in society continue to ask themselves. What requires urgent attention and prioritization is answered as one ponders the consequences of inequities on young children and their families.

Time to reflect … *Building an action agenda*

Moving into action requires a clear agenda detailing and prioritizing the issues to address. Every community is unique and may have responded differently to immigrants. Consider the nature of events and circumstances surrounding immigrant children in your community. If you were to create an action agenda, what issues would you include? How and why would you prioritize these issues?

Current times continue to pose a variety of challenging issues facing children and their families. They continue to urge actions on behalf of immigrant children. Many are ongoing issues and some involve government actions. Others emerged in recent times. Overall, they call for attention and efforts from advocates for children. Among those calling to be addressed, some that we have considered critical are highlighted in Figure 6.3. They bring to attention issues impacting the nature and quality and overall experience of programs and services for young children.

Many decisions and actions remain as society seeks fairness for child immigrants. Existing and continuing issues give shape to an agenda of actions encompassing circumstances demanding structural changes. Each of those major issues remains hindering opportunities and high-quality experiences for young immigrant children.

Immigration: An unresolved issue

Before addressing the issues listed, there is one that continues influencing the wellbeing and lives of close to a third of US children (Yoshikawa and Kholoptseva 2013), immigration policies. At the core of many of the inequities and challenges facing children is the need for addressing the issue that current policies about immigration have created. This is an issue where actions from the government are needed. While those decisions and considerations are made, as educators we continue to point out that as an unresolved issue, thousands of children whose parents entered unofficially, continue to experience the challenge of their immigration status (Box 6.4). The call remains for attention while advocates continue to emphasize the need for some effective solutions to alleviate the social and emotional toll that children and parents are experiencing.

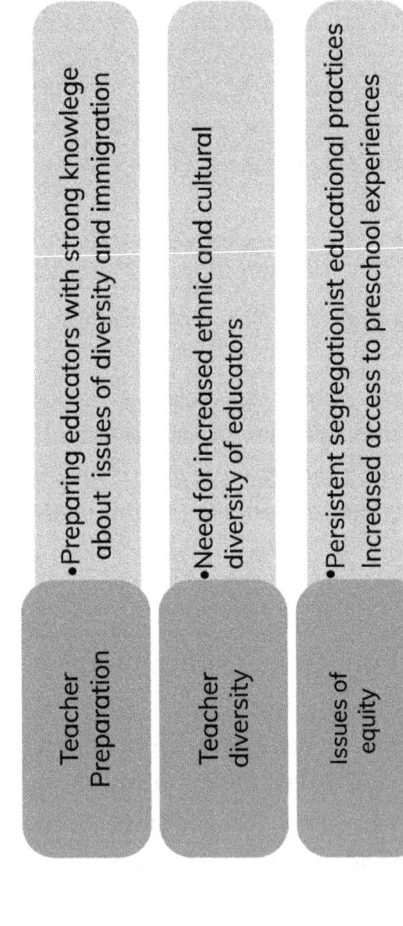

Figure 6.3 Some issues challenging young child immigrants and their families.

Box 6.4 Immigration policies and families: *An ongoing issue*

Immigration policies pose many overlapping ramifications for the well-being of children and society (Yoshikawa and Kholoptseva 2013). Unresolved issues about legality of entry into the country of thousands of families with parents or family members who entered unofficially continue to challenge the welfare of many children who are US citizens themselves. Consideration to the fact that in 2016 over five million children under age 18 had a parent with an unauthorized immigration status (Zong, Batalova, and Burrows 2019) prompts and demands action. It is even more when one realizes that nearly 90 percent of these children are citizens. Beyond politics, there is a need for a serious revision and reform that will better align its tenets and provisions with the events and needs of twenty-first-century US society (Pierce 2019; Pierce, Bolter, and Selee 2018). Voices urging actions to address the immigration situation of thousands of parents with unofficial entry have been loudly advocating for an answer. Given the changing needs and realities of immigrants in the nation, clear and more realistic pathways to citizenship require immediate attention and action. Efforts demanding to update regulations based on current immigration circumstances continue as an essential step addressing the status of thousands of immigrants. In particular, a pathway to citizenship has been pointed out by advocates and scholars as a critical need to address the immigration status of over five million undocumented immigrants (Capps, Fix, and Zong 2016; Yoshikawa and Kholoptseva 2013). Though details about the political debate are beyond the scope of this work, it is relevant to mention that at the time of writing, discussions related to immigration have been mostly absent from the congressional agenda (Pierce 2019). Meanwhile, it remains as a definite factor in need of attention to bring clarity and attain fairness to the immigration circumstances of thousands of immigrant children and families.

Quality as a matter of equity for immigrant children

A report from The Annie Casey Foundation concluded that "We need all children to reach their full potential if we are to reach ours as a nation" (2017, 17). Meeting such goal depends and demands quality programs. Quality is what is always aspired to define practices in early childhood education. As elusive as the construct of quality is, one fact continues to be true: teachers are key to the success of children. Research has indicated that teachers remain as the crucial factor for excellence in programs and services for young children (Copple and Bredekamp 2009; La Paro et al. 2012; Winton and McCollum 2008). Quality of experiences and teaching are among the paramount indicators leading to successful outcomes for young children (Winton, McCollum, and Catlett 2008). Accordingly, federal education mandates require highly qualified educators. If we are to achieve equality and high quality of experiences for all children, the need for appropriate preparation is vital to this end.

Quality is a composite of various factors all vital to achieve excellence in practices and services to children and their families. Unpacking the concept of quality in education exposes multiple angles among which teaching practice is central to achieving equity in learning experiences. Though for decades quality has been heralded as one of the aspirations, still, "access to quality teaching is unequally distributed ... in different contexts and that serve different population of students" (Hollins 2011, 395). Visions of quality in programs and services remain critical to support the well-being of thousands of immigrant children in our communities, especially in low-income households where children's schooling success depends on the nature of their experiences (Greenberg, Rosenboom, and Adams 2019). The road to achieve excellence in experiences for children is long and continues as there is always a need for improvement, especially as society responds to the circumstances and needs of our youngest learners.

Teacher preparation for equity

How ready are teachers to address the needs of children and their diverse realities? What knowledge do they bring about socially just actions to support their work with children with diverse backgrounds? Similar questions have been asked before by proponents of preparation for diversity, an imperative given today's social and demographical realities (Banks 2015; Delpit [1995] 2006; Ladson-Billings 1994; NAEYC 2019; Nieto and Bode 2018). Furthermore, the question remains about teachers' preparation to effectively address the children's changing demographics and diversity across classrooms (Gomez, Kagan, and Fox 2014; Mader 2015; Samson and Collins 2012). Tied to successful teaching practices, teacher preparation is undeniably one of the factors contributing to achieving quality in the classroom (Hollins 2011). The issue as stated by Winton, McCollum, and Catlett is that "Obviously, practitioners 'readiness' to implement an effective program for children is influenced by their education and training" (2008, vii). Teacher educators agree that the nature and quality of experiences responsibly provided are determining factors in preparing educators to address realities and learning needs of students.

The challenge of teacher preparation and of support for practicing teachers continues to be raised in teacher education (Abo-Zena 2018; Goodwin 2017; Suárez-Orozco 2017; Tarozzi 2014). Mindful of the need to appropriately respond to the evolving societal and diversity needs of young immigrant children, they demand attention to strengthen the knowledge base to avoid continuation of the "prevalent deficit-oriented perspective" (da Silva and Reyes 2017, 34). Similarly concerned, the recent NAEYC position statement on equity (2019) provided recommendations for teacher preparation and professional development. Specifically, it underlined the importance of addressing socially just and equitable practices as integral knowledge for teacher candidates as well as for practicing educators.

The issue of teacher preparation and development consonant with society's reality remains high on the agenda for addressing diversity and immigration. Takanishi (2010) posited teacher preparation in her call to level the field for immigrant children, describing it as "the most serious current challenge … to educate newcomer children more effectively" (25). More recently, NAEYC (2019a) in its position statement on equity underlined the importance of teacher preparation guided at building knowledge about fairness in teaching practices. Posed as a social justice issue, attention to diversity continues to call for training and formative experiences with emphasis on practices centered on what is rightful for children (Sims 2015). Similar concerns were also raised in a report from the Center for American Progress about preparation to address the needs of English language learners (ELL) (Samson and Collins 2012). In the report, the reality of the changing demographics stemming from immigration was pointed out given its concomitant teaching implications. It pointed out that "The fact that the nation's teachers are and will increasingly encounter a diverse range of learners requires that every teacher has sufficient breadth and depth of knowledge and range of skills to meet the unique needs of all students, including those who struggle with English" (1). Referring to the language needs of ELL children, the report concluded that the need for explicit teacher preparation was vital to address and meet the leaning needs of a growing diverse student population (Samson and Collins 2012). Meanwhile, challenges facing teachers without the required professional development continue as a main priority (Banks 2015; Quintero and Hansen 2017). Of concern to everyone is the fact that while attention to issues of diversity is not properly focused, many will continue to enter the profession without the proper knowledge tools to effectively drive their practices.

Absence of topics about immigration

The topic of immigration still continues to be absent or hardly addressed in the preparation of future educators. Concerns about the preparation of teachers working with immigrant children guided Goodwin (2017) to conduct her research. In her earlier study, she conducted a literature analysis of teacher preparation related to immigrants. Results identified a "noticeable silence surrounding the preparation of new teachers to work with immigrant children" (438). Replicating the study almost fifteen years later, this time her results revealed that despite changes in immigration patterns, there was "scant attention" (439) to the topic. Outcomes of her research exposed a serious issue pointing to, what Goodwin called, the virtual absence of immigrants and their children's experiences in the literature germane to teacher preparation. In her analysis, she pointed out that the apparent absence of topics about immigrants could signal "that these concerns are not making their way into teacher education curriculum" (439).

Time to reflect … *Teaching child immigrants*

Teacher development and preparation are vital to address the needs of an increasing enrollment of child immigrants in schools. Reflect on your own knowledge and professional development. How ready are you to teach children with diverse experiences and cultures? What areas do you consider in need of professional development or growth?

Implications are clear about the lack of attention to immigration realities in teacher preparation. We are not effectively preparing teachers with the understanding necessary about issues of diversity and specifically about those of immigration. In the meantime, empowering teachers with the knowledge and skills required to work with young immigrant students continues as a critical factor if we are to achieve educational equity in the nation's classrooms. The greatest concern should come given the current and projected demographics. As teacher educators ourselves, we the authors share these concerns. We know from our own experiences that consideration of the specific realities of immigration is not explicitly addressed in teacher preparation. A review of national teacher preparation standards[1] showed that specific attention is absent to issues of immigrants or to immigration. It was found that, while facets about diversity are integrated in teacher preparation standards, immigrant experiences were not included as a facet of diversity, leaving this to remain mostly at the discretion of instructors if these are to be investigated and addressed. Even if topics about diversity are included, concerns on how diversity is approached and examined have been voiced many times. Valentin (2006) pointed out her concern about the fragmented way in which the concept is presented. Similarly, other authors have revealed the need for consideration to the lack of consistency in how cultural diversity concepts are addressed in teacher education (Beutel and Tangen 2018; Hinojosa Pareja and López 2018; Swindler Boutte 2008). While diversity is expected to serve as the thread throughout course experiences for teacher candidates, little or no attention is typically placed on aspects about immigration. Indeed, the need to place emphasis on immigration realities and its implications for practice calls for a more defined approach.

Interest of teachers to acquire and further their knowledge about immigrants is well known. This has become evident whenever the authors hear students' comments, questions, and concerns about children and immigration experiences. The challenge is for the subject of immigration to be integral to discussions, not as an isolated theme but as a central topic itself in teacher preparation and in systematic professional development. An understanding about the realities of diversity and of children of immigrant backgrounds continues to be a factor in empowering early childhood educators to deliver and ensure equity in their practice. Specificity about the implications of immigration for the child and family demands attention to fully appreciate its repercussions on children's learning and overall development. Meanwhile, it is relevant to remember that immigration is projected to steadily continue to influence the demographic character of the nation. This prompts the question, will we be ready to equitably address the needs of immigrant children?

---

[1] The review of teacher preparation standards for early childhood candidates included those from the Interstate Support and Assessment Consortium (InTASC), Council for the Accreditation of Educator Preparation (CAEP), and the NAEYC.

Time to reflect … *Committed teachers*

Early childhood educators are known for their commitment to young children, which denotes their ethical conduct and strong commitment. Their commitment is evident in their daily work. Working with immigrant children and their many diverse realities calls for a strong commitment. Reflect on what guides your commitment to work with young children. What drives you to overcome any obstacles children may face?

Preparing teachers to address children's needs is not accomplished through one course or workshop. Teacher preparation and development is an ongoing and systematic process carefully planned and clearly targeted at addressing and clarifying the implications of immigration. It demands attention to issues of diversity in its broadest sense. Quality of teaching oriented to deliver equitable practices depends on the experiences preparing educators to work with the multiple realities of children and families. To make this happen, we need:

1. Teacher preparation and professional development that effectively builds an understanding about the realities of immigration and its pedagogical implications (Abo-Zena 2018) using the lens of what is socially just for children (Christman 2010; NAEYC 2019b). Integration of experiences examining immigration and its multiple circumstances (da Silva Iddings and Reyes 2017), underlining what is essential to support the needs of children.

2. Experiences that consistently provide early childhood educators with the critical lenses of culture and development allowing children to be viewed through the dimensions of their overall developmental potential together with their individual cultures and experience (Davis 2006; Nieto and Bode 2018; Robles-Meléndez and Driscoll 2017; Sánchez and Thorp 2008). Activities of experiential nature would be especially necessary to gain knowledge about the nature of realities in children's contexts.

3. Consistent emphasis and opportunities preparing teachers as reflective educators to consciously consider needs, actions, and responses as part of educational practice. In fact, this is what leads professionals to focus on the needs and circumstances unique to the child. This is what the authors have intentionally conveyed through the reflection capsules, found throughout the chapters.

Segregation and isolationist practices

Equity raises the need for consideration of practices that today isolate immigrant students (Ryabov and Van Hook 2007). It is difficult to understand the existing segregation practices considering the landmark ruling over sixty-five years ago in the 1954 *Brown* v. *Board of Education* case where segregationist practices were ruled unconstitutional. Educators and advocates for the rights of immigrants have raised attention to issues segregating immigrant children in some communities that continue to accentuate underlying discriminatory practices. This practice has been found in communities with high concentrations of immigrant groups and lower income levels (Camera 2016). Social and economic factors and immigration status have contributed to the segregation of immigrant families and their children. Race has also contributed to segregationist practices in current times. Findings reported in 2016 by the Government Accountability Office (GAO) concluded that certain schools "were more racially and economically concentrated" (GAO 2016, 1). They found that these schools had a disproportionate percentage of students ranging from 75 to 100 percent from ethnic minorities, predominantly African-Americans and Hispanics. Also reported was the fact that secondary level schools had lower academic offerings to prepare students for college versus other schools, which evidently placed students at a disadvantage. At the same time, the fact is that some primary schools in communities with higher immigrant population also face fewer resources and opportunities for the younger students. Findings identify that particularly Hispanics, who in many cases account for the majority of a school's enrollment, experience greater segregation.

Generally, isolation has been evident in primary schools where enrollment in many communities is mostly of immigrants as we have both witnessed in our years of experience. Language diversity and family immigration status have also contributed to their isolation (Box 6.5). The reality is that educators cannot remain quiet about this fact given the implicit disadvantage that young immigrant children experience. The authors echo the words of McArdle, Osypuk, and Acevedo-García, who, in their analysis about school segregation, stated that "The fact that such gross levels of disparity continue in American public schools must not be met with apathy or acceptance, but be confronted to ensure that our children and our nation can thrive in an increasingly diverse and challenging world" (2010, 22). Failure to end this isolation hurts all children irrespective of their cultures and ethnic or racial groups (Frankenberg et al. 2019). Interactions and experiences in the community of the school prepare all children for life and successful future as members of a diverse society. A need to erase the conditions perpetuating separation urgently demands action given their adverse effect on children.

Box 6.5 Language and family immigration status, two factors also contributing to isolate children

Many children also experience isolation and segregation due to linguistic diversity and their families' immigration status. Both tend to isolate families and their children in their communities. Children in these situations end up in schools that are more constrained by fewer resources and lower quality of teaching experiences (Villalobos et al. 2018). Many of these schools are also categorized as low performing. This further impacts the children's experiences as they are excluded from comparable high-quality practices and resources found in other locations (Crawford 2017; Crosnoe 2013). Additionally, children are also impacted by their own vulnerabilities and challenges, stemming from their situations and by lower levels of necessary ancillary supports at their schools and communities. Family immigration status may also exclude children from what peers experience, such as home stability, higher levels of participation in early childhood programs and services, and better economic situations (Abrego 2006; Crawford 2017; Yoshikawa and Kholoptseva 2013). Though immigrant children are legally entitled to equal educational services and programs, living in mostly ethnic communities and with parents fearful of deportation increases their separation rather than integration into the community of the school.

Time to reflect ... *Isolationist practices*

Issues of segregation are found across many communities. Is it present in your community? Take time to examine the early childhood enrollment in your community and determine if this is a challenge for centers and primary schools in your community. What steps would you propose to erase this reality?

Access to preschool experiences: Another reality demanding attention

As addressed earlier in Chapter 4, living in communities with limited or no access to affordable preschool programs is a contributing factor to segregation of many young immigrant children who end up excluded from experiences necessary to support their development and well-being (Ayón 2015). Lower or no participation has also been identified as a factor placing children at risk and limiting opportunities for future schooling success (Crosnoe 2013). Takanishi (2010) pointedly stated in her report that participation in preschool experiences is necessary to evenly level the playing field for every child. This is what democracy implies where everyone has equal opportunities. Still, though most preschool-age immigrant children are US citizens, their enrollment "continues to lag behind that of their peers with U.S. born parents" (Greenberg, Michie, and Adams 2018, v).

Access and participation in preschool programs have been shown to be significantly challenged in some ethnic groups. In 2012, reports showed that Hispanic children were less likely to be enrolled in preschool programs (Child Trends Databank 2014; NCES 2019). Though public school programs for 4-year-olds have increased preschool options and participation, variation in access and availability "significantly vary from state to state" (Pasquantonio 2017). There are still many communities where affordable or available preschool programs remain out of reach for many immigrant families.

Evidence abounds concerning the role and impact of preschool experiences on school achievement (Copple and Bredekamp 2009; Winton, McCollum, and Catlett 2008). Outcomes from program models, such as the Perry Preschool and Abecedarian projects, conclusively demonstrated that preschool experience is a significant factor for higher schooling success (Lamy 2013). Limiting children from accessing preschool programs is a factor affecting their learning outcomes and expanding learning gaps among young children. Targeted efforts are needed to end practices that, directly or indirectly, continue to perpetuate separating and excluding children from receiving equitable opportunities to participate in high-quality programs. From the perspective of consciously centered practices, adopting and fostering inclusiveness to eliminate discriminatory practices is essential. This begins with an honest appraisal of what children are experiencing in the community and with deliberate steps to eliminate inequities.

Time to reflect ... *Addressing equity in quality practices*

Segregationist practices are discriminatory and remain as a challenge to equitable experiences for young immigrant children. Consider the existing programs in your community or state. What practices would you consider as segregationist? What would you propose to extinguish segregationist practice?

Teacher diversity: Who is teaching our immigrant children?

Teaching children of immigrants requires thoughtful understanding of their circumstances and experiences. As an increasing segment of the student population, children of immigrants are projected to become over 55 percent of the public schools' enrollment. Practically half of all children under age 5 are from diverse ethnic groups. The question is, who is teaching these children? This is a question many have asked given the lower diversity of the teaching force. With an increasing immigrant growth trend, teachers should reflect the nation's demographics. The fact is that "Young people need to see who they can become—you can't be who you don't see" (Bianco, cited by Long 2017). Ladson-Billings in *Dreamkeepers* (1994) showed the powerful influence of teachers who shared the same ethnic background of their students. The social and cultural connections made are influential in their overall experiences. They believe in their children and are able to connect with their realities, as one of the teachers reveals stating, "When I look at my children I see myself" (Ladson-Billings 1994, 42). Clearly, teachers of similar ethnic backgrounds are important role models for students, which further justifies the need for increasing diversity in the classroom.

Emphasis on increasing teacher diversity, a continuing issue, has been pointed out over the years. Culturally responsive and highly knowledgeable educators are essential to meet the needs of children of immigrants as well as those of all children, irrespective of race or ethnicity. This is what the authors strongly believe. We also recognize children need to have teachers they can see as role models, particularly for immigrant children who can inspire them by their example as to what is possible to accomplish. Evidence from research studies has revealed that when children are taught by teachers who share their same ethnic backgrounds, their responses, outcomes, and performance are positively influenced (Cherng and Halpin 2016; Dee 2004; Figlio 2017; Gershenson et al. 2017). This positive influence was particularly evidenced in a study with primary school children taught by same-race teachers (Gershenson et al. 2017). In the study, findings revealed that children demonstrated academic gains and were less likely to drop out from schools when taught by teachers of their same ethnic group. Overall, results from research suggest the importance of teacher diversity as a factor supporting experiences of children who are culturally and linguistically diverse.

With increasing evidence about the positive result of teacher diversity on children's experiences, the question arises concerning steps to increase the diversity of teachers in the nation's classrooms. Meanwhile, reports show that the teacher pool in the nation continues to show a lower representation of ethnic minorities (National Center for Education Statistics 2019). Data about teacher diversity indicate that mainstream teachers still predominantly represent most of the teaching force. It makes people wonder why minorities are not entering the education profession. During 2015–16, 80 percent of teachers were White (National Center for Education Statistics 2019). The report also reflected a slight increase in the number of teachers from diverse ethnic groups from previous years. This growth appears still minimal when one considers that it accounted for only 20 percent of public school teachers. Despite the increase in teachers' diversity, it is projected that continuing "underrepresentation of teachers of colors will likely persist or even grow in the coming decades" (Hansen and Quintero 2019). The challenge is evident as projections continue to show an increasing immigration. Data from the Census shows that almost 4 percent (3.9) of children enrolled in schools were foreign born (U.S. Bureau of the Census 2017). This trend is expected to increase in the coming decades. The U.S. Department of Education has recognized the need for teacher diversity and its importance for supporting student's performance. A report in 2016 about the diversity of the teacher workforce cited John King, secretary of education, who stated that

> We've got to understand that **all students benefit from teacher diversity**. We have strong evidence that students of color benefit from having teachers and leaders who look like them, as role models, and also benefit from the classroom dynamics that diversity creates. But it is also important for our white students to see teachers of color in leadership roles in their classrooms and communities. The question for the nation is how do we address this quickly and thoughtfully? (2016, 1) (emphasis added)

Increasing teacher diversity

Steps to encourage greater teacher diversity are essential to be more ethnically consistent with the student enrollment. Incentives, new programs, and practices to attract future teachers are essential to increase the number of teachers from diverse ethnic groups. In the authors' experience as teacher educators, financial support emerges as one of the challenges faced by aspiring teachers from diverse ethnic groups. Teaching in a minority serving institution, both authors have witnessed the aspirations and the barriers encountered by many of our own students. Funding continues to be limited for teachers from diverse ethnic groups aspiring to teach in early childhood education.

Language barriers are another challenge for aspiring teachers as well as for practitioners with languages other than English. This is a particular barrier for immigrant educators wanting to continue teaching or for those entering the early childhood profession. While many aspiring teachers are in the process of learning English, some still find themselves challenged by course options delivered only in English. In countless instances, bilingual supports are minimal or nonexistent, discouraging many. Efforts have begun to respond to language challenges facing student teachers and practitioners across several states. In response to the needs of Spanish-speaking preschool practitioners in southeastern Florida, a bilingual early childhood program was designed. Participants were all immigrants who needed to comply with new licensing expectations. The program, a collaboration between a county early childhood quality initiative and a private university, was specifically designed for the participants using a culturally based teacher training model (Robles-Meléndez and Valdes-Diaz 2011). Details about the program appear in Box 6.6. Similarly, more program options are needed if we are to expand the representation of teacher from diverse ethnic groups in our classrooms and schools.

Box 6.6 Connecting ideas: *Growing to help children grow and supporting Hispanic early childhood practitioners*

Language should never be a barrier when someone wants to perform optimally, especially for children. This premise was what guided the development of a bilingual early childhood certificate program. With new quality initiatives aimed at increasing the quality of programs, additional requirements for practitioners have also emerged. The program evolved in response to the challenge of Spanish-speaking preschool practitioners working in private centers who needed to comply with new credentialing requirements. At the time, no training options delivered in Spanish were available in their local area. Facing the possibility of losing their jobs, a local private university was contacted by the director of the county early childhood quality initiative. Motivated by the situation, the university early childhood program coordinator quickly responded, ensuring that language barriers were not going to be an obstacle. Rather than just translating coursework, the university college faculty engaged in the design of strategies tailored to the needs of the Spanish-speaking students. A culturally based training was designed for the audience of practitioners, all immigrants from Latin America, the majority of whom were teachers with degrees from their own countries. Crafted to meet the required credentials, the program included an experienced group of bilingual faculty and resources to support the emerging English language skills of the participants. Readings and resources were intentionally selected to address expectations and also reflect the cultures of the children who were served by the practitioners. Delivered as cohort-based groups, weekly meetings using a blended format with online and onsite meetings responded to the needs of working professionals, honoring and acknowledging their experiences. An emphasis on funds of knowledge, culture, and reflection on their professional growth was woven throughout the coursework. Follow-up activities were also included in the design of the program, which allowed faculty to visit students once they had completed the program. When the first group met in 2007, the anxiety that many of the students experienced was evident. For some students, it signified the first time enrolling in a US-based university and the feeling of the challenge was clear. Months later, in 2008, their success was celebrated, as evidence of what they had accomplished. Most importantly, it reaffirmed, as later shared by practitioners, their commitment to children. Over three hundred students benefited during the duration of the program.

Moving into action for child immigrants

At present, reports and the media continue to inform the public about the ongoing journeys of immigrants and of immigrants living in our communities. This is a story that for our nation is continuous. Projections indicate that immigration remains as a critical part of the nation's society and history. For the authors, writing at a time of graduations and grade promotions, once again they witness the joyful celebrations and successful accomplishments of a generation of young children and youth who are growing up in our classrooms, many of them children of immigrants. Reminding everyone about what they can accomplish, their faces are as diverse as the stories they represent.

We are reminded that the agenda for children of immigrants remains as a priority for everyone's support and action. Andrew and Ewen posit that "Meeting the needs of the growing population of young children of immigrants presents a challenge for the early childhood field. It is a challenge, however, that is essential to meet" (2010, 15). Throughout the preceding chapters, present issues weaved into the discussions have prominently focused on urging early educators to expand their views about the realities of immigration. Previously highlighted were some points to be considered and prioritized in the educational agenda for immigrant children. They include those in Figure 6.3, which were presented earlier in this chapter. They serve as action areas to frame efforts directed to bring equity and social justice to the experience of immigrant children. By no means are these inclusive of all that requires action. Long-standing issues such as the needed revision of immigration policies are among those presenting continuing challenges.

Action is necessary to address the ensuing unfairness and discriminatory practices experienced by immigrants that persist currently. Perceptions about immigration continue to be distorted or enthralled in misleading arguments. What is warranted as key action items in an agenda for the immigrant children begins with an understanding that every child merits our attention and care, as ingrained in society. Beyond awareness, knowledge about circumstances challenging children is critical for early childhood educators as they consciously and effectively respond to children's needs. Conscious consideration to current circumstances, both individual and systemic, can guide decisions and actions on behalf of immigrant children. Responding to the needs of child immigrants and of their diverse experiences demands vigilant understanding to inform and guide actions. This also entails knowledge about the capacity that educators have to address the needs of the immigrant child. Through reflective practice, early childhood educators can become consciously mindful about the needs of the youngest immigrants and about their professional responsibility to assist. No action is ever too small for children.

Looking ahead

Over two decades ago, Hernandez (1999) remarked that "no group of American children is expanding more rapidly than those in immigrant families" (1), observing their important role "to the vitality of this nation" (2). Today, his comments resonate, continuing to describe the significance of immigration as a societal changing force in the United States. In the midst of the debates about immigration, early childhood educators are reminded about the ever-increasing and diverse needs of the youngest immigrants we teach in our classrooms. Their presence is a reminder about the continuous search and need for equitable opportunities and experiences (Abo-Zena 2018; Adair 2015; Ayón 2015; Suárez-Orozco and Suárez-Orozco 2018). Equity in the experience of a child remains, challenging everyone to make it happen as another defining trait of their journey in the nation's classrooms.

Immigration is a very complex state of affairs. It demands serious and concerted efforts in need of address for families and children coming to our country and for the many who presently live in our country, the country they also call home. Our classrooms are the place where thousands of young immigrant children, where the majority are US citizens, continue to grow and develop in spite of current challenges and immigration debates. While waiting for policies and government decisions to be made about immigration, many actions remain in our hands as early childhood educators. In our daily practice, in classrooms and programs for young children and their families, consciously determined actions are what continue to support children and give hope to families, hope that is placed in each of us.

The time for responses and actions is always now if we are to meet the needs of a young child. How can early childhood educators respond to the needs of young immigrant children? Here are some suggestions to begin drafting an agenda moving forward:

As an early childhood educator:

- *Build your knowledge about immigration*: Make a personal decision to learn more about immigration. Whether individually or together with colleagues, search for information and resources that can expand your knowledge about immigration status and regulations. Search out about workshops or webinars to help build your knowledge on immigration. Keep yourself aware of new decisions, practices pertaining to immigrants, and their implications for children and families in your community.

- *Become informed about the educational rights of child immigrants*: Locate information about the educational rights that child immigrants are legally entitled to receive. Familiarize yourself with confidentiality practices pertaining to enrollment and child/family information. Consult with school administrators or locate official information from your school district or state on services and programs for young children who are immigrants.

- *Become informed about the diversity of immigrants in the community*: Find information about the demographic traits in your community as well as in the community of the school where you work. Learn about their languages, traditions, and practices. Start a conversation with colleagues and explore views, happenings about diversity and immigration in your community. Talk with those whose experience can help provide direction and ideas to assist immigrant children and their families.

In the classroom or in your program:

- *Make your classroom or center/program into an emotionally safe environment for children*: Take time to consciously determine the social and emotional environment of your classroom or center. Consider arrangement and materials and ensure fair access and participation for everyone. Purposefully observe interactions and note any actions or words that exclude children because of their diversity.

- *Deliberately respond to prejudice and biased comments*: Respond to any biased or prejudiced behavior as these occur. Remember that young children are learning and may use comments heard from others. Check materials for any biases or misleading illustrations. Make sure items are inclusive and reflect cultures of children. Carefully ponder decisions about children's academic needs. Keep in mind that some may have experienced traumatic situations. Encourage learning and show your confidence in what they can do.

- *Deliver experiences following consciously centered practices*: As a practice, make a decision to intentionally provide support and learning experiences that address the culture and diverse needs of immigrant children. Make consideration to the individual needs and circumstances of children a parameter guiding your activities, planning, and decisions for children and their families.

- *Engage immigrant families in your classroom/program*: Plan ways to engage families in the classroom activities. Find ways to address any linguistic barriers to ease communication. Take time to talk to them about their children and learn about their aspirations for their children. Become aware about their strengths and abilities. Share information about resources and programs available in the community they may need.

- *Demonstrate an understanding about the child and family's realities:* Consider that some families may be experiencing difficult circumstances, which may prevent them from participating or attending meetings. Rather than making assumptions, find out about their needs and consult with school professionals if assistance is needed.

Projecting into the future

Every day, experiences with children across classrooms and communities take early childhood educators closer to learn and personally know their stories and realities. With the fluidity of events and circumstances in present times, the agenda for children is a working one, calling for adjustment as events evolve. What remains ahead is overwhelming but indeed not impossible. Efforts are needed from everyone in the early childhood education community as we strive with empathy, knowledge, and understanding to view children and consciously work to fulfil the responsibility of supporting their development.

In *Dreamkeepers* (1995), Ladson-Billings showed us that when practices are meaningful and relevant, learning is encouraged, and success follows. Key to each child's success, as she revealed, are teachers who can make those dreams happen. This is precisely what early childhood educators and the authors envision for immigrant children—educators that inspire, challenge, and motivate children to grow and develop successfully. Also envisioned is understanding and disposition to support equitable and socially just actions for young immigrant children. This is what each and every child rightfully deserves.

Early childhood educators' visions of hope for immigrant children remain strong. They guide their efforts and determination to provide children with what is consciously responsible. In the story *The Big Umbrella* (Bates 2018), everyone finds there is always room to shelter together. This is what we envision in our classrooms, centers, schools, and society in general—enthusiastically welcoming the future seen in every child. Today they are the best hope we have for what is to come in the future.

Much work continues to remain ahead. Continued and determined action by early childhood educators along with advocates can make possibilities a reality for immigrant children. Every effort counts and makes a difference for a child. Children are counting on us.

Key points

- Advocacy is essential to ensure fair and equal access to education and related services for children of immigrants and their families. Advocating efforts for children contribute to ensuring their access to services and programs essential to their well-being. Advocates for immigrant children include efforts from individuals as well as from groups and organizations. They all play a significant role in identifying situations, calling for action, as well as ensuring immigrant children receive legally entitled services and programs. Advocacy is an ongoing process guided to address current and emerging situations facing immigrants.
- In early childhood education, advocacy is an ethical responsibility. Efforts of early childhood professionals are guided by their sense of what is critical to safeguarding children. Teachers' efforts play a leading role in daily experiences as they strive for what is unquestioningly right for children. Actions of many early educators demonstrate their commitment and are examples of their dedication to children.
- Several issues remain hindering child immigrants from receiving equitable services and high-quality experiences. These issues continue to call for advocates' efforts to build awareness and support equitable practices. Together, they form an agenda for action to ensure fair and equitable services for child immigrants.
- Teacher empowerment to address the needs of child immigrants remains as a relevant need in the agenda for action. The need exists for intentional teacher preparation addressing the realities of immigration and its influence on children's development and its subsequent educational implications. Concerted actions and efforts are required to fully appreciate the impact of immigration on the nation and the ensuing responsibilities for early childhood education.

To think, do, and reflect …

1. Reflect on the variety of responsibilities to safeguard the rights of child immigrants in your community. What actions would you propose to ensure the attention and support to children's needs?

2. Advocacy is a rather difficult term to define. Based on the discussion in this chapter and your own experiences, draft a definition of advocacy reflective of your own views about advocacy.
3. Consider programs in your community and identify any inequitable practices that are denying immigrant students from receiving equal experiences. What actions would you propose to correct these inequitable practices?
4. What compelling arguments would you employ to support the need for immigration and diversity-specific professional development for early childhood educators?
5. What actions or issues would you propose to be added to the advocacy agenda for immigrant children?

References

Abo-Zena, Mona. 2018. "Supporting immigrant-origin children: Grounding teacher education in critical developmental perspectives and practices." *The Teacher Educator* 53(3): 263–76.

Abrego, Leisy. 2006. "I can't go to college because I don't have papers." Incorporation Patterns of Latino Undocumented Youth. *Latino Studies* 2(3): 212–31.

Adair, Jennifer. 2015. *The Impact of Discrimination on the Early Schooling Experiences of Children from Immigrant Families*. Washington, DC: Migration Policy Institute.

American Association of Pediatricians. 2013. "Policy statement: Providing care for immigrant, migrant, and border children." *Pediatrics* 131(6). doi:10.1542/peds.2013–109.

Andrew, Hannah, and Danielle Ewen. 2010. "Early Education Programs and Children of Immigrants: Learning Each Other's Language." Paper presented at the *Young Children in Immigrant Families and the Path to Educational Success Roundtable*. The Urban Institute. June 28. Retrieved from https://www.fcd-us.org/assets/2016/04/Matthews_Ewen-Early-Education-Programs-and-Children-of-Immigrants.pdf.

Ayón, Cecilia. 2015. *Economic, Social, and Health Effects of Discrimination on Latino Immigrant Families*. Washington, DC: Migration Policy Institute.

Banks, James. 2015. *Multicultural Education: Issues and Perspectives* (9th ed.). New York: Wiley.

Bates, Amy. 2018. *The Big Umbrella*. New York: Simon & Schuster.

Beutel, Denise, and Donna Tangen. 2018. "The Impact of Intercultural Experiences on Preservice Teachers' Preparedness to Engage with Diverse Learners." *Australian Journal of Teacher Education* 43(3). Retrieved from http://ro.ecu.edu.au/ajte/vol43/iss3/11.

Brammertz, I., Mendez, R., Eklund, J., and Moonan, M. 2012. *Wendell Rollason: A Life of Purpose.* Immokalee, FL: RCMA.

Camera, Lauren. 2016. "More than 60 years after Brown v. Board of Education, school segregation still exists." *Education News. U.S. News.* May 17. Retrieved from https://www.usnews.com/news/articles/2016-05-17/after-brown-v-board-of-education-school-segregation-still-exists.

Capps, Randy, Michael Fix, and Jie Zong. 2016. *A Profile of U.S. Children with Unauthorized Immigrant Parents. Fact Sheet.* Migration Policy Institute. Retrieved from https://www.migrationpolicy.org/research/profile-us-children-unauthorized-immigrant-parents.

Cherng, Hua-Yu Sebastian, and Peter Halpin. 2016. "The importance of minority teachers: Students perception of minority versus White teachers." *Educational Researcher* 45(7): 407–20. doi: 10.3102/0013189X16671718.

Chezare, Warren. 2017. "Empathy, teacher dispositions, and preparation for culturally responsive pedagogy." *Journal of Teacher Education* 69(2): 169–83.

Child Trends Databank. 2014. *Early Childhood Program Enrollment.* Retrieved from https://www.childtrends.org/?indicators=early-childhood-program-enrollment.

Child Stats. 2019. *America's children: Key indicators of wellbeing, 2019.* Retrieved https://www.childstats.gov/americaschildren/family.asp.

Christman, Dana. 2010. "Creating social justice in early childhood education: A case study in equity and context." *Journal of Research on Leadership Education.* 5(3.4): 109–37.

Copple, Carol, and Sue Bredekamp. 2009. *Developmentally Appropriate Practice in Early Childhood Programs Serving Children from Birth to Eight* (3rd ed.). Washington, DC: National Association for the Education of Young Children.

Crawford, Emily. 2017. "The ethic of community and incorporating undocumented immigrant concerns into ethical school leadership." *Educational Administration Quarterly* 53(2): 147–79.

Crosnoe, Robert. 2013. *Preparing the Children of Immigrants for Early Academic Success.* Washington, DC: Migration Policy Institute.

Cummins, Lauren, and Bridget Asempapa. 2013. "Fostering teacher candidate dispositions in teacher education programs." *Journal of the Scholarship of Teaching and Learning* 13(3): 99–119.

da Silva, Idings, Ana Christina, and Iliana Reyes. 2017. "Learning with immigrant children, families and communities: The imperative of early childhood teacher education." *Early Years* 37(1): 34–46.

Davis, Bonnie. 2006. *How to Teach Students Who Don't Look Like You: Culturally Relevant Teaching Strategies.* Thousand Oaks, CA: Corwin Press.

Dee, Thomas. 2004. "Teachers, race and student achievement in a randomized experiment." *Review of Economics and Statistics* 86(1): 195–210.

Delpit, Lisa. [1995] 2006. *Other People's Children: Cultural Conflict in the Classroom.* New York: New Press.

Driscoll, Wayne. 2017. "Wealth equity and education: Rhetoric, politics or dreams realized?" In S. Natale and A. Labatella (eds.), *Wealth Equity Dynamics: Economic and Education Challenges*, 131–9. New York: Global Scholarly Publications.

Feliciano, Cynthia, and Yader Lanuza. 2017. "An immigrant paradox? Contextual attainment and intergenerational mobility." *American Sociological Review* 82(1): 211–41.

Fenech, Marianne, and Mianna Lotz. 2018. "Systems advocacy in the professional practice of early childhood teachers: From antithetical to the ethical." *Early Years* 38(1): 19–34.

Figlio, David. 2017. "The importance of a diverse teaching force." *Brookings series. Evidence Speaks*. November 16. Retrieved from https://www.brookings.edu/research/the-importance-of-a-diverse-teaching-force/.

Florida Department of Education. 2019. *Consent Decree*. Retrieved from http://www.fldoe.org/academics/eng-language-learners/consent-decree.stml.

Frankenberg, Erica, Jongyeon Ee, Jennifer Ayscue, and Gary Orfield. 2019. *Harming Our Common Future: America's Segregated Schools 65 Years after Brown*. The Civil Rights Project. Center for Education and Civil Rights. Retrieved from https://www.civilrightsproject.ucla.edu/research/k-12-education/integration-and-diversity/harming-our-common-future-americas-segregated-schools-65-years-after-brown/Brown-65-050919v4-final.pdf.

Freire, Paulo. [1974] 2013. *Education for Critical Consciousness*. London: Bloomsbury.

Gay, Geneva. 2000. *Culturally Relevant Teaching* (2nd ed.). New York: Teachers College Press.

Gershenson, Seth, Cassandra Hart, Constance Lindsay, and Nicholas Papageorge. 2017. *The Long-run Impacts of Same-race Teachers*. IZA Institute of Labor Economics. Discussion Paper Series. Retrieved from https://www.iza.org/publications/dp/10630.

Gomez, Rebecca, Sharon L. Kagan, and Emily Fox. 2014. "Professional development of the early childhood education teaching workforce in the United States: An overview." *Professional Development in Education* 41(2): 169–86.

González, Jeremiah, Stacy Kula, Verónica González, and Susan Paik. 2017. "Context of Latino students' separation during and after immigration: Perspectives, challenges, and opportunities for collaborative efforts." *School Community Journal* 27(2): 211–28.

Goodwin, Lin. 2017. "Who is in the classroom now? Teacher preparation and the education of immigrant children." *Educational Studies* 53(5): 433–49.

Greenberg, Erica, Molly Michie, and Gina Adams. 2018. *Expanding Preschool Access for Children of Immigrants*. The Urban Institute. Retrieved from https://www.urban.org/research/publication/expanding-preschool-access-children-immigrants/view/full_report.

Greenberg, Erica, Victoria Rosenboom, and Gina Adams. 2019. *Preparing the Future Workforce: Early Care and Education Participation among Children of Immigrants*. Urban Institute. Retrieved from https://www.pgpf.org/us-2050/research-projects/

Preparing-the-Future-Workforce-Early-Care-and-Education-Participation-Among-Children-of-Immigrants.

Hansen, Michael, and Diana Quintero. 2019. "The diversity gap for public school teachers is actually growing across generations." *Brown Center Blackboard*, March 7, 2019. Retrieved from https://www.brookings.edu/blog/brown-center-chalkboard/2019/03/07/the-diversity-gap-for-public-school-teachers-is-actually-growing-across-generations/.

Hernandez, Donald. 1999. "Children of immigrants: Health, adjustment, and public assistance." In National Research Council and Institute of Medicine (1999). *Children of Immigrants: Health, Adjustment, and Public Assistance.* Committee on the Health and Adjustment of Immigrant Children and Families, Donald J. Hernandez (ed.), Board on Children Youth and Families. Washington, DC: National Academy Press.

Hinojosa Pareja, Eva, and M. Carmen López. 2018. "Interculturality and teacher education: A study from pre-service teachers' perspective." *Australian Journal of Teacher Education* 43(3): 74–92.

Hollins, Etta. (2011). "Teacher preparation for quality teaching." *Journal of Teacher Education* 2(4): 395–407.

International Organization for Migration. 2020. *World Migration Report 2020.* Retrieved from https://publications.iom.int/books/world-migration-report-2020.

Kieff, Judith. 2008. *Informed Advocacy in Early Childhood Care and Education: Making a Difference for Young Children and Families.* Boston, MA: Pearson.

Ladson-Billings, Gloria. 1995. *The Dreamkeepers: Successful Teachers of African-American Children.* New York: Jossey-Bass.

Lamy, Cynthia. 2013. "How preschool fights poverty." *Educational Leadership* 70(8): 32–6.

LaRocco, Diana, and Deborah Bruns. 2005. "Advocacy is only a phone call away: Strategies to make a difference on behalf of children and their families." *Young Exceptional Children* 8(4): 11–18.

La Paro, Karen, Amy Thomason, Joanna Lower, Victoria Kintner-Duffy, and Deborah Cassidy. 2012. "Examining the definition and measurement of quality in early childhood education: Review of studies using the ECERS-R from 2003–2010." *Early Childhood Research and Practice* 14(1). Retrieved from http://ecrp.uiuc.edu/v14n1/laparo.html.

Linton, Julie, Marsha Griffin, Alan Shapiro, and AAP Council on Community Pediatrics. 2017. "Detention of immigrant children. Policy Statement." *Pediatrics* 139(5). doi: 10.1542/peds.2017-0483.

Long, Cindy. 2017. "Experts discuss how to find—and keep—teachers of color." *neaToday.* June 2, 2017. Retrieved from www.neatoday.org/2017/06/02/experts-discuss-teacher-diversity.

Lovato, Kristina, Corina Lopez, Leyla Karimli, and Laura Abrams. 2018. "The impact of deportation-related family separations on the well-being of Latino children and youth: A review of the literature." *Children and Youth Services Review* 95: 109–16.

LULAC. n.d. *LULAC's milestones.* Accessed May 21, 2019. Retrieved from https://lulac. org/about/history/milestones/.

Lynch, Eleanor, and Marci Hanson. 2011. *Developing Cross-Cultural Competence. A Guide for Working with Young Children and Their Families* (4th ed). Baltimore, MD: Paul Brookes.

Mader, Jackie. 2015. "Teacher prep fails to prepare educators for diversity, child trauma, panel says." *The Hechinger Report.* Retrieved from https://hechingerreport.org/ teacher-prep-fails-to-prepare-educators-for-diversity-child-trauma-panel-says/.

McCardle, Nancy, Theresa Osypuk, and Dolores Acevedo-García. 2010. *Segregation and Exposure to High-Poverty Schools in Large Metropolitan Areas: 2008–09. Special Report.* Diversitydata.org. Accessed June 1, 2019. Retrieved from https://school-diversity.org/pdf/school_segregation_report.pdf.

Mevawalla, Zinnia, and Fay Hadley. 2012. "The advocacy of educators: Perspectives from early childhood." *Australasian Journal of Early Childhood* 37(1): 74–80.

NAEYC. 2011. *Code of Ethical Behavior and Statement of Commitment. A Position Statement of the National Association for the Education of Young Children.* Washington, DC: Author.

NAEYC. 2019a. "NAEYC's Statement on families belong together." Blog. June 26. Retrieved from https://www.naeyc.org/resources/blog/statement-families-belong-together.

NAEYC. 2019b. *Advancing Equity in Early Childhood Education: Position Statement.* Retrieved from https://www.naeyc.org/resources/position-statements/equity.

National Center for Education Statistics. 2013. *School and Staffing Survey. Table 1. Total Number of Public School Teachers and Percentage Distribution of School Teachers, by Race/Ethnicity and State: 2011–12.* Retrieved from https://nces.ed.gov/surveys/sass/ tables/sass1112_2013314_t1s_001.asp.

National Center for Education Statistics. 2019. "Preschool and kindergarten enrollment." In *The Condition of Education,* 1–5. Retrieved from https://nces.ed.gov/ programs/coe/indicator_cfa.asp.

Nieto, Sonia, and Patty Bode. 2018. *Affirming Diversity: The Sociopolitical Context of Multicultural Education.* Boston, MA: Pearson.

Office of Head Start. 2010. *Revisiting and Updating the Multicultural Principles for Head Start Programs Serving Children Age's Birth to Five.* Washington, DC: Author.

Office of Head Start. 2019a. *Head Start Services Snapshot. National 2017–2018.* Retrieved from https://eclkc.ohs.acf.hhs.gov/sites/default/files/pdf/no-search/ service-snapshot-hs-2017–2018.pdf.

Office of Head Start. 2019b. *Head Start Timeline.* Retrieved from https://eclkc.ohs.acf. hhs.gov/about-us/article/head-start-timeline.

Pasquantonio, Victoria. May 26 2017. "A record number of kids now attend public preschool, so why has inequality grown?" *Education.* Retrieved from https://www.pbs.org/newshour/education/record-number-kids-now-attend-public-preschool-inequality-grown.

Pew Research Center. 2015. *Modern Immigration Wave Brings 59 Million to U.S., Driving Population Growth and Change through 2065: Views on Immigration's Impact on U.S. Society Mixed.* Washington, DC: Pew Research Center.

Pierce, Sarah. 2019. *Immigration-related Policy Changes in the First Two Years of the Trump Administration.* Washington, DC: Migration Policy Institute.

Pierce, Sarah, Jessica Bolter, and Andrew Selee. 2018. *U.S. Immigration Policy under Trump: Deep Changes and Lasting Impacts.* Washington, DC: Migration Policy Institute.

Quintero, Diana, and Michael Hansen. 2017. "English learners and the growing need for qualified teachers." June 2, 2017. *Brown Center Chalkboard.* Brookings. Retrieved from https://www.brookings.edu/blog/brown-center-chalkboard/2017/06/02/english-learners-and-the-growing-need-for-qualified-teachers/.

Robles-Meléndez, Wilma, and Wayne Driscoll. 2017. "Here I am! Listening to the voices of immigrant children and their families: An analysis of socially just practices supporting immigrant children's sociocultural development." Paper presented at the Annual conference of the European Early Childhood Research Association, Bologna, Italy, August 30.

Robles-Meléndez, Wilma, and Wayne Driscoll. 2018. "Poverty and immigrant children: Moving ahead with *esperanza*, with hope." *Dimensions of Early Childhood* 46(2): 21–4.

Robles-Meléndez, Wilma, and Wayne Driscoll. 2019. "Teacher, teacher, I am here! Addressing the well-being of young immigrant children: Preparing culturally and socially responsive early childhood educators." Paper presented at the Annual conference of the European Early Childhood Research Association, Thessaloniki, Greece, August 21.

Robles-Meléndez, Wilma, and Mabel Valdés-Díaz. 2011. "Creciendo para hacer crecer: Un modelo bilingüe para promover calidad y desarrollo profesional apropiado a las necesidades culturales de los educadores del nivel infantil." [Growing to help children grow: A bilingual model to foster quality and culturally responsive professional development of early childhood teachers]. Paper presented at the Annual conference of the National Association for the Education of Young Children, Orlando, Florida, November 2–5.

Royea, Amber, and Dolores Appl. 2009. "Every voice matters: The importance of advocacy." Guest editorial. *Early Childhood Education Journal* 37: 89–91. doi 10.1007/s10643-009-0335-y.

Ryabov, Igor, and Jennifer Van Hook. 2007. "School segregation and academic achievement among Hispanic children." *Social Science Research* 36(2): 767–88.

Samson, Jennifer, and Brian Collins. 2012. *Preparing All Teachers to Meet the Needs of English Language Learners.* Washington, DC: Center for American Progress.

Sánchez, Sylvia, and Eva Thorp. 2008. "Teaching to transform: Infusing cultural and linguistic diversity." In Pamela Winton, Jeannette McCollum, and Camille Catlett (eds.), *Practical Approaches to Early Childhood Professional Development: Evidence, Strategies, and Resources*, 81–97. Washington, DC: Zero to Three.

Sanna, Francesca. 2016. *The Journey*. London, UK: Flying Eye Books.

Sims, Margaret. 2015. "Social justice, children's needs and rights: An approach to planning." *Journal of Curriculum and Planning* 4(2): 122–9.

Spears Brown, Christia and Hui Chu. 2012. "Discrimination, ethnic identity and academic outcomes of Mexican Immigrant children: The importance of school context." *Child Development* 83(5): 1477–85.

Suárez-Orozco, Carola, and Marcelo Suárez-Orozco. 2001. *Children of Immigration*. Cambridge, MA: Harvard University Press.

Suárez-Orozco, Marcelo, and Carola Suárez-Orozco. 2018. "Like it or not, immigrant children are our future." *WorldPost Opinion. Washington Post.* Accessed May 18, 2019. Retrieved from https://www.washingtonpost.com/news/theworldpost/wp/2018/09/20/immigrant/?noredirect=on&utm_term=.ebd1e3569d7f.

Sugarman, Julie. 2019. "Legal protection for K-12 learner and immigrant background students." *Issue Brief.* Migration Policy Institute. Retrieved from https://www.migrationpolicy.org/research/legal-protections-k-12-english-learner-immigrant-students.

Super, Charles, and Sarah Harkness. 1986. "The developmental niche: A conceptualization at the interface of child and culture." *International Journal of Development* 9(4). doi: https://doi.org/10.1177/016502548600900409.

Swindler Boutte, Gloria. 2008. "Beyond the illusion of diversity: How early childhood teachers can promote social justice." *The Social Studies* 99(4): 165–73.

Takanishi, Ruby. 2008. "Children in immigrant families: All our children?" In "Children in immigrant families: looking to America's future" by Donald Hernandez, Nancy Denton, and Suzanne Macartney. *Social Policy Report* 22(3). Retrieved from https://files.eric.ed.gov/fulltext/ED521704.pdf.

Takanishi, Ruby. 2010. *Leveling the Playing Field: Supporting Immigrant Children from Birth to Eight*. Washington, DC: Foundation for Child Development.

Tarozzi, Massimiliano. 2014. "Building an 'intercultural ethos' in teacher education." *Intercultural Education* 25(2): 128–42.

Taylor, Martha. 2006. "Advocating for young children: A preservice teacher education project." *Journal of Early Childhood Teacher Education* 27(4): 391–9.

The Annie E. Casey Foundation. 2017. *Race for Results. 2017 Policy Report. Kids Count. Building a Path of Opportunity for All Children*. Baltimore: The Annie E. Casey Foundation. Accessed October 20, 2019. Retrieved from http://www.aecf.org/m/resourcedoc/aecf-2017raceforresults-2017.pdf.

Thompson, Lauren. 2008. *Hope Is an Open Heart*. New York: Scholastic.

Toczydlowska, Emilia, and Bina D'Costa. 2017. "Migration and inequality: Making policies inclusive for every child." *Innocenti Research Brief* 2017-14. Retrieved from https://www.unicef-irc.org/publications/pdf/IRB%202017-14%20FINAL.pdf.

UNESCO. 2007. *The Right to Education for All: Ten Reasons why the Convention against Discrimination in Education Is Highly Significant in Today's World*. Retrieved from https://unesdoc.unesco.org/ark:/48223/pf0000153765.

UNICEF. 2016. *Uprooted. The Growing Crisis for Refugee and Migrant Children*. Retrieved from https://www.unicef.org/publications/files/Uprooted_Executive_Summary_Sept_2016.pdf.

UNICEF. 2018a. *Child Migration*. Retrieved from https://data.unicef.org/topic/child-migration-and-displacement/migration/.

UNICEF. 2018b. *A Right to Be Heard*. Retrieved from https://data.unicef.org/resources/youthpoll/.

U.S. Bureau of the Census. 2017. *American Community Survey 2017 1-year Estimates*. Retrieved from https://factfinder.census.gov/faces/tableservices/jsf/pages/productview.xhtml?pid=ACS_17_1YR_S0201&prodType=table.

U.S. Government Accounting Office (GAO). 2016. *K-12 Education. Better Use of Information Could Help Agencies Identify Disparities and Address Racial Discrimination*. Report to congressional requesters. April 2016. GAO-16–345.

Valentin, Sylvia. 2006. "Addressing diversity in teacher education programs." *Education* 127(2): 196–202.

Vaughn, Michael, Christopher Salas-Wright, Matt DeLisi, and Brandy Maynard. 2014. "The immigrant paradox: Immigrants are less antisocial than native-born." *Social Psychiatry and Psychiatric Epidemiology* 49(7): 1129–37. doi: 10.1007/s00127-013-0799-3.

Villalobos, Cristobal, Ernesto Treviño, Ignacio Wyman, and Consuelo Béjares. 2018. "School segregation of immigrant students." In Andrés Sandoval-Hernández, María Magdalena Isaac, and Daniel Miranda (eds.), *Teaching Tolerance in a Globalized World*. IEA Research for Education, vol. 4. Springer.

Votruba-Drzal, Elizabeth, Rebekah Levine Coley, Melissa Collins, and Portia Miller. 2017. "Center-based preschool and school readiness skills of children from immigrant families." *Early Education and Development* 26(4): 549–73.

Wagner, John. 2019. "House members visiting migrant detention centers amid reports of deplorable conditions." *The Washington Post*. July 1. Accessed July 1, 2019. Retrieved from https://www.msn.com/en-us/news/politics/house-members-visiting-migrant-detention-centers-amid-reports-of-deplorable-conditions/ar-AADHmUe?ocid=spartanntp.

Winton, Pamela, and Jeannette McCollum. 2008. "Preparing and supporting high-quality early childhood practitioner: Issues and evidence." In Pamela Winton, Jeannette McCollum, and Camille Catlett (eds.), *Practical Approaches to Early Childhood Professional Development: Evidence, Strategies, and Resources*, 1–12. Washington, DC: Zero to Three.

Winton, Pamela, Jeannette McCollum, and Camille Catlett. 2008. *Practical Approaches to Early Childhood Professional Development. Evidence, Strategies, and Resources*. Washington, DC: Zero to Three.

Wright, Amy, and Kenneth Jaffe. 2014. *Six Steps to Successful Child Advocacy: Changing the World for Children*. New York: Sage.

Wright, Pam, and Pete Wright. 2016. *From Emotions to Advocacy: The Special Education Survival Guide* (2nd ed.). Hartfield, VA: Harbor House Law.

Yoshikawa, Hirokazu, and Jenya Kholoptseva. 2013. *Unauthorized Immigrant Parents and Their Children's Development*. Migration Policy Institute. Retrieved from https://www.migrationpolicy.org/research/unauthorized-immigrant-parents-and-their-childrens-development.

Zong, Jie, Jeanne Batalova, and Mycayla Burrows. 2019. *Frequently Requested Statistics on Immigrants and Immigration in the United States. Spotlight*. Migration Policy Institute. Accessed May 17, 2019. Retrieved from https://www.migrationpolicy.org/article/frequently-requested-statistics-immigrants-and-immigration-united-states#Children.

Index

Lightning Source UK Ltd.
Milton Keynes UK
UKHW010414141020
371550UK00005B/102